Praise for
The New Writer's Handbook 2007

"Editor Martin begins a new annual anthology and from the preface by Erica Jong to the closing piece by Mary Pipher, it surprises and satisfies ... If you purchase only one book from this list, make it this one."
—Stacey Rae Brownlie, *Library Journal* (Starred Review)

"The most evident indication of the quality of Philip Martin's book is its wide and various array of authoritative contributors ... Their individual voices invigorate the work as a whole, making it a more appealing read than most how-to books."
—Harold Cordry, *ForeWord*

"Expertly compiled and deftly edited ... A critically important and strongly recommended addition to personal, professional, academic, and community library reference collections."
—*Midwest Book Review*

"It's an impressive debut."
—Erika Dreifus, *The Writer*

"If you love [a] variety of topics and [authors'] voices about writing, you will enjoy this title. I recommend it."
—W. Terry Whalin, *ASJA Monthly* (American Society of Journalists and Authors)

"It's a worthwhile volume and I look forward to reading next year's edition. *The New Writer's Handbook* inspires writers to brush up and branch out, explore and think differently about their work, their skills, and abilities."
—Amy Brozio-Andrews, *Absolute Write*

> *The New Writer's Handbook 2007* is winner of *ForeWord* Magazine's Book of the Year Award (Career category).

The New Writer's Handbook:

A Practical Anthology of Best Advice
for Your Craft & Career

Volume 2

EDITED by PHILIP MARTIN

PREFACE by TED KOOSER

SCARLETTA PRESS

MINNEAPOLIS

Scarletta Press

10 South Fifth Street, Suite 1105, Minneapolis, MN 55402, U.S.A.

Visit our website at www.scarlettapress.com

Publisher's Cataloging-In-Publication Data

The new writer's handbook : a practical anthology of best advice for your craft & career, volume 2 / edited by Philip Martin.

v. ; cm.

Includes bibliographical references.

ISSN: 1936-7104

1. Authorship—Handbooks, manuals, etc.—Periodicals. I. Martin, Philip, 1953-

PN151 .N49

808.02

ISBN: 978-0-9798249-2-0

Book design by Mighty Media Inc., Minneapolis, MN
Cover: Chris Long, Anders Hanson and Tracy Kompelien
Interior: Chris Long

10   9   8   7   6   5   4   3   2   1

Printed in Canada

Contents

Pitching Your Work

Internet Marketing Skills

Business Savvy

Last Words & Literary Thoughts

Appendices

Ordinary Things

by Ted Kooser

IN MY WORK, I try to look at ordinary things quite closely to see if there isn't a little bit of something remarkable about them. By habit, most of us go through our lives without paying much attention. Surely it's happened to you: at the end of a day, you drive several miles home and when you get there you can't remember a single thing you saw along the way.

When I was beginning to write, Robert Bly once criticized a poem of mine, saying, "You're just making this up." He meant that I'd created the scene from my memory, sitting in my comfortable chair. What I'd written were the predictable things, the kinds of details the imagination finds easily. The imagination makes a lousy realist; it places in its scenes only those that it prefers to see there. Bly was encouraging me to write from life, to go out and actually experience something and then write about that while its particular and unique detail was fresh in my mind.

It won't be the birthday cake covered with twinkling candles that will make readers feel you were really at the party, but the bone-handled serving fork with one tine missing and the place where the lace has pulled loose from the hem of the tablecloth.

Father

Today you would be ninety-seven
if you had lived, and we would all be
miserable, you and your children,
driving from clinic to clinic,
an ancient fearful hypochondriac
and his fretful son and daughter,
asking directions, trying to read
the complicated, fading map of cures.

But with your dignity intact
you have been gone for twenty years,
and I am glad for all of us, although
I miss you every day—the heartbeat
under your necktie, the hand cupped
on the back of my neck, Old Spice
in the air, your voice delighted with stories.
On this day each year you loved to relate
that the moment of your birth
your mother glanced out the window
and saw lilacs in bloom. Well, today
lilacs are blooming in side yards
all over Iowa, still welcoming you.

My father was known as a wonderful storyteller. I recall once a neighbor told me, "I would rather hear your father describe someone than see the person myself." So at some level, the selection of details becomes something wonderful of its own, like a painting that becomes of interest for its own shapes and character, beyond the reality of the original object.

Besides images, I also look for the metaphor, the bridge to connect two things.

Sometimes, in a metaphor, it's not the things being connected that are of most importance, but the grace and lift of the bridge between them, flying high over the surface.

Too often I find students who can come up with a metaphor that's pretty good, but they don't follow it through. They just drop it in like a bead on a string. It's important to weave it into the poem so it reaches all the corners.

Here's a short poem, "August."

The cicada shell
clings to a day in the past,
its broken lantern
dusty with evening light.

Walking alone toward the house,
my life is a moon

in the frail blue branches
of my veins.

Where do the ideas come from? You sit with your notebook, and after a while something begins to interest you. The poet William Stafford described it as being like fishing: you throw out your line and wait for a little tug. Maybe all you get is a minnow, three or four words that seem to have magic, but even that can be enough to get the writing started. And a minnow can be pretty good bait for bigger fish.

Whenever something happens to catch your attention, and you feel like making a note about it, you can usually trust your impulse. Many of the freshest and most engaging poems come from little glimpses of life.

I'm always revising away from difficulty and toward clarity. I used to read my poems to my secretary at the insurance company where I worked to see if they were clear enough. I'd write every morning very early, and then I would bring my work in and I'd say, "Joanne, does this make any sense to you?" And if she said, "Well, no, it doesn't," then I would try to find out where it fell down for her.

You might ask one or two people to read your poem aloud to you. Don't let them rehearse. Ask them to read it aloud without looking at it first. Listen carefully for where they stumble, for places where they trip over the vocabulary or the rhythm. Samuel Taylor Coleridge said poetry is the best words in the best order. That's part of what you're listening for.

My wife is a retired newspaperwoman, the former editor of Lincoln's *Journal Star*, and we talk about newspaper readers a lot. I think I have a good sense of what an average reader will read and enjoy, and that's my objective. I try to write in what I might call the William Carlos Williams strain of poetry, in which poems of simplicity and clarity are valued. If your work is hard to decipher or if it doesn't do anything for a reader, he or she will just move on to read something else.

When I wrote *The Poetry Home Repair Manual*, I wanted to suggest that in some way writing is something that you put together with tools of one kind or another. I don't know that a writer can be made, but one who is already writing in some way can be helped, I think, to write better.

I write to the best of my ability, and that's all I do or can do. Nine out of ten days I write, and nothing good happens. In a sense, I fail, day after day. But for me, writing every day is finding something in your world to celebrate. It's a variety of devotional activity.

At its best, good writing may touch on greater themes, on some sort of universal design or order, and if at some time I touch upon a big issue, it's not because I set out to do so but because I stumbled over it along the way. Any poet who sets out to write poems about big issues is going to have a really hard time. In some way everything is related, and the small can relate to the grand. I pay attention to things, and enjoy the joy and play of language, and I write every day, looking for things that connect.

> *The quarry road tumbles before me*
> *out of the early morning darkness,*
> *lustrous with frost, an unrolled bolt*
> *of softly glowing fabric, interwoven*
> *with tiny glass beads on silver thread,*
> *the cloth spilled out and then lovingly*
> *smoothed by my father's hand*
> *as he stands behind the wooden counter*
> *(dark as these fields) at Tilden's Store*
> *so many years ago. "Here," he says smiling,*
> *"you can make something special with this."*
> —opening poem in *Winter Morning Walks*

Is there sentiment involved? It is a fine line, touching on emotion or sentiment. Overdone, sentimentality becomes gushiness, something we all can recognize. The only way to be completely safe from the charge is to write with so much restraint that emotion is virtually excluded. And that of course leads to poetry that has no feeling, which has no "human heat," as my friend Jim Harrison says. We want some of that human heat. Each of us who writes must find a balance between restraint and expressions of feeling.

I once wrote to the late Richard Hugo, who from time to time had been accused of sentimentality. I told him of having seen a silent movie in which Charlie Chaplin played a night janitor in a department store. There was a mezzanine above the main floor, with no safety rail. The dark store lay far below. To impress the young woman who was with him, Chaplin roller-skated back and forth, smiling and waving, altogether oblivious of the danger of plunging over the edge. The entire audience held its breath with every pass.

I told Hugo I thought his best poems managed to skate along the edge.

Seamus Heaney, winner of the Nobel Prize, writing on William Butler Yeats, said, "The aim of the poet and the poetry is finally to be of service, to ply the effort of the individual work into the larger of the community as a whole." That's good enough to cut out and pin over your work space.

Ted Kooser, US Poet Laureate (2004–2006) is a professor of English at the University of Nebraska–Lincoln. He worked for many years in the life insurance business, retiring as a vice president in 1999 to teach and write poetry. His writing is known for its clarity, precision and plainspoken style. Many of his poems speak to the discovery of beauty in ordinary things.

He is the author of eleven full-length collections of poetry, and his works have appeared in many periodicals including the *Atlantic Monthly*, *New Yorker*, *Poetry*, *The Nation*, *American Poetry Review* and elsewhere. He is also director of the American Life in Poetry project, which provides a free weekly column for newspapers and online publications featuring contemporary American poems.

Kooser is co-author with Steve Cox of a book of advice for writers, *Writing Brave and Free: Encouraging Words for People Who Want to Start Writing* (2005), and has his own acclaimed book, *Poetry Home Repair Manual: Practical Advice for Beginning Poets* ("Useful to poets at any level of achievement"—*Booklist*).

He and his wife, Kathleen Rutledge, former editor of the *Lincoln Journal Star,* live near the village of Garland, Nebraska.

"Father" is from *Delights and Shadows* (Copper Canyon Press, 2004). "August" is from *Sure Signs* (University of Pittsburgh Press, 1980). The poem that begins "The quarry road tumbles before me" is from *Winter Morning Walks: 100 Postcards to Jim Harrison* (Carnegie Mellon University Press, 2000).

Ted Kooser's website is www.tedkooser.com.

CREATIVITY & MOTIVATION

Three Creative Exercises

by Lisa Firke

FOR ME—and I don't really suppose I'm unique—the writing work-day is frequently spent struggling to find a balance point on the creative seesaw. On one end is my best friend, *Inertia*, the sweetest but most stolid kid on the playground. It seems as though her end of the seesaw is weighed to the ground with rocks and just won't budge.

On the high end of the seesaw, tiny, scrappy *New Work* tries valiantly to kick off, but her end is so high she is kicking off from air, and to no effect.

What New Work needs is someone or something to come sit with her on her end, to counterbalance dear Inertia. What you'll find here is my own growing set of counterweights—blockbusters, if you will—developed out of my own attempts to find a balance point.

Mix & Match

Brainstorm. This word gets used often, but just what does a person do to get their brain to *storm*? Where do ideas *come* from?

Everywhere and nowhere. All around you and only from inside you.

Our minds have a handy habit of disdaining lonely, unattached fragments of information. Sometimes all you need to do is juxtapose two wildly unrelated bits and then see what kind of connection your mind forms between them. You can give this process a nudge by intentionally sitting down with some random input (where's that list you made yesterday?), stipulate a time limit (set a timer, say 15 minutes?) and/or a length requirement (at least five sentences?), and *go*.

Here's an example, below, if you need one. The words were chosen randomly from the dictionary:

> *crucible*

> *bowl*

> *Briton*

> *gay*

> *plummet*

> *fairyland*

> *nationality*

> *roughen*

> *oxbow*

> *pullet*

I was the first person in our high school he told: "I'm gay." I don't know what I expected when Phil sat me down on the grass and then stared at his shoes, but this wasn't it. What I knew then about gayness could fit in a fingerbowl. At least I knew enough to know that this conversation was a crucible and what we were refining was courage (his) and forbearance (mine). Still, my confidence plummeted; what could I say? I was a pullet waiting for a skillet. "How do you—um—know?" was the best I came up with. "There was this Briton ..." he told me, shyly. That confused me since gayness was enough of a topic without bringing in subtleties of nationality. The whole conversation became like an oxbow lake, cut off from the flow of its beginnings. I mentioned how once I had ridden through the lowlands of Scotland in a dense fog. "It was almost like fairyland," I prattled, and then clapped my hand over my mouth. What had I said?

(1 paragraph, 15 minutes; 9 out of 10 random words used)

Pick a Bird

Pick a bird. This expression from Anne Lamott's priceless writer's guide (the one writer's manual you must take with you to a desert island) helps me remember the hardest and most basic thing:

> *Thirty years ago my older brother, who was ten years old at the time, was trying to get a report on birds written that he'd had three months to write. [It] was due the next day ... he was at the kitchen table close to tears, surrounded by binder paper and unopened books on birds, immobilized by the hugeness of the task ahead ... My father sat down beside him, put his arm around my brother's shoulder, and said, "Bird by bird, buddy. Just take it bird by bird."*
>
> —Anne Lamott, *Bird by Bird*

You don't write books, or screenplays, or even chapters or acts. You write words and sentences, passages and moments. All you have to write today is what you can see in the work at hand. Pick a bird. Give it your full attention. Show us.

Keep a Copy Book

I'm not talking about swiping someone else's creative expression. That's bad.

No, what I mean is getting out the old quill and pretending you're a monk, copying down scripture and other great literature and saving civilization while you're about it.

The idea behind this is very old-fashioned and yet it's also quite modern. What you copy—not photocopy, not cut-and-paste, not download, but *write out*, preferably by hand—somehow moves into your brain through the concert of your eyes and fingers. What you copy will stick with you, will become part of you, ready to call upon in your own way, as a more powerful syntax, a more muscular delivery, when you need it.

Copy passages you admire—fragments of dialogue, chapter openings, cliffhangers, flashpoints between characters—whatever you need. This is a practice that pays dividends over time. If you're stuck for something to copy today, try the passage below from Annie Dillard's essay, "Living Like Weasels."

A weasel is wild. Who knows what he thinks? He sleeps in his underground den, his tail draped over his nose. Sometimes he lives in his den for two days without leaving. Outside, he stalks rabbits, mice, muskrats, and birds, killing more bodies than he can eat warm, and often dragging the carcasses home. Obedient to instinct, he bites his prey at the neck, either splitting the jugular vein at the throat or crunching the brain at the base of the skull, and he does not let go. One naturalist refused to kill a weasel who was socketed into his hand as deeply as a rattlesnake. The man could in no way pry the tiny weasel off, and he had to walk half a mile to water, the weasel dangling from his palm, and soak him off like a stubborn label.

—Annie Dillard, from *Teaching a Stone to Talk*

Lisa Firke is a writer and designer who enjoys encouraging creativity in others. She publishes poems, short stories and essays, and is the author of "Blockbusters and Balancing Acts," the set of creativity prompts on her website from which this article is drawn.

Her web design company, Hit Those Keys (www.hitthosekeys.com) has designed sites for dozens of authors from Cynthia Leitich Smith to Brian Yansky. Firke also speaks to groups on the topic of making effective author websites.

Great Faith. Great Doubt. Great Effort.

by Rhonda Abrams

ON MY DESK, I have a small book of quotations that I look at from time to time for inspiration. The one that I refer to regularly as I run and build my business: "Great Faith. Great Doubt. Great Effort."

"Great Faith. Great Doubt. Great Effort." It takes all three to bring anything meaningful to fruition, and it's good to keep those in mind if you're trying to start or grow your own company.

1. Great Faith

To build a business—or start anything new—you have to believe in yourself and your ideas. You can envision something that others cannot. You think up a new business, process, design, technology, that hasn't existed before.

It is not only the quality of your ideas, but the strength of your faith in your ideas that will help you succeed. Moreover, it is your faith in yourself that attracts others to work with you, invest in your vision, support you as you pursue your dreams.

Great faith is exhilarating. But it is also exhausting.

Great faith is also exhausting. It's impossible to stay on an emotional high, even if things continually go well. And the reality is they will not always go well. When your business encounters the inevitable pitfalls, detours, slowdowns, you will be the one others will look to for reassurance.

That's when you have to have *great* faith. You will then have to call on the reserves of your own faith in your project to bring back the momentum, to reassure others. Your vision and dedication has to be strong enough to withstand the doubts of others and your own doubts as well.

When others believe you are drowning, you have to be the one who can still see the shore.

2. Great Doubt

Even the best-laid plans and the best-planned businesses can fail. You have to allow yourself to clearly see and anticipate potential problems. If you do not bring a healthy and respectful appreciation of the challenges you'll face when building a new business, you'll be unable to withstand the difficult times.

I have met many would-be entrepreneurs who have "fool-proof" ideas for businesses or inventions who will never succeed, because they do not have a sufficient level of doubt. Nothing is "fool-proof."

If you believe you cannot fail, then you won't be emotionally prepared to deal with the inevitable setbacks. Instead, you have to recognize that there will be great difficulties, and you need to be able to adapt, regroup, re-energize.

Moreover, you must challenge yourself. You must be willing to take a clear-headed look at your plans, your abilities, the strength of your competition so you can respond accordingly.

Great doubt is part of the process of building a success, not necessarily an indication of failure. I remind myself of that every time I find myself at 3 A.M., sleepless, daunted by all the things we have to do to make our business a success.

3. Great Effort

Nothing succeeds without hard work. I've seen hundreds of people with great ideas who have never made a dime.

Thoreau was wrong; if you build a better mousetrap, the world will not beat a path to your door. No, you've got to work hard to make your mousetrap a success. You've got to find financing for your mousetrap company; produce, market, and ship those mousetraps; deal with the personality conflict between your marketing manager and CFO; fight with the patent office over your patent. Then, you have to figure out how to respond when a competitor brings in cheaper, foreign imitations. Some days you'll wish you never thought up a better mousetrap!

No great businesses are built on ideas alone—they take perseverance and long, hard work. Late-night infomercials and email spam may offer "get rich quick" schemes, but don't be misled. One of Rhonda's Rules is "The way to be an overnight success is to work at it for years."

Great faith. Great doubt. Great effort. It takes all three. Others will challenge your ideas and question your chances of success. Without great faith, you'll be shaken. Without great doubt, you won't listen. Without great effort, they'll be right.

Rhonda Abrams directs The Planning Shop (www.planningshop.com) and has provided business planning expertise to hundreds of thousands of entrepreneurs for more than 15 years. She is author of the bestselling *The Successful Business Plan: Secrets & Strategies*, now in its 4th edition, and other books. Her nationally syndicated column on small-business strategies reaches 20 million readers a week in over 130 newspapers, and she is frequently invited to speak at conferences, corporate meetings and workshops.

This article is found at www.RhondaOnline.com, along with many others on business planning topics.

Baby Steps
by Bill O'Hanlon

MANY THERAPISTS related to the movie *What About Bob?* and laughed at the pop psychiatrist's prescriptive program called Baby Steps. Take small steps out of problems and into mental health. As silly as it sounded, many writers have successfully used the same strategy to get their writing done. A Chinese proverb makes the point: Enough shovels of earth—a mountain. Enough pails of water—a river.

You *can* break up the task of writing a novel into smaller pieces and smaller increments of time, take small actions, and break the mental barrier. Here's how:

Small Assignments

First, focus not on the whole task but on the smallest piece of the task. "I've been struggling with 'bookus interruptus' for years," says Sandy Beadle, a coauthor of one of my books. "My next book got waylaid when the energy went away. It had taken far too long and I lost focus. I knew that there was nothing like a deadline to get me focused, so I asked someone in my seminar if I could send her a page or a chapter every week. She didn't have to comment, or even read it—just catch it. That was 83 weeks ago, and I just mailed her my 79th file. Sometimes it's just a paragraph; sometimes it's a whole chapter. I recently told her I was going to arbitrarily call it finished when I got to 100 items, so that's not far off."

To divide your project up into bite-sized chunks, first make a simple outline. Next, make a more detailed outline with ideas for anecdotes, quotations, exercises, scenes, plot points, which characters are in the scene, and where it takes place. Then transfer each of those detailed points onto index cards that you can carry with you everywhere and write on. Keep them bundled with a rubber band in chapter or section order. "It's like driving at night in the fog," E.L. Doctorow once said. "You can only see as far as your headlights, but you can make the whole trip that way."

Small Increments

Big things can get done in small amounts of time. Max Barry wrote two novels—*Company* and *Jennifer Government*—during his lunch hours while working at Hewlett-Packard. It took him several years but he finally made enough money writing that he could quit his job and begin writing full time.

The most common strategy to get yourself to write when you're not writing is to commit to small amounts of time. Choose five or fifteen minutes. You can write more if you want. But you must write at least that amount of time per writing session. Writing begets writing, and not writing begets not writing. If you can trick yourself into writing a little, that trickle often creates a bigger flow.

Decide on a minimal amount of time and a realistic number of words or pages you're willing to commit to writing each week. Because the human mind often works better with a limited and achievable finish line, make limited time commitments as well. Decide you'll write every day for one month, or that you'll write three times per week for two weeks. If it works for you and is producing the writing you want, you can recommit or commit to a longer time period.

An experiment: For the next week, sit down with a kitchen timer and write for five minutes without lifting your fingers from the keyboard. Write on a particular pre-selected part of your book. No matter how busy you are, devote five minutes. Most people can write about 250 words in five minutes. That's about one page of a double-spaced manuscript. Do that every day for a year and you'll have a book.

Break the Mental Barrier

One of the reasons the small-steps method can be so useful is that it makes big projects seem less mentally and emotionally daunting. When my friend, psychologist Stephen Gilligan, was an adolescent, his father was an alcoholic. They would occasionally exchange harsh words, and his father's favorite put-down was, "Who the hell do you think you are?"

Many years later, his father sobered up and their relationship much improved, Stephen discovered that he had internalized his father's criticism. As he sat down to write his first book, he was stopped by a voice that asked, "Who the hell do you think you are, that you could write a book?" The voice stopped Stephen for some time until one day it occurred to him that if the question wasn't used as a put-down, it was actually a pretty useful question for self-exploration. "Who the hell do I think I am?" Stephen began to wonder. This take on the question broke the mental barrier and Stephen finally completed the first of several books he's written.

One way to change your counterproductive view of writing is to discover where you're focusing your attention and shift that attention to something else. For example, if you're focusing on the idea that you'll never get published or get an agent, and that stops you from writing, shift your focus to writing for the pleasure of it or getting the words down on paper. If you're focused on how you're not as good a writer as John Irving and that stymies you, compare yourself to a writer you think is bad but who still got published. If you're focused on getting all the words and ideas perfect and that paralyzes you, focus instead on the number of words you write each day.

In psychotherapy we use a technique called externalizing. First, identify unhelpful inner voices or ideas that mess up your motivation to write. Then, begin to consider them as external. That is, instead of thinking, I really sabotage myself by telling myself I'm not a good enough writer to get published, think of that voice or idea as an external influence. Try thinking, self-doubt is trying to convince me that I'm not good enough. Or, self-criticism is whispering unhelpful things into my ear today. This change can help you shift your relationship to those undermining voices and ideas and, at times, make it easier to challenge them.

For a more physical way of dealing with your internal criticisms, write your unhelpful thoughts or ideas on a piece of paper or draw some representation of them, and then burn, tear up or bury them. For example, if you're having writer's block, write the words "Writer's Block" on a piece of paper, burn it, and flush the ashes down the toilet.

Here's another variation on this idea: carry a heavy rock around with you (in your purse, backpack, or briefcase) to represent your barriers, fears, or problems in your writing. Carry it for several days until you become really annoyed with the burden. Then—without getting caught—place the rock in the garden of someone who annoys you. Or, on a more positive note, throw the rock in a lake and enjoy watching your fears symbolically sink out of sight.

There's something in the human psyche that can actually use this method to purge unhelpful influences. (If you want to find out more about this method, search the term "narrative therapy" on the Internet.)

Develop Your Identity as a Writer

Before I wrote my first book, I'd never known anyone who had written a book and published it. I was clueless about how to proceed. But these days, I think of myself as a writer.

That identity shift took time. At first I thought of myself as "someone who had written books," not "a writer." I kept thinking I wouldn't be a writer until I developed writerly habits: writing every day from 8:00 A.M. to noon; wearing corduroy blazers with patches on the elbows; smoking a pipe and sipping bourbon while pounding at the typewriter keys. None of these things ever happened and yet I kept cranking out books. Eventually I began to list "writer" on my immigration and customs cards when returning from overseas—that was the first element in stepping into an identity as a writer. Next I began to say "I write books" when someone asked me what kind of work I did. That gradually shifted to "I'm a writer."

You may have known early on that you were a writer. Or maybe you weren't so lucky or clear. You have to move toward thinking of yourself as a writer. It really supports the process of writing—opens the possibilities of writing and completing books—if you begin to think of yourself as a writer. One of my friends says she thinks of herself as "a thinker, not a writer." She has, at times, shared her thoughts and ideas with someone, only to later see them in print with the person taking credit. She gets annoyed when she sees them writing what she didn't, but still can't imagine herself as a writer. She's afraid no one will read what she writes. Contrast her self-image with that of Isaac Asimov, who once said: "If my doctor told me I had only six minutes to live, I wouldn't brood. I'd type a little faster."

Do whatever it takes to convince yourself you're a writer. Get a mock-up of a book cover with your title and name. Get published in the local rag. Whatever it is, start doing those things and someday, in the near future, you'll live your dream of being a writer.

To do that takes action.

Don't just dream it, do it.

Bill O'Hanlon (www.billohanlon.com) has authored or co-authored 28 books. He regularly speaks about writing and offers seminars for people who want to write and publish books. This article was excerpted from *Write Is a Verb* (Writer's Digest Books, 2007), and appeared in the February 2008 edition of *Writer's Digest* magazine.

Writing and Mothering:
How I (sort of) Do Both

by Shannon Hale

AT SOME POINT in the young and hopeful stage of my writing career, I realized that two things rarely went together—successful writer and successful mother. Oh, there are plenty of father writers, successful in at least one of those trades, but many of the great literary women I could think of, and most of my women writing professors, did not have children. I read a quote by Jamaica Kincaid saying that she could not have produced her earlier works if she'd had children at the time. The thought frightened me. There was nothing in this world I wanted as passionately as having a family and being able to write books, and I feared that the two just could not go together.

Happily, I was wrong! Let me confess that I am by no means an expert at this subject. At this writing, I have one child, age 15 months. I've met fabulous women who somehow mother six children and create great works of fiction, and I'm tiny and shivering in their shadows. But quite often I get the question: How do you write and be a mother? So here are my thoughts.

I got a head start. Obviously, this tactic won't help everyone. I know many women who did not start to write until their littlest one was in school, but in my case, I was quite lucky to figure out at a young age that I had to be a writer. By the time I got married, I had received an MFA in Creative Writing and been in the habit of writing every day (except I take Sundays off). Habits are powerful and much easier to form, I've noticed, when I have leisure time. When my first child was born, *The Goose Girl* had been published, and the week before I'd sent my final draft of *Enna Burning* to my editor.

I make and meet goals. I really know of no better way for any writer to finish a book, with or without children. In a mother's case, it's a non-negotiable. My goals change. Before Max, it was 1500 words/day, when he was a newborn, it was 800/day, and now it's 1000/day. I find a goal that is challenging but possible, and I keep it. If I don't make my daily goal, I stay up at night writing, and if I simply can't do it one day, I make it up on Saturday. I don't think I've missed a weekly goal in a couple of years. It's like dieting—the first time you cheat, it's that much harder the next time you see a Snickers.

My writing time is sacred time. Not everyone understands this one. I know I've come across as *uncooperative* to many folks as I turn down lunch invites and requests for author visits, but I have to be so firm with myself. Max's naptime is my writing time. I turn off the phone (repeat: I turn off the phone, non-negotiable), I resist responding to emails or exploring websites or playing mind-numbing rounds of computer solitaire (Vegas game rules). I don't even eat, often getting around to lunch at 4 P.M. This is not especially healthy, I know, but those two to three hours are my writing time. If I didn't set aside a certain time every day and stick with it, I'd probably be well fed, but my books would be starving.

I make Max my world. There are days when I have to leave Max with a sitter to go do author visits or even go out of town, so I make sure that my mornings and afternoons alone with my boy are wonderful fun. We play hard, we talk and read books, putter around, go outside, visit dogs. It makes it easier to have my writer times when I feel confident I am devoting myself the rest of the time to my family.

I accept the fact that my house will never be clean. OK, really I should say, I plan on accepting that fact any day now. I wish my carpets were vacuumed weekly, that I had a meal plan and didn't panic when 6 P.M. rolls around and the kitchen is stone cold. Our backyard is literally a back *yard*, and I still can't manage to keep it weed free and full of happy plants. Really, you'd be shocked. And don't look under my bed. But my priorities are: Max's needs, husband time, writing, feeding self, sleep, bathing self, church volunteer responsibilities, paying bills … housework comes somewhere down here, maybe after essential grooming.

I know I need to write. It's easy to feel guilty as a mother. There are endless demands on us, particularly as the number of children grow and as they grow up and are expected to be taking piano lessons, dance lessons, nuclear physics lessons. Children need their mothers to read to them, do homework, listen, anticipate disaster and chop off its head. But I also know that Max will always need a mostly sane mother, a happy mother, a mother to be proud of. And I know that when I'm not writing, I'm not happy, and the unwritten stories start to haunt me and tug on my sleeves and demand words on a page, and I cease to be the functioning kind of sane and start swatting at invisible characters. Mamas need our creative output, too. My finger painting is books.

Update: November 2007

Before I begin, let me acknowledge that there are superstar moms who have nine children and still write, so I know I'm not particularly harried. But I have reached that new stage, that more awkward stage, where there is more than one child and one never naps. How do I keep writing? When do I find the time? Here's the truth: there's always time. It is not easy. If you wanted a nice easy hobby, you wouldn't have picked writing books. You'd be knitting scarves or raising an orchid. You want to write books because you must, because those stories and characters and words won't leave you alone. So you will find the time. Here's some more thoughts on how I've adapted to my new situation:

I mostly fail. It feels like that most days. And I have to let myself be okay with it. My output is significantly decreased, my word-count goals very tiny. But I am first a mother and second a writer. And I love being a mother of small children. Life is very, very good. Times and seasons for everything, my mother-in-law reminds me. Times and seasons.

I try to know my limits. I'm not going to keep up a book a year. I can't do as many book tours, I can't answer email and do local school visits and book clubs. I can't make homemade Halloween costumes or keep my scrapbook up to date. I can only be a mother and write a little on the side, and occasionally take a shower.

I get my 15 minutes a day. Everyone can make this a reality. Fifteen minutes. That's reachable. And sometimes opportunity allows for more. Sometimes the baby is napping and my toddler will sit still and play by himself while I write for 45 minutes. And sometimes he sits beside me and holds down the space bar. Ah, helpful, helpful lad. You win some, you lose some. And it's okay.

I use my brain. Whenever I have some space for thought, I've trained my brain to return to the story. Showers are particularly productive. Driving. Folding laundry. I can keep writing even when I don't have time to sit at my computer because my brain keeps working on the story. This, for me, is absolutely essential. I could not be a writer if I didn't allow (and insist upon) daydreaming about the stories.

Keep notes! You get an idea for a line, a scene, a character, and you think you'll remember. You won't. I have to make myself write it down. Sometimes they're bad ideas, many I'll never use, but I write them all down. Keeping a notepad in my purse (a.k.a. diaper bag) and by my bed really helps. This helps me focus on my kids more, because once I write the idea down, I know it's safe, and I can let my attention leave worrying about it and return to them.

I keep reading. I know so many people who give up reading once they start writing, but I find reading good books (besides being a blast) inspires the same part of my brain where I create stories and sentences. I really believe being a reading writer will make you a better and more productive writing writer.

I take advantage of what I can *now* and not try to wait for a mythical era of free time. Megan Whalen Turner, fabulous writer and mother of school age children, recently told me, "a number of people warned me that I shouldn't expect to get any real work done until my youngest child was in school full time. But, I didn't find small children any impediment to writing. I hired a babysitter (several great ones, actually, thank you Trisha Falvey, thank you Nancy Schaffstall!) and wrote *The Thief* and *The Queen of Attolia*. It wasn't that hard to find someone to feed babies, change babies, and take babies to the park. Then they grew up and went to school. You can't pay someone else to go on field trips for you, or help them with their homework. Never mind that when you hire a babysitter you get to set the schedule and hire them when it is convenient for you. The elementary school is just not as accommodating. So write, quick! Quick!"

The truth is, if I wasn't a mother, I could get so much more done. For one thing, I could say yes to all the local school visits and book clubs and signing requests I get. I could tour the country more, doing 20-city tours instead of four-city tours. I'd sell a lot more books. I'd make more money, have a wider fan base ... and I wouldn't have my amazing little sweethearts. Sheesh. Not even worth it. I'm so so so happy to be a mother, so honored to have these little people in my family. Whatever your passion is, you can see it through and still be a mother. Somehow. Bit by bit. And all the rest of us working mothers, creative mothers, fitting-it-in mothers will be hooting for you and shouting, "You rock."

Shannon Hale started writing books at age ten and never stopped. After 19 years of writing and many rejections, she published her first book, *The Goose Girl*, chosen by the ALA as a Teens' Top Ten book. *Enna Burning* and *River Secrets* followed as companion books to *Goose*. She is now the author of five award-winning young adult novels, including the bestselling Newbery Honor book *Princess Academy*. *Austenland* is her first book for adults. She and her husband are co-writing a series of graphic novels, and live with their two small children in Salt Lake City, Utah.

Her website, at www.squeetus.com, offers advice for writers drawn from her own experience, including this article.

Keeping the Faith

by Kirby Larson

My Newbery (Honor) year has been magical ... but it has kept me away from my writing. My friend, Roland Smith, has lectured me that it *is* possible to write on the road. I have no doubt that it is possible to write on the road ... for him. Not for me.

Finally, there I got a break in the tour schedule. Home sweet home! Nothing to do but apply a liberal dose of bum glue and stick myself in my writing chair. I knew there was an important reason for telling the story I'd been working on but it was resisting any of my efforts to get it whipped into shape. Last week, I spent every single day like a modern day Jacob, wrestling with words. And I produced thousands, one or two of which aren't bad.

But I still didn't know exactly where I was headed. I recalled the words that had inspired me so while writing *Hattie Big Sky*, words shared by YA author Randy Powell: "You've got to write through the bad stuff." I forced myself to stay in my chair and plunk away, even when I could hear the junk drawer calling me to come reorganize it.

Last night, my sheer stubbornness paid off. Though it kept me awake much of the night, I finally figured out what I couldn't see before. I had the hook, the theme, the raison d'etre of my story. It was the classic example of what Picasso and others have said: "Inspiration only finds you when you're working."

Maybe my epiphany will help you. If you are stuck, dedicate the next few weeks to writing away, no matter what. This sounds trite but keep the faith. There is a reason you've been led to write a particular story. Honor that impulse with the hard work needed to bring the story to life.

Then, you can go clean out the junk drawer.

Kirby Larson is the author of the 2007 Newbery Honor book, *Hattie Big Sky*, a young adult novel she wrote inspired by her great-grandmother, Hattie Inez Brooks Wright, who homesteaded by herself in eastern Montana as a young woman. In addition, Larson has written three books for children, including the award-winning picture book, *The Magic Kerchief*.

This is based on a December 2007 entry from her blog, which can be found at her website, www.kirbylarson.com.

Brainstorming

by Laini Taylor

WRITERS ARE ASKED all the time, "Where do you get your ideas?" Well, getting ideas is the easy part. They just come. They come from stray thoughts and tidbits gleaned from dusty old folklore books; they come from dreams and memories, from headlines and bizarre facts and conversations overheard in the street; they can come from writing prompts, and perhaps from one perfect, shining sentence that emerges from the middle of a wild, jumbled freewrite.

And, this is important: they come *when you make them come.*

Louis Pasteur said "Chance favors the prepared mind," and I find that ideas favor a prepared mind too. The more you cast your mind out into thoughts and dreams, the more you observe and read and wonder and think, the more ideas you will "chance upon." A writer is on safari for ideas every single moment of his or her life, waking and sleeping. And when an idea alights upon you, you capture it. Write it down. It's yours now, to do with what you will.

But where to begin? That's the hard part—not getting ideas, but doing something with them.

Brainstorming

Ideas have developmental stages. For me, they usually begin not as a full-blown premise or plot, but as a small "seed," perhaps just enough to scrawl down in the margin of a notebook. It might be a general idea like, "a faerie who hunts devils," or a random line like, "Avery Dry, who put her soul in the collection plate," or it might be a single evocative word, like "wishbone."

The seed of my graphic novel, *The Drowned,* was an image from a dream. In it, a desolate village sat at the very edge of the sea. It was hidden beneath the water most of the time, and only at the lowest ebb tide was it exposed to the air. It was barnacle-covered and lonesome, with a thin wisp of music drifting from it. I know whence this dream-image most likely arose—years ago I traveled to Cornwall, where the tides are so dramatic that even the roots of islands are exposed so you can walk all the way around them. It was magical, and I guess it kicked around in my mind until one night it worked its way into a dream, with a village thrown in.

It still didn't qualify as an "idea." It was only a seed. The next step was to ask myself questions. Here, the obvious one was: Who might live in such a village? Figure that out and there might just be a story in it.

This is where brainstorming comes in, and I *love* this part of the process. It amazes me anew each time a simple word or image grows from a seed into a big, complex idea, and into a *story*.

A good place to start "brainstorming" is just by freewriting every-thing you know about your idea so far. Don't worry at all about the "writing" at this phase. This is just about getting ideas out—every pos-sible idea, not just the first ones to come to mind. Write those down and reach past them. Think and daydream and brainstorm.

You want to know about your characters, their motivations, the world of your story, the why of your plot. You want to know when, where, you want to begin to feel texture, to see color, for the story to begin to come alive. You want stray ideas to bump into each other and coalesce, to begin to give depth and detail to your story. The chil-dren's book writer Sid Fleischman said, "You need two ideas to rub together to start a fire," and I have found this to be true. And not just two, but many. Brainstorming is about herding ideas, matchmaking ideas, swirling ideas together and seeing what, by alchemy and magic, merges to become something new, vibrant, and exciting.

At this stage, be open. Think of it like the auditions for *American Idol*. You have to listen to the terrible singers—you have to listen to *all* the singers—to ferret out the tiny handful of good ones.

As you're writing down everything you know about your idea, you'll start to see how much you *don't* know. So, start asking yourself questions and trying to answer them. Answer them with "maybes." Really cross-examine your ideas. Ask "What if?" a hundred times, ask "Why?" and "How?" Don't settle for the first thing that pops into your head. Cast your imagination out far and deep, like a fishing net that is going to haul up strange and unexpected things. Yes, you will have to toss a lot of these things back, but there will be, glimmering among them, treasures you never could have found up on the surface.

And when your brainstorming yields the right idea, you'll know. You'll feel "the snick."

The Snick

How I love the snick. It's the sound and feeling of a puzzle piece fitting into place. You know what I mean: you instantly feel the rightness of it, the ease. When you're forcing a piece, you know it too. It's awkward, you have to work too hard to jam it in. Pay attention to those feelings and never settle for a piece that doesn't fit, even if it *almost* does. Keep brainstorming. Demand "the snick" every time, to every question.

You know when you're reading a book and you feel the intrusion of the author all of a sudden, you feel them trying to *make* something happen. Characters might behave in unbelievable ways; a plotline or dilemma might get wrapped up in an awkward manner. As soon as you feel that, you know the author gave up too easily, stopped brainstorming, and went ahead with something wrong, artificial, awkward. You don't want that. If you work hard enough and think long enough, you'll find the right puzzle piece. You'll *invent* the right puzzle piece.

Plus, the great thing about "the snick" is that when it comes, the story has a tendency to spurt forward with exuberant ease, to get unstuck, to get *fun*. And that's the best thing a writer can wish for!

More Brainstorming

And, it's not like I do all brainstorming at the beginning of the writing process and then the rest of the writing is smooth sailing. I come back to brainstorming again and again all along the way, addressing issues as they arise. When a plot point that seemed like it would work turns out to feel wrong and forced, I resort to brainstorming. When a scene doesn't feel as rich and alive as I want it to, I brainstorm. When I need to figure out what a character would say or do, I brainstorm.

It's a different mindset, a free place where you can stand back and see clearly, like a painter stepping away from the canvas, deciding his next brush stroke, or indeed, seeing mistakes that were not visible up close. I write down these ponderings and "what ifs," this spew of possible ideas, in a "working document" I have open beside my manuscript document. It is an unprecious place that exists for just this purpose, and it is crucial to my process, so that my manuscript might stay relatively pristine, with all the mess and jumble of wild ideas happening elsewhere.

There's so much that you will discover as you write and brainstorm and write and brainstorm. So much will come up that you never could have anticipated. You need to keep your ability to come up with new ideas every step of the way. Never feel that you're "married" to an idea, even if it was the original seed that sparked the whole story. You might find that it has to go, like a scaffolding that comes down after a mural is painted. Maybe that was its only purpose, to hold you up while you found the real idea.

Be open. Be rigorous. Think hard. Daydream relentlessly. Stretch your imagination. Audition thousands of ideas. Write them all down, use some, and keep others for later.

And have fun!

Idea-Generating Exercise

Make a long, long list of things that "light your mind on fire," juicy, colorful things that particularly appeal to *you*. Think of the kinds of story elements and details and settings that, if you read them on a book jacket, would make you instantly hungry to read that book. Have a freewriting mindset as you do this, and do not discriminate.

Your list might have simple snippets like *carnivals, ballet, ornithology, tattoos, cupcakes,* and it might have more complex ideas like *possessing hidden gifts* or *seeing someone with new eyes,* and it might have the seeds of plots that run to paragraphs.

Open and open and open your mind.

Set out to write down 500 things, so you will have to get past the obvious and into the strange and unexpected.

Let these ideas and images mingle, let them spark new ideas and images.

Choose some to use as prompts for freewriting exercises. Stories *will* come.

Laini Taylor is a writer of children's and young adult fantasy novels. Her first book, *Faeries of Dreamdark: Blackbringer* (Putnam) was published in 2007 and will shortly be followed by *Silksinger*. Her first book for teens, *Goblin Fruit* (Arthur A. Levine Books, Scholastic), will be out in 2009. Each of its three tales of supernatural romance emerged from writing prompts, in which she is a true believer.

Taylor lives in Portland, Oregon, with her husband, illustrator Jim Di Bartolo. You can find out more about Taylor and her books, blog and writing website Not For Robots at www.lainitaylor.com.

Sock Monkeys and Stegosauruses

by Eve Porinchak

I'VE HAD a hideous headache since Friday. For me, this is rare and can only mean one thing. No, not a hangover. I don't even drink (that much ... on Mondays ... in the summer ... during months that end in 'gust).

No, I've self-diagnosed a Writer's Blockage.

It's not that I'm at a loss for ideas for my YA romance-in-progress. Problem is that there are too many ideas swimming aimlessly around my brain, clogging up the place. It's more like a Writer's Clot, a literary aneurysm, if you will. The pressure is building, causing my head to feel like it might, at any second, explode *Scanners*-style all over my white carpet.

Believe it or not, a random blog comment from Lisa Yee led to the most bizarre of cures. She said, and I quote, "One time I couldn't write until I had a sock monkey. I know it sounds weird now, but I swear the lack of a sock monkey shut me down."

Hmm. Sock monkey. Sock monkey. Where on earth could one get a sock—?

Then I remembered that last time I was in Florida visiting my family, my eight-year-old nephew gave me ... wait for it ... wait for it ... *a sock monkey!* (Dressed as "Heidi" with yellow braided pigtails and, for some odd reason, a lasso. But, hey, a sock monkey nonetheless.)

When I put Heidi sock monkey next to my computer today, strange things happened.

A sense of calmness took over.

Ideas began to flow and make sense.

I took copious notes on my main theme.

Just as I was staring at the ceiling trying to figure out how to weave this theme with the others, a link to a random *Salon* article popped up on my computer ... and it was perfect! It pretty much summed up (in a strangely scientific way) my main character's belief system and motivation for acting the way she does, which hadn't occurred to me before today.

Soon, I could feel the swelling in my aneurysm shrinking.

While writing my first book, *Ring of Fire*, I suffered a severe three-month blockage. One day I woke up and felt better, and the story began to unfold and write itself like buttah.

In retracing my steps to figure out what changed for me back then, I remembered Robin's son, Luke, brought me a rubber toy stegosaurus and left it on my dining table one day. If I remember correctly, it wasn't until that rubber dinosaur appeared that I actually got a firm handle on what exactly I was doing with my book.

Sock monkeys? Stegosauri? Who knew??

As I'm proofreading this post, I realize how outlandish it sounds. But, on the other hand ... *whatever works, man.* J.K. Rowling has her Potter-ites. John Green has his Nerdfighters.

And I got my sock monkeys!

Eve Porinchak is a young adult writer whose work in progress, *Ring of Fire*, is "a modern day *Lord of the Flies* set in a mountain summer camp for inner-city kids, where a friendly game of Capture the Flag develops into a war over boundaries and reputation, and ultimately parallels the evolution of contemporary Los Angeles street gangs." This piece was posted August 2007 on the group blog The Disco Mermaids, found at www.discomermaids.blogspot.com, featuring Porinchak and fellow writers Robin Mellom and Jay Asher.

THE CRAFT OF WRITING

Action Is Boring

by Tess Gerritsen

IN THE AIRPORT in Zurich, I bought a paperback novel for the flight home. I wasn't looking for heavy literature, just something to keep me entertained for the seven-hour flight, so I chose it based on the back-cover description, which promised a fast-paced thriller with an international setting. Within the first chapter, bam, someone died a violent death. About every other chapter after that, there was a gun battle or a car chase or a fistfight. The protagonists were chased across several countries, by a relentless cabal of bad guys, and everyone was after a piece of evidence that would change the world. There was a fall off a cliff, some death-defying escapes, and countless ambushes.

I was bored out of my mind.

I wanted to stuff the book in the seat-back pocket for some other hapless airline traveler, but I still had five hours left in the flight and nothing else to read, so I persevered, more as a writers' exercise than for entertainment. When I finished the book, I thought about why the book didn't work for me. On the surface, you'd think it should be exciting, with all the chases and derring-do. Yet it lacked tension. It was all action, and no suspense.

I have the same reaction while I'm watching films. I find that the most boring part of a thriller movie is often the car chase. That's when I yawn and glance at my watch, waiting for something more interesting to happen. During the most recent James Bond film, I thought the action sequences were okay, but what really got me to perk up was the dialogue between Bond and the Eva Green character on the train ride. The verbal sparring, the double entendres, the undercurrent of sexual tension—that's what I call suspense.

When it comes to books, I've come to realize that action on the page is sometimes the least interesting part of the whole story. Real suspense lies in the buildup toward conflict or danger, the threat of something terrible happening. When it finally does turn into action, all that tension is released and leaks out of the story like a deflating balloon.

A lot of writers confuse suspense with action. They think that for a book to be thrilling, it needs lots of fights and gun battles and falling bodies. Well, let me tell you about four books that kept me riveted to the page, books that were loaded with heart-pounding suspense, yet weren't overstuffed with action. *No Time for Goodbye* by Linwood Barclay and *Remembering Sarah* by Chris Mooney were by male authors who managed to inject amazing suspense just by the conflicts and crises of their characters. Once I'd started these two books, I couldn't stop. They didn't need action scenes dripping with testosterone. Instead, they relied on something far more difficult to achieve: characters whose lives are in such crisis, you have to keep reading to see what happens.

I can think of two other books that managed this feat. One is an older book, *Killing Me Softly* by Nicci French. I can't even remember any violence in the book, but I remember almost unbearable tension toward the end, as the heroine finally discovers the truth about her lover. Another memorable book is *Ice Trap* by debut author Kitty Sewell. It has no violence that I can recall, yet the author manages to set up so much psychological conflict and that I didn't really care if it was a thriller, a murder mystery, or just a novel about twisted characters in the far north—I had to find the answer to the puzzle that the author introduces within the first few chapters.

I think it takes far more skill to write a suspenseful novel with no action. Action scenes are easy. Anyone can write a chase scene or a murder scene, and less skillful writers confuse action with suspense. They think a gun battle is all you need to make a chapter exciting. Instead it may have the opposite effect. It may bore readers like me, readers who just flip past all the running and shooting and screeching tires.

Pay attention the next time you read a thriller novel. When does your heart pound, your hand go sweaty? Is it during the gun battle? Or is it during the pages leading up to the gun battle? Is it the dread and impending doom? Or is it when the bullets actually start to fly?

Internationally bestselling author Tess Gerritsen was trained as a physician and holds an MD. While on maternity leave, she began to write fiction. In 1987, her first novel, a romantic thriller, was published, followed by eight more romantic suspense novels. Her first medical thriller, *Harvest*, was released in hardcover in 1996, and quickly rose to the *New York Times* bestseller list.

Subsequent suspense novels include: *Life Support, Bloodstream, Gravity, The Surgeon, The Apprentice, The Sinner, Body Double, Vanish, The Mephisto Club,* and most recently, *The Bone Garden* (2007). Her books have been translated into 31 languages, and more than 15 million copies have been sold around the world. She has won both mystery's Nero Wolfe Award and romance's Rita Award. *Publishers Weekly* has dubbed her the "medical suspense queen." Now retired from medicine, she writes full time.

Her website is www.tessgerritsen.com.

Storytelling Techniques

by Ira Glass

ONE OF THE THINGS that's really important if you're making stories is to understand the building blocks of stories. One of the things you *don't* want to do is to think about it the way you learned in high school. In high school, we're all taught that the way that you write is that there's a topic sentence. And then there's the facts, which fill out the argument.

Instead, in making stories, you have two very powerful basic building blocks.

One is the anecdote. The anecdote is literally just a sequence of actions. What is a story in its purest form? A story in its purest form is somebody saying: this happened, and that led to this next thing, and that led to this next thing.

The power of the anecdote is so great that in a way, no matter how boring the material is, in a story form, an anecdote has a momentum in and of itself.

Okay, I'm going to think of the most boring possible story. There's a guy ...

> ... and he wakes up. And he's lying in bed.
> And the house is very, very quiet. Just unearthly quiet.
> So he sits up, and he puts his feet on the floor. And he walks to the door of his bedroom.
> Again, it's just very, very quiet.
> He walks down the stairs, looks around ...
> It's just unusually quiet.

This is the most boring possible fact pattern. And yet, there's suspense in it. It feels like something's going to happen.

The reason why is that it's a sequence of events. He's moving from space to space. You can feel through its form, as one thing leads to the next … that you're on a train that has a destination. That he's going to find something.

The other thing about that little anecdote: it's raising a question from the beginning. You want bait. You want to constantly be raising questions. In that little story, the bait is that the house is very quiet.

So the question that's hanging in the air is: why?

And it's implied that any question you raise, you're going to answer. You want to constantly be raising questions and answering them—from the beginning of the story. The whole shape of the story is that you're throwing out questions, to keep people watching or listening, and then answering them along the way.

The other big building block, your other tool, is to have a moment of reflection. By that I mean, at some point, somebody needs to say: Here's why the hell you're listening to this story. Here's the point of this story. Here's the bigger *something* that we're driving at.

The bane of my existence is that often you have an anecdote that just *kills* … and it's so surprising … and so many things happen, and you meet these great characters …

And it means absolutely nothing. It's just completely predictable. It doesn't tell you anything new.

It's your job to be ruthless, to understand when either you don't have a sequence of action that works, or you don't have the moment of reflection that works.

You're going to need both. The two, together, interwoven, will make something that's larger than the sum of its parts.

Ira Glass is host and executive producer of the nationally syndicated show *This American Life* (www.thislife.org), produced on radio since 1995 by Chicago Public Radio and more recently on television by Showtime. Glass has been in public radio for more than thirty years, working as everything from tape-cutter and newscast writer to editor, producer, reporter and host.

He is also editor of *The New Kings of Nonfiction* (Riverhead, 2007), an anthology of examples of outstanding journalism rooted in good storytelling.

This piece is transcribed from a video produced by Current TV as part of a training module for beginning video producers (http://current.com/producerResources.htm). Current is a global peer-to-peer news and information network, the first to feature Viewer Created Content, which now comprises over one-third of its programming.

Sweat the Small Stuff

by Stephen Delaney

THEN WE NOTICED *that in the second pillow was the indentation of a head. One of us lifted something from it, and leaning forward, that faint and invisible dust dry and acrid in the nostrils, we saw a long strand of iron-gray hair.*

Why does this paragraph, the emotional hammer-blow of Faulkner's classic story "A Rose for Emily," still reverberate so forcefully after so many readings? Even detached from the story as it is here, we sense the author's presence as he leads us on, gently planting that impression on the pillow to flit across our brain's synapses and then drawing out the last sentence toward that inevitable, brutal word.

I *know* how the story will end. I've read it in countless anthologies, and the ending *still* works its magic. It's not just suspense that holds me, I think, but something smaller, in the details themselves. A faint impression, floating specks of dust, that single, wavering strand. We've entered the realm of the small, the invisible or the barely visible.

It's this realm I'd like to explore. How are small things treated in fiction, and what purposes do they serve?

Of course, it's a truism that good writing depends on the details. Scan any page of fiction and it's hard to miss at least some sensory details. But I'm not talking about just *any* details here. I'm talking about things that are *physically small*. How small? That can get tricky. Faulkner didn't tell us the dimensions of Emily's hair (he does tell us it's long), but I don't think anyone would argue that a strand of hair isn't small. For simplicity's sake, we'll say that if seeing the thing strains human eyes (notice everyone leans forward as the hair is lifted), we'll say it's small.

Why should I care about something so trivial? you ask yourself. Small. Tiny. Minute. Humble. Unimportant. Petty. *Unworthy*. These are some of the synonyms for "small," according to my dog-eared thesaurus. And I think they say a lot. Our perspective is the only correct one. Things we can't see don't exist, unless they happen to make our eyes water and noses dribble, or if that small insignificant thing happens to be whining in our ears and is *out for blood.*

Today, more than 300 years after Leeuwenhoek stuck that water droplet under his lens and saw his "wretched beasties," with the knowledge that trillions of microbes within us do much of our inner housework for us, we're all aware that small doesn't always mean petty. And I think our literature bears this out. If we imagine a work of fiction as a house, small things aren't just the clapboard and trim (though they often are), but they can be structural elements as well. A single hair can make our emotions peak. When sketching a character, that hair can add vertiginous perspective and depth.

Although small things are more commonly used in poetry, since they lend themselves to brief insights and emotional flashes more easily than to sustained narrative drama, I think in fiction they've been overlooked. Let's separate a few of them out from their contexts—focusing on those that influence the plot or have particular resonance—and see what they might do for your *own* writing.

The Many Uses of Small

Small things that irritate: a pebble in one's shoe, the tree root you trip over (again) in the front yard, a flicker of condescension in a friend's smile. The seemingly insignificant intersects with one's own path, forcing itself into view. In fiction, the small thing presses on the character's consciousness, becomes as real as anything else. It threatens and agitates. It's not an enemy—it's just following instincts or physical laws, or doesn't show enough to judge by—but it isn't exactly a friend, either. It's more *out of place* than anything else. This type is a convention in ghost stories, of course—the creak on the stairs, the waft of cold air. The small thing only seems small, but something larger and potentially dangerous looms behind it. In W.W. Jacobs' "The Monkey's Paw," the sergeant-major visiting the Whites' house states, "To look at … it's just an ordinary little paw, dried to a mummy." Of course, nothing could be further from the truth! Its ordinariness is its perfect disguise, preventing the characters—though not the reader—from seeing its true nature.

Small things can be used to startle, to intensify an already troubled emotional field. In Edgar Allan Poe's story "Ligeia," after Rowena has died from a mysterious illness and the narrator stands by her corpse, he says, "At length it became evident that a slight, a very feeble, and a barely noticeable tinge of color had flushed up within the cheeks, and along the sunken small veins of the eyelids." These details offer little reassurance, however, since his imagination and senses can deceive him. In an instant, these flickers of life are withdrawn: her "lips doubly shriveled and pinched up in the ghastly expression of death."

There's always an unstable element to the very small, since they might at any moment (like the Cheshire cat with his smile) wink themselves out of existence. Things at the edge of perception are suspect, dwelling in the realm of fancy, hallucination or even madness.

Small things aren't always unfriendly. They are often in league with the poor, the working class, the economically and socially powerless. Children notice them because they haven't yet learned *not* to notice them. Small things can trigger the imagination, lending them special powers. They can provide means of escape, of discovery, of gaining prestige in the eyes of other children. They offer themselves as (relatively) safe companions. In his story "The Grasshopper and the Bell Cricket," Yasunari Kawabata conveys a child's values through both repetition and detail:

> "Oh! It's not a grasshopper. It's a bell cricket." The girl's eyes shone as she looked at the small brown insect.
>
> "It's a bell cricket! It's a bell cricket!" The children echoed in an envious chorus.
>
> "It's a bell cricket. It's a bell cricket."

By readjusting our own (possibly) jaded values, Kawabata makes us re-see familiar things, revealing their inherent drama. He makes them glow with an inner light—the light of potentiality, their power to influence people and events. They illuminate their own being as well as the things around them. A cricket is dramatic because the children *believe* it is; their belief—and the author's—is what grants it narrative force. A small thing can overcome fiction's creaky resistance to quiet, seemingly unremarkable moments.

Women in traditional roles are surrounded by the small, whether they be the needle and thread to sew the hem of a skirt or a dusty film forming on top of a curio shelf. But small things can also balk at tradition's bounds. In Charlotte Perkins Gilman's "The Yellow Wallpaper," the wallpaper's patterns extend to the narrator an escape route, a place for her imagination to roam. The practical man (her husband) has no need for small things. What good are they to me? he asks. His wife's mental retreat is ultimately an act of defiance: She *won't* deny small things their imaginative pull, which artists and children naturally acknowledge.

In Nathaniel Hawthorne's "Young Goodman Brown," the appearance of Faith's pink ribbon is the turning point of the story: "But something fluttered lightly down through the air and caught on the branch of a tree. The young man seized it, and beheld a pink ribbon." At this moment, he knows in his heart she's lost. As in "A Rose for Emily," an emotional bang is announced with a whisper. The reader closes his eyes, expecting a blow, a figurative punch in the gut, only to feel something else: something so light and airy, it's even more unsettling. The ribbon is animated by qualities Hawthorne grants it—Faith's innocence and gentle grace. But the fact that it's found in the woods shifts its meaning, as it takes on the devil's subtle guise.

Sometimes, small things are noticed out of simple habit or need: the father panhandles on the street as his son, dizzy with hunger, strains to see the word "oysters" written on a restaurant's tiny placard (Anton Chekhov's "Oysters"), or the bellboy stoops down for the champagne cork in Raymond Carver's "The Errand."

People also turn to the small objects in times of stress or grief. Because of their scale, small things seem detached from our world and its problems. They're half in this world, half in another. In fact, for those confronting serious illness or death—their lives reeling—small things can offer glimmerings of spiritual hope. In this case, a "small" thing can be a gesture, a word or a sign. It's small in relation to the universe but still deserving of loving attention.

In Tolstoy's story "The Death of Ivan Ilych," in which a respectable prosecutor faces his death, small things take the form of both objects and small gestures. Once all hope of recovery fades, Ivan's anguished thoughts insistently turn to his past, to the French plums and toys of his childhood, and he remembers a scene in which he and his brother were punished and their mother comforted them with tarts. Small things also reflect the concerns tragedy brings, when details are magnified to encompass life and death. Gerasim, the butler's assistant, acts as a sick nurse for Ivan, selflessly caring for him. At one point Gerasim raises Ivan's legs on a chair, then adds a cushion; finally, he props them on his shoulders to ease Ivan's pain. When Ivan apologizes, Gerasim states, "Don't you worry, Ivan Ilych. I'll get sleep enough later on," and, "If you weren't sick it would be another matter, but as it is, why should I grudge a little trouble?" It's a moment of human contact, a small reprieve from Ivan's suffering. The implication at the end, with his newfound peace and redemption, is that spiritual meaning can be gathered from just such moments.

Let's return for a moment to Emily's strand of hair. Someone's lifting it up, but as yet no one else has seen it. It's still invisible, clouded by a faint haze of dust. Particles swirl in the room, in dim light that glows through rose curtains. We lean forward to get a better look. We see. And as much as we try, we're unable to turn away.

Stephen Delaney is a Texas-based teacher and freelance writer. He has had work published in *Crazyhorse*, *Pedestal Magazine* and the *San Francisco Chronicle*. This article first appeared in the January 2006 issue of *The Writer*.

Autobiography or Imagination?

by Joshua Henkin

MY FRESHMAN YEAR at college was the inspiration for *Matrimony*, though I changed many of the details. But which details, and why? What's the role of autobiography in fiction?

How do you balance lived experience with imagination to come up with art?

I teach writing to undergraduate and MFA students, and that's one of the questions that I get asked most often.

Should you be writing about yourself? How personal should it be?

There's of course no easy formula (if only there were!), but I think there are ways to think about the question that can be helpful to people starting to write. Among the students I've taught, I've seen a whole lot of talent, but also at times a real underconfidence (What writer isn't insecure? Believe me, that feeling never ends, even if you encounter some success)—this feeling that you're young and what do you have that's important to write about that could interest anyone but you and your friends?

There's a grain of truth there, in that I think it takes time even for a really talented writer to mature. You don't see eight-year-old writing prodigies the way you see eight-year-old violin prodigies or eight-year-old ballerinas and figure skaters. It's a different learning curve, and some people think that as long as you're under 50 you're still considered a young writer.

At the same time, I like to remind my students of what Flannery O'Connor said—that anyone who has lived until the age of ten has enough material to write about for a lifetime.

The question, though, is how to turn that material into art? Do you write what you know or what you don't know? That's always the question a writer faces, and it's the question my students ask me.

And what I like to say is that you should write what you *know* about what you *don't know* … or what you *don't know* about what you *know*.

I know—that sounds like some nightmare GRE (Graduate Record Examination) problem. But conceptually, it's not as complicated as it sounds. Writing what you *know* about what you *don't know* is taking a situation that's unfamiliar to you and imagining yourself in it. And writing what you *don't know* about what you *know* is taking a situation that's familiar to you and imagining someone different from you experiencing it.

The idea is to have the benefit of both closeness and distance. You want what you're writing about to be close enough to your own experience that there's heart in it, but not so close that you aren't able to realize the ways you can use imagination to get at a deeper, more authentic truth.

It's this balance between closeness and distance that's essential to me as a writer and that I try to convey to my students.

Joshua Henkin is the author of the novel *Swimming Across the Hudson* (Putnam, 1997), named a *Los Angeles Times* Notable Book of 1997. His recent novel, *Matrimony* (Pantheon, 2007), a 2007 *New York Times* Notable Book, was also highly praised ("In the tradition of John Cheever … a beautiful book" —Michael Cunningham). His short stories have been published in *Glimmer Train, Ploughshares, The Southern Review, The Yale Review* and elsewhere. He is recipient of the James Fellowship for the Novel, the Hopwood Award, and the PEN Syndicated Fiction Award. He teaches in the creative writing programs at Sarah Lawrence College and Brooklyn College, and at the Unterberg Poetry Center of the 92nd Street Y.

This piece appeared October 2007 on his website's blog, www.joshuahenkin.com.

Revision Strategies

by Brandi Reissenweber

THERE ARE AS MANY approaches to the writing process as there are writers. No one set formula stipulates the best, most direct route to a completed work. Just because Ernest Hemingway wrote standing up doesn't mean the words will flow while you're on your feet. Still, it can be useful to learn about other writers' techniques so you can try them out and see if they'll work for you.

In the particular practice of revision there are two main camps: revise as you go or get it all out and revise later.

Robert Olen Butler, author of numerous books, including the Pulitzer Prize–winning short story collection *A Good Scent From a Strange Mountain*, swears by the importance of revising as you go. His reasoning is that each and every detail must work with everything else in the story, and it's not possible to move forward until you have those details set.

"And if I make an approximation in this sentence," he said, "it's impossible to write an accurate next sentence. And if that one's also approximate, the third sentence gets farther and farther away."

Some writers may take this approach with bigger chunks of text, rather than revising sentence by sentence. Revisiting a chapter or a scene can help you clarify your intentions in those passages before moving forward.

Some writers, however, find that revising as they go hinders their progress. How can an author set the words with conviction when she doesn't know exactly where the story will end up? For these writers, the early drafts are ones of discovery, where the writer is learning about the characters and the plot.

Will Allison, author of *What You Have Left*, advises writers to "throw up, then clean up." That first draft might be messy, but getting through it can help clarify and define the terrain of the story. This approach can also be useful for the writer who finds herself stopped too early in the process by the internal critic. A writer who doubts her work or ideas may not have a chance to let them live and develop on the page if she tosses them out at the internal critic's first furrowed brow.

Revision, like most other aspects of the creative process, resists compartmentalization. So, you may end up being the sort of writer who hovers in between these two categories, writing forward for the most part, but occasionally going back to flesh out a character or add in a scene. And that's fine. Give yourself the opportunity to try each approach and, more importantly, listen to your own writerly demands. Keep in mind: some impulses are useful to resist, such as researching every facet of a police procedure, when you really just need to know how a gun would be handled as evidence.

And resisting other impulses can even give you momentum. Ending a writing session mid-scene instead of finishing it may help you pick up smoothly when you return.

You'll have to figure those strategies out by trial and error. Stay aware of what slows you down or distracts you from the real work of pushing forward to your strongest writing.

Once you figure out how to revise, how do you know when you're done? Writers often develop a gut feeling about this, understanding when they've taken the piece as far as it can go. Still, knowing whether you're done can be elusive. And you can certainly over-revise by worrying and reworking until you've written all the energy out of it.

Some writers maintain that a fiction is never finished, but rather a writer hits a point where he's finished with it. When you lose the intrigue for a story, it may be time to move on. At this point, you need to decide if the piece is strong. Has your exhaustion with it coincided with the pinnacle of its quality?

If not (or you're not sure), put it aside. Time can reinvigorate the writer's energy.

If that enthusiasm doesn't return when you pick it up again, and you know you can do better, don't stress. You may truly be done with it, even though it isn't up to muster. Remember, you learn something from every writing experience.

If you do stay interested and continue revising, be careful of falling into the familiarity trap. Fresh lines may begin to sound inevitable because you know them too well, not because they're predictable. Gaining objectivity, then, is vital. The best way to do this is to take time away from the story. It's the oldest trick in the revision book, but it's essential to seeing the story anew.

It may take you a few weeks to gain this distance, or several months. Once you do, you will be able to see the quality of the writing and the originality of the ideas for what they are, rather than for what they've become in your mind.

Brandi Reissenweber has published fiction in many literary journals and authored the chapter on Character in *Writing Fiction* (Bloomsbury), part of Gotham Writers Workshop's series of writing guides. She also writes an online column for *The Writer* magazine and edits *Letterpress,* a monthly newsletter on fiction writing. She was an assistant editor for *Zoetrope: All-Story* and has taught writing at New York University, St. John's University and Il Chiostro in Italy. She currently teaches at Gotham Writers Workshop and Illinois Wesleyan University.

A version of this article first appeared in *The Writer* magazine's online Q&A column.

The Pen and the Artful Edit

by Susan Bell

IT IS TRUE: Shakespeare had no editor and, well, he wrote just fine. But at the risk of stating the obvious, we do not all possess Shakespeare's gifts. Besides, Shakespeare penned his immortal lines in the relative quiet of sixteenth-century Britain, untempted by iPods and mobile phones. The blinding pace and complexity of the modern world may just keep writers from literally seeing all they need to in their manuscripts. Take computers. Nearly every author in the Western world, and a good many beyond, uses a computer—a device that makes the editorial enterprise both more appealing and more troublesome. People tend to think the computer is the supreme editing tool. Sure, editing on a computer is easy to do physically. But that gloriously easy machinery may well soften the editorial muscle mentally.

For Gerald Howard, executive editor at Doubleday, "word processors have made the physical act of producing a novel so much easier that you can see manuscripts that have word processoritis. They're swollen and [the writing] looks so good, arranged in such an attractive format that how could it not be good? Well, it's *not* good, and there's too much of it!" When a writer had to deal with the laborious task of pounding out seventy-five or a hundred thousand words on a manual typewriter, Howard went on, he would "be a lot more careful about the sentences he allowed to get into manuscript form."

Most of us who write on computers are facing and continually accessing a global Internet lodged in our writing instrument. Shakespeare's world was neither small nor simple, but he didn't have to face nearly every aspect of it on the Web, nor a full inbox of personal and junk mail, each time he set to write. A pen was, after all, just a pen. In conditions of creativity that are increasingly complex, stringent editing can focus the multitasker's scuttling mind.

Judith Freeman is emphatic about sustaining a flow of imagination when she writes. By handwriting her novel *Red Water*, Freeman found detachment in the act of writing itself, not simply at the end of the draft. In the past, typing into a computer had made the writing process choppy. The flow of her imagination was continually blocked by frequent checking of sentences, paragraphs, words. By the end of a first draft, she would feel confused and drained by the continual rereads and minor adjustments she'd made along the way, and she would need a dramatic break from the text to see it clearly.

Freeman wanted to try another path to clarity: longhand. "When writing longhand," she explains, "the brain and the hand are connected. Once you begin to let an idea unfold, you keep unfolding it. Ink flows, ideas flow with it. When writing longhand, I am not tempted to constantly go back, scroll up, stop and reread. When you type, especially into a computer, you don't give your imagination the chance to really follow things through."

Clean and professional-looking, the typed page can induce the illusion that the sentences on it are finished and ready to be inspected. It is impossible to make that mistake with a hand-scrawled notebook. Moreover, the scroll mechanism of the word processor was a gilded invitation to Freeman's inner censor. Without the scroll, without clean type, Freeman relinquished her grip on her text. At the end of a draft, her words were essentially new to her. She hadn't read them to death by then, but just recorded them directly from her imagination. Or to use writer Albert Mobilio's phrase, it was "as if [her] hands were the actual agents of composition." After she had finished the handwritten draft, Freeman transferred it from her notebooks into her computer, then used the ease of a computer processor to edit further drafts.

Not everyone will be willing or able to write in longhand. Using a pen will seem too anachronistic, quaint, and above all, inefficient. But don't form rash conclusions before you give it a try. Freeman proved that longhand can be as or more efficient than a word processor. Her editor made far fewer suggestions on *Red Water*, for instance, than on her previous computer-written manuscripts. For Freeman, there were three advantages to longhand:

1. Slowing down in the writing stage made her first draft more thought-out.

2. Because she didn't constantly reread as she wrote, her first reread was fresh, so she saw more clearly and more quickly what needed adjustment.

3. The kinetic link from a writer's mind to ink to page seemed to make Freeman's first draft truer to what she wanted, so there were fewer changes than usual. Freeman credits the pen with her ability to see her manuscript clearly and edit it well herself before handing it to an editor.

Whereas Freeman gave up the computer to write more fluidly, D.S. Stone, who uses one, says, "I never reread what I'm working on while I'm working on it. The less I look at [my writing], when it is time to edit it, the fresher I am." He follows Freeman's dictum, but goes at it differently. Stone has taught himself, after years of application, to type with a flow reminiscent of Freeman's longhand. The potentially alienating machine that divides hand from word does not disturb him. "You do the thing and get it done," he says, the ultimate pragmatist.

Echoing Stone, Jonathan Franzen says, "I've learned to avoid rewriting on the computer screen until I have a complete draft of a section or chapter. By then, a good deal of time has passed, and I can see the pages more clearly. Generally, if I find myself trying to achieve perspective prematurely … it's a sign that the section isn't working and that I don't want to admit this to myself."

To avoid rereading as you type, try writing with a pen. If you resist writing with a pen, try harder to resist the scroll mechanism on your computer.

Susan Bell is the author of *The Artful Edit: On the Practice of Editing Yourself* (W.W. Norton & Co., 2007), and co-author with Jason West of *Dare to Hope: Saving American Democracy,* essays on political activism (Miramax, 2005). A former editor at Random House and *Conjunctions* magazine, she has edited both fiction and nonfiction for 20 years. She also collaborates with her husband, Mitch Epstein, a visual artist, on books and exhibitions. In 2001, she created a seminar on self-editing for the New School's graduate writing program, and continues to teach there.

This piece is excerpted from the introduction and chapter one of *The Artful Edit* ("Short, helpful, original."—William Safire, *New York Times*). For more, visit her website, www.artfuledit.com.

The Metaskills of Journalism

by Gerald Grow

EVERY PROFESSION is based on both skills and metaskills. Skills are the activities people have to perform well—like reporting, writing, attributing quotes properly and avoiding libel. Metaskills are higher-order skills that enable journalists to use their skills effectively. Metaskills—such as critical thinking—are what make the skills effective. Without metaskills, skills are like a hammer in the hands of a child.

Journalism education programs agree widely on the basic skills of the profession, but the metaskills are so seldom discussed that there is no agreement on what they are, how to teach them, or whether students are learning them.

Students sometimes ask why they need to study so hard, when much of what they learn will become obsolete. The answer points to the meaning of "metaskill." Though students will have to re-learn many skills, it is only through learning skills that they can learn the metaskills. Even if the skills become obsolete, the metaskills empower students to continue to update their skills. By learning skills that will become obsolete, students can learn metaskills that endure.

This article considers a list of metaskills in relation to the practice of journalism, in order to open a discussion on metaskills and how to teach them.

Clarity

Clarity is the ability to give attention, and to give it when needed. It means always having access to a clear channel in the mind. Clarity is the skill that underlies all efforts at research and reporting, for without clarity, you look at the world and see either yourself reflected back, or a muddled haze.

Ideal clarity means seeing without preconceptions, without agendas, without filters, without interpretations. It means just being there, and being there fully, with all the skills and purposes of a journalist.

Curiosity is the active form of clarity, the form that asks, that goes out and looks, that returns for a second look.

Another aspect of clarity leads to openness, to freshness of perception, to the ability to recognize that no two things are ever alike, no two people ever do the same things. This is the clarity of innocence.

To maintain clarity, journalists have to renew their ability to see—to see doubly as both adult and child; to see at once in the full context of everything you have ever known, and yet to see as if for the first time, anew.

Clarity can cause problems, because journalists see so many difficult things, all the hard realities of human life on this earth. Journalists have to live with what they see.

Compassion

Journalists have to live with what they learn. Unless they anticipate this need, they may find that the very clarity of vision that makes good journalists also leads them toward cynicism, irony, disillusion, detachment, or an empty relativism. Like medical students, journalists may go through a spiritual crisis as they learn more about human beings than they can assimilate. Few other people have to know so much—especially so many bad things—about being human. Few other people are exposed hour after hour to tragedy, disaster, loss, betrayal, murder, robbery, rape, death, exploitation, decrepitude, ineptness, and suffering.

Seeing too much too clearly easily leads to a world-weary attitude. Journalists may oscillate between an aloof superiority from which they criticize, and the grimy guilt that comes from turning their pitiless honesty upon their own imperfect selves.

Clarity needs another metaskill to manage it. Compassion can help sustain and renew the task of repeatedly seeing oneself and others in the nakedness of truth. Compassion begins with the deep and repeated awareness of one's own web of self-delusion and imperfection, learning to look upon one's lumpiness gently, kindly. From this self-kindness, one can learn to look upon others kindly—not ignoring anything, not softening their failures, not ignoring their destructiveness.

Seeing it all, seeing it clearly, seeing it from the perspective of the other person, and feeling compassion. Compassion requires clear seeing, and clarity of vision can be sustained through compassion.

Commitment

Clarity and compassion bring the danger that, in seeing all, one will be tempted to forgive all. By themselves, clarity and compassion tend toward an all-seeing, all-forgiving perspective that can be grounded only by a keen sense of standards in life.

Journalists are sworn to principles of accuracy and fairness. They are committed to going beyond clarity and exposing what they find, no matter where it leads. In an ethic similar to that of the scientist, journalists are committed to the truth as their methods reveal it and as their media permit its expression. They uphold the freedom of expression for themselves and for everyone. They subject everyone's free expressions to the same scrutiny—including their own. You could call it honor.

Clarity and compassion tend to a life of reflection; those metaskills make a difference in the world only when they are impelled into action by someone who is committed to high standards yet has the courage to act—which means, the courage to be imperfect, the courage to fail. In this world, the only people who fail are those who do things. Journalists act, and they act imperfectly—again and again, committed to a cumulative, self-correcting body of work that, within its constraints, strives for integrity.

Context

In our multidimensional world, few things have simple meanings. It is rarely enough to learn the facts of an event, because meaning comes only when the event is placed in a context. Journalists do not always have the obligation, or the luxury, of placing things in context. Their day-to-day job is to report events, not to interpret them.

Yet the day-to-day job of readers is to interpret events, and in this task readers need help. One of the crucial roles of journalism is to equip readers to bring to the news contexts that make sense out of the news. Most journalism seems to presume that readers will pick up such contexts on their own, but, increasingly, journalism recognizes that readers need reminders, summaries, maps, histories, explanations, definitions, biographies, theories, and other tools with which to place important events in richly useful contexts that help readers understand life. Events do not explain themselves. Journalists can help readers through articles that try to make sense out of the world—

analysis, commentary, and background. Opinion pieces can be valuable—but chiefly those pieces that do not focus on the opinion of the writer, but rather help equip readers to form their own opinions on complex issues.

In order for journalists to help readers by providing context, journalists must themselves learn enough to bring context to the news. This means continuously working to understand how to understand this world. To do this, journalists need more opportunities to consider, reflect, integrate—and to write reflectively. Reflecting on the meaning of events, bringing perspective—these are the essential skills of context.

Creativity

Even clarity, compassion, commitment and context are not enough to deal with the repetitiveness of journalism—the endless, day by day production of reports, one after the other, in the same small number of formats, with the same small vocabulary, in the same limited range of music and voice.

The crucial metaskill here is creativity.

To keep from becoming dulled in their perception and writing, journalists need to take things in deeply enough that they are no longer manufacturing their work out of the ordinary tools of consciousness. They need to be able to tap the creative mind, to feed it material and to learn to listen to what it does with that material. Creativity is intimately tied not only with inventiveness, but with freshness, with the ability to see things like a grown-up child—with "clarity."

But creativity brings its own kind of strain. The incessant newness of news, combined with the dulling sameness of news, stresses anyone's ability to find fresh ways to say what you have already said a hundred times.

Centering

Journalism is a particularly demanding profession, one that constantly pulls journalists away from themselves, thrusting them into the lives of others, yanking them out again, and thrusting them elsewhere.

Only by having one's own life to live, and living it simply and whole-heartedly, can one bear the burden of clarity, compassion, commitment, context, and creativity. To use these skills, one must also be able to turn them off, trust, and just let life happen.

There has to be a place where one can stop being a journalist and just be a person. Journalists need a life outside of work. This can be difficult, because when journalists become members of the community, they come to know and love the very people about whom they may later have to report difficult truths.

They may find that friends are reluctant to be candid with them for fear their words will appear in the paper. People may try to manipulate their views in order to advance their own, or to hide something. They may always wonder when they are seeing people as they are and when people are acting with the journalist as their audience.

So that they won't be whirled away by the pace of the profession, the sameness of method, the incessant quest for the scoop, the repetitive frenzy of so much of journalism, journalists need to know how to center. They need to know how to nourish their own lives—for the task of the journalist and the task of the reader are essentially the same: How to live with what we know so that we act more humanely in the world.

Clarity, compassion, commitment, context, creativity, and centering: six metaskills that journalism depends on. If you are a journalism student, look for ways to cultivate these. If you are a journalism teacher, look for ways to teach them.

Gerald Owen Grow is professor of magazine journalism at Florida A&M University. A graduate of Harvard with a PhD in English from Yale, he has taught at Yale, San Francisco State, St. Mary's College of California, Florida State University and Florida A&M University. He is also the author of *Florida Parks: A Guide to Camping in Nature* (a nature-lover's guide to the Florida outdoors, now in its sixth edition).

This article is from a collection of articles on his website, www.longleaf.net/ggrow.

Fluff, Guff, Geek, and Weasel

by Tom Sant

Have you ever been reading something, only to lose your train of thought halfway through? Often we go back to the beginning of a sentence or paragraph and tiptoe through it, trying to figure out what it's saying. But why does that happen?

Or have you ever read a routine email or report, only to find yourself getting more and more irritated with the writer? What's up with that?

What's up can be summarized in two words: bad writing. In both cases, the writer failed to communicate. And that's our subject this time: how to write successfully.

In my recent book, *The Language of Success,* I focus on the two aspects of writing that determine our success or failure. The first aspect is the use of "pseudo-languages" that people lapse into without even being aware of it. We need to avoid these artificial, clumsy, ugly ways of writing. (The second aspect consists of the various characteristics that make writing work—five characteristics that must be present for our writing to communicate successfully.)

In this article, I'll discuss the first aspect.

What do you need to avoid? This is simple. You need to avoid imitating people who can't write. You need to speak and write in your own voice.

Unfortunately, we are surrounded by four ugly, ineffective "pseudo-languages"—I call them Fluff, Guff, Geek, and Weasel—that don't work. Because we're bombarded with examples of them every day, we begin to imitate them. *Stop!* They will cause your writing to fail.

Fluff

Fluff, for example, is the kind of bombast we often get from marketing:

We provide world-class products that combine best-of-breed hardware with state-of-the-art software to deliver leading edge performance.

By partnering with our customers, we leverage the synergies inherent in the relationship to deliver competitive advantage at an affordable price.

Blah, blah, blah. Grandiose claims. Vague generalities. You've seen this kind of writing on websites, in marketing brochures, in proposals, and a dozen other places. And you've seen that it doesn't work. In fact, it quickly makes you suspicious that you're dealing with somebody who is trying to put one over on you.

Guff

Guff is the pretentious, self-important prose we get from bureaucrats, politicians, attorneys, academics, and others who think their most important job is convincing us that they're a lot smarter than we are. Sometimes they're actively trying to mislead us, confuse us, or hide the truth.

Guff uses long, complicated sentences, complex words, and lots of passive voice, like this:

The dimensionality of anticipated project problems coupled with the limited time available for preparation means that choices will have to be made to assure viability of the most critical analytical processes.

Now I'm willing to bet you knew we were in trouble as soon as you saw the word "dimensionality," right? But what else is wrong here? First of all, the sentence is too long. It contains 31 words, when 15 to 17 words is a good average sentence length for educated adults. Second, it uses too many big words, words that have three or more syllables. And, third, the sentence uses a passive voice construction in the second half—"choices will have to be made ..." By whom? One of the problems with passive voice is that it often obscures who's doing what and who's responsible.

Geek

Geek is the language of choice among engineers, programmers, healthcare professionals, and others who work in technical fields. It functions pretty well when they're talking to each other, but when they use it to communicate with a non-technical audience, it's a disaster. Here's an example:

> Attached are the Prioritized P3 tickets for FIMS. Note that the BIM has raised questions whether the 3274609 should be logged as an "enhancement." More to come.

"More to come"? Gosh, let's hope not. I didn't understand the first dose. To get rid of Geek, challenge the use of jargon and acronyms. Use everyday language or define the terms before using them.

Weasel

Weasel is writing that avoids saying anything definitive, that qualifies everything to death: It may be that further study of the side effects could be warranted and would not represent a nonproductive use of resources. Weasel sounds wishy-washy, even sneaky. This kind of writing habitually uses words and phrases like "may," "might," "could," "can," "can be," "virtually," "up to," "as much as," "possibly," and similar qualifiers that create enough wiggle room for a rhino. Weasel also uses hypothetical and subjunctive constructions:

> If I were you, I would consider diversifying.

Well, you're not me, so does that mean you don't recommend diversification?

The most irritating use of Weasel occurs when politicians and celebrities make non-apologies for their outrageous behavior:

> I would like to express my sincere regret to anyone who might have been injured and for any damage that may have been done.

Injuries that "might have" occurred? Damage that "may have" happened? We're not exactly stepping forward to admit the error of our ways here, are we?

Those are the four pseudo-languages that you must avoid. Instead, you need to speak and write in your own voice and to do so as clearly and concisely as possible.

Tom Sant is recognized as one of the world's foremost experts on effective business communication. He is the founder of the Sant Corporation, the world's leading proposal automation firm, and Hyde Park Partners (www.hydeparkpartnerscal.com). He has received numerous awards, including a Gold Medal at the New York Industrial Film Festival for best script and the Platinum Award from the MarCom Association for best electronic newsletter.

His books include the bestselling *Persuasive Business Proposals,* a fresh look at how proposals are written, and *The Giants of Sales,* linking modern sales techniques to key principles of human psychology. His most recent book, *The Language of Success*, identifies nonfunctional modes of writing—Fluff, Guff, Geek, and Weasel—that prevent people from communicating effectively, then shows how to overcome them. It focuses on techniques for writing emails, letters, memos, reports, appraisals and proposals clearly, concisely and effectively.

This article is drawn from *The Language of Success* (2008), and appeared in his free newsletter, available on his website.

Creative Nonfiction

by Melissa Hart

"FOURTEEN YEARS AGO, I started a journal to publish narrative nonfiction," says Professor Lee Gutkind, editor of *Creative Nonfiction*. "Everyone thought it was a stupid idea. Now, at least fifty MFA programs offer degrees in the genre."

Creative nonfiction, or literary nonfiction as it's sometimes known, owes its beginnings to immersion journalists such as Gay Talese ("Frank Sinatra Has a Cold") and Tom Wolfe (*The Right Stuff*). The form defies easy description. It's not just memoir. Nor is it simply a research-driven article. Rather, it's an exciting hybrid which offers writers the chance to explore life-changing personal issues through investigation and revelation.

As Gutkind says on *Creative Nonfiction*'s website, the genre "allows a writer to employ the diligence of a reporter, the shifting voices and viewpoints of a novelist, the refined wordplay of a poet and the analytical modes of the essayist." His journal publishes both established and emerging writers who can craft taut, compelling narrative in essay form.

A recent issue of *Creative Nonfiction* explores the ways in which literature may change by the year 2025. In a witty selection titled "Best of Times, Worst of Times," Philip Lopate explores the possibilities of ESP publishing and cyber-residuals, while in her darkly humorous piece, "The Writers in the Silos," Heidi Julavits describes a "text bioweapon" that causes—literally—the death of a reading culture. "I look for narrative, first and foremost," Gutkind explains. "Creative nonfiction is narrative—and it starts at an exciting place, whatever the story is."

The stories in the journal aren't theme-based; however, donors occasionally fund a particular theme. JPMorgan Chase enabled Gutkind to offer a $10,000 prize for the best issue exploring the subject of diversity. "In 2006, we had an anonymous grant from a New York Italian woman who wanted to see more New York Italian women being published," Gutkind explains. The funding, shared with contributing writers, resulted in an issue titled "Our Roots Are Deep With Passion," with essays exploring everything from Italian history to a celebration of garlic. "I really believe that creative nonfiction is supposed to tell our readers something, teach our readers something," Gutkind says of the journal's themed issues, "and so I like to pick a subject and see writers explore it deeply."

Gutkind notes that ninety percent of the submissions he sees are overly personal. "It's too bad your grandmother died," he says, "but what are you going to tell the millions of people whose grandmothers die every day? Creative nonfiction teaches readers something."

He points to the importance of the "three Rs" in this genre, the first of which is Reality. "I like discovering a narrative that captures someone's real life with intimacy," he says. "The second R is Research. Readers need to know how your grandmother differs from other grand-mothers. She might have been the only shoemaker in the western US. She might have worshipped leather. This makes her unique and allows you to share something special."

The final R stands for Reflection. Gutkind notes *Creative Nonfiction* writers must tell readers how to think about a subject. "So your grand-mother was a great bootmaker," he says. "What does that mean to you, and what should it mean to readers?"

Gutkind himself has performed as a clown with Barnum & Bailey and scrubbed in with organ-transplant surgeons—both in the service of the creative nonfiction essay. "If you look at the essays and books that are selling, they're often the products of immersion," he says. "They're about people who spend a lot of time with other people. This is a great opportunity to look at the world through other people's eyes. You can learn about a subject, and introduce that subject in an inti-mate way."

He notes that writers can be gun-shy about attempting the genre after a watchdog website titled The Smoking Gun called foul on events in James Frey's bestselling (and partially fabricated) memoir, *A Million Little Pieces*. In response to the 2006 debacle, issue 29 of *Creative Nonfic-tion* bears the title "A Million Little Choices," offering readers "every-thing you need to know to avoid the James Frey jinx."

"The issue almost sold out because it was so popular," Gutkind notes. In 2008, Norton expanded and republished the issue as a book titled *Keep It Real*.

Potential contributors to *Creative Nonfiction* can further hone their skills through the journal's mentorship program. "So many writers want help," Gukind notes. "They can only attend MFA programs with twenty people in a class. They need targeted one-on-one time and attention." He explains that one of the most common mistakes made by writers new to creative nonfiction lies in focusing too much on their own experiences and on their emotions about those experiences.

"We're writing for the reader, not ourselves," he says. "A good essay should have one strong point it's making. I want a reader to be moved to say, 'I've learned something, and now I feel like doing something.'"

Creative Nonfiction's mentoring program pairs writers with professional editors or authors who review manuscripts, offer writing assignments, and suggest publication options for polished work.

"We've tried hard to give the field dignity," Gutkind concludes. "We're an organization dedicated to making a significant literary art form."

Melissa Hart is author of a memoir, *The Assault of Laughter* (Windstorm, 2005), and teaches Introduction to Memoir for University of California–Berkeley's online extension program. Her website is www.melissahart.com.

The quarterly journal *Creative Nonfiction* (www.creativenonfiction.org) publishes essays with strong voice and reportage that show "compelling, focused, sustained narrative" and "an instructional element that offers the reader something to learn."

Asking the Hard Question:
Top Ten Interview Tips
by Michelle Vranizan Rafter

NOT LONG AGO, a writer in a freelance group I belong to posted a question on the group message boards. She had an interview scheduled with a subject who had a reputation for being grouchy and wanted to know how to prepare.

It's a great question. Reporters are thought of as thick-skinned hacks who can take just about anything, and dish it out too. While I've known some like that, most aren't and they'd just as soon avoid confrontation as the next person.

So if you're not Mike Wallace, how do you ask the hard questions? Here's my top ten tips for conducting tough interviews:

> **Do your homework.** The more information you have, the better prepared you'll be to ask any kind of question, hard or easy. And it's easier to steer the conversation back to tough topics when you've got your facts down cold.
> **Write questions down.** In an age when everyone seems pressed for time, it's not uncommon for interview subjects or their PR handlers to ask for questions in advance. That's fine, especially since it forces you to prepare. But once you're talking, don't feel obliged to stick to the script. When you've got a subject comfortable, go with the flow and toss out a couple juicy questions that aren't on the list.
> **Don't ask "yes" or "no" questions.** Don't give an interview subject the opportunity for monosyllabic answers, otherwise you'll be stuck with no good quotes. Ask open-ended questions that make them think, such as "What led you to that decision?" or "How did you solve that problem?" or "What else can you tell me about that?"

> **Don't be afraid to look stupid.** What if you have the opposite problem and your subject is a know-it-all who talks in circles all the better to intimidate you? If what they're saying isn't obvious to you, it won't be obvious to your readers either. So swallow your pride and ask, "Can you run that by me again?" or "I'm not sure what you mean by that?" or "Can you explain why?"

> **Don't let a subject off the hook.** You ask a question, they won't answer. Ask a different way. Or ask why they won't answer. I get this a lot because I interview executives at private companies who don't want to talk about revenue or other money matters—and if they're privately held, there's nothing forcing them to divulge it. Coax it out of them by asking "Can you give me a range?" or "What do companies in your industry generally charge?" or "How much did sales increase over last year?"

> **Get specifics.** Don't be satisfied with pat answers or industry jargon. This is especially true if you're writing about a field or subject with a language all its own, like business, medicine or technology. If you don't understand the terminology an interview subject is using, don't be afraid to ask "Can you explain that for me?" or "I'm not familiar with that term, what does it mean?"

> **If you're pressed for time, front load.** If you've only got a celebrity or CEO for a couple minutes, cut to the chase. Ask your three or four most important questions right away so you're sure to get the information that you absolutely positively have to have or your editor will kill you—or your story.

> **Play good cop/bad cop.** Interview subject not cooperating? Or do you have to ask someone about something they've been blamed for or accused of? Start out polite and only get more assertive or aggressive if you need to. In these cases, save hardball questions for the very end, so you have time to soften them up and they let their guard down. What's the worst thing that could happen? They refuse to answer or walk out of the interview—at least you got answers to your other questions.

> **Circle back.** The subject won't answer a question the first time around. Let it go, move on to your other questions, then come back to it at the end. Approach it by saying, "Now that you've had more time to think about it, what did you really want to say about Topic XXX?" or "I'd like you to reconsider talking about XXX." All they can

say is no. Then again, your solid interview skills may lead them to reconsider.

> **Psyche yourself up.** Football players get pumped for the big game by listening to a pep talk or their favorite upbeat song, praying, jumping up and down or performing some other ritual. Figure out what psyches you up and use it. Then pick up the phone.

Michelle Vranizan Rafter is a Portland, Oregon, freelance writer covering technology, workplace issues and business. Her current clients include *Inc.* magazine's tech website, IncTechnology.com, Workforce Management, and Oregon Business. She's written for the *Los Angeles Times*, *Chicago Tribune*, *The Industry Standard*, *Internet World* and Reuters, and was previously a staff writer at the *Orange County Register*.

This piece was posted February 2008 on WordCount (http://michellerafter.wordpress. com), her blog about freelance writing in the 21st century.

Five Steps to Successful Email Interviews

by Terry L. Stawar

NEED A QUOTE from some national authority to wrap up your latest masterpiece on business communication? How will you get some experts for that round-up article on healthcare reform and where can you possibly find a couple willing to tell the story about how swing dancing broke up their marriage? Look no further than your computer terminal. All of this and much more can be obtained through email interviews (e-views) which promise to replace the more familiar face-to-face and telephone genre for some writers. To enhance both credibility and salability of your nonfiction writing, try following these five simple steps.

1. Develop your contact list.

Unless you already have the email address of a specific person you want to quote, the first place to start is a series of Web searches for the person's name. If you don't even have names yet, search the topic areas.

Consider using a top search-engine site for these initial inquiries such as Google or alltheweb.com. Google Scholar has become increasingly useful for locating experts. You might be lucky enough to find a home page for some experts and even a direct email link. If not, you can at least begin your potential contact list. Don't overlook bookseller sites to get the names of authors who have written in the field you're researching. If you already have existing articles or literature, add names from these sources to your list.

Make your initial list as large as you can and prioritize it with the best-known or most important contacts at the top, knowing that you may be able to locate email addresses for only a small percentage of the names. Also don't overlook specialized search sites for specific disciplines, such as the Medline search engine for medical topics and PsycINFO for psychological topics.

2. Locate your contacts.

The next step is finding the email address of your contact. There are several people-find search sites which usually include email addresses, although they are only marginally useful for this purpose. You will have much better luck searching for work/business websites and especially university faculty directories, which are usually accessible through the university's home page. Searching through the faculty directories from several major universities can identify many potential experts who are not so well-known to the general public. Professional associations and speaker bureaus are other places to seek out experts on the Web, not only to find specific people but also to add new possibilities to your list.

3. Compose the first contact letter.

Contact letters should contain at least four basic sections: First, an introduction: explain who you are, describe your current project, and identify your reading audience. It is best to say outright that you are looking for experts to quote.

The second section is a series of questions for the purpose of eliciting usable quotes. Keep the number down to fewer than five questions and always have some open-ended questions like, "What is the burning issue in this field?" or "What are the most important things my reader should remember?" Ask your experts to answer any of the questions they would care to address and to feel free to skip any items they wish. If you have sufficient background on the experts, ask specific questions about their research or their special areas of expertise.

Many nonfiction articles can be structured around a series of questions you intend to answer for your reader. If you ask these questions in your email interviews with several experts, you can selectively pick the best quotes for each question. This can make for better copy and increased credibility as you have more authorities to cite.

In the third section, request identifying information in order to make an accurate attribution. Ask for the experts' full names, titles,

business and academic affiliations, degrees, cities and states of residence, and if they wish, websites or email addresses.

The final section should contain a heartfelt thank-you and identifying information, including your day and night phone numbers. You
should also ask for snail-mail addresses if they would like to receive
tearsheets when the article is published.

4. Process replies.

In about ten to fifteen percent of your inquiries, you can expect a fairly
prompt reply with usable quotes. Consider staggering your initial contacts so that you can change the questions if you find yourself over-
loaded with quotes on a particular topic.

Often you will get a polite turndown ("I don't have the time.") or
rarely an impolite rejection ("I don't work for free."). Rarer still you
may get a paranoid reply ("How did you get my address?") or an outright hostile one ("What makes you qualified to write this article?").

Some experts will offer phone interviews instead and provide
times and phone numbers were they can be reached. Although the
email responses are often easier to manage (the quotes are always
accurate and you don't have to take notes), take advantage of these
phone interview offers if you need deeper background or the expert is
a high-profile authority who would add prestige to your piece. Be prepared to receive an influx of clippings, articles, video tapes, CDs, books,
and even product samples in response to your inquiries.

5. Wrap it up.

Finally, always send a prompt thank-you (even to turndowns—"Maybe
next time?") and when appropriate, ask specific follow-up questions
or clarifications. These dialogues can be especially productive and help
build a future source list. Download all usable email quotes into a separate data file that you can later cut and paste into your piece. Finally,
be scrupulously polite and remember to send tearsheets to the people
you quote as soon as the article is published. Don't overuse or abuse
your sources—you're dependent upon them.

Newsgroups and special-interest bulletin boards can be used to obtain
first-person stories, which can enhance a variety of nonfiction works.
When I completed piece on children's sleep disturbances, I included

a wealth of well-written and poignant anecdotes that were emailed to me in response to a request posted on a parenting site bulletin board.

The potential of e-views to reach authorities from around the world is staggering. Crank up that modem and remember, "It never hurts to ask."

A Successful E-view: An Example

Below is a ten-question email interview conducted with Jean Donaldson, bestselling author of *Dogs Are From Neptune*, for a round-up article on aggressive behavior in dogs. I ended up using several of her excellent quotes in my *DOGworld Magazine* article, "Decoding the Many Faces of Aggression." Professional writers such as Donaldson often make the best e-view prospects, since they are so comfortable with written expression.

The original questions are included, as are her responses (in italics).

Dear Ms. Donaldson:

My name is Terry Stawar and I'm a psychologist and freelance writer working on a round-up piece for *DOGworld Magazine* on diagnosing and managing aggressive behaviors in dogs. It is a comprehensive overview of the area and as usual, I am looking for experts to quote. I am familiar with some of your writings and work in this area and feel your comments would greatly enhance my article.

The following questions summarize the areas in which I need expert opinion. I would appreciate your responses to any of these questions that you are inclined to address.

1. How serious a problem is canine aggression and what are the most common sources of canine aggression?
   Her answer: *Canine aggression is an extremely serious problem. It bears repeating that dogs are animals and animals bite when they feel threatened or are defending resources. There is a dangerous head-in-the sand attitude from many dog owners that if a dog has a "nice" temperament (i.e., is "normal") he is at low or zero risk for ever behaving aggressively. Statistics do not bear this out. The vast majority of dog bites are example of dogs behaving normally, for dogs ...*

2. What treatment or training strategies seem to work best with aggressive dogs?

   In the case of resource guarding and handleability (which encompass the vast majority of intra-familial bites), systematic desensitization to the tricky scenario(s) achieve the best results. Things like object exchanges, food-bowl desensitization, placement-command practice have excellent track records ...

3. What kinds of canine aggression are easiest to treat and which kinds are most resistant to treatment?

   In general, younger animals are easier to resocialize than older. Also, there is a clear genetic predisposition to both resource guarding and ease of socialization. Relative to virtually all other types of behavior problems (except fear and anxiety type problems, also emotionally based), all types of aggression are tricky to treat ...

4. Can medications help treat aggressive dogs? What medicines work the best? Which should be avoided?

   Yes, there are promising initial results with SSRIS. My only reservations are that 1) the long-term effects of dogs being kept on them are not yet in and 2) if drugs like Prozac work—too—well, they will diminish incentive to breed for non-aggressive animals as well as good overall husbandry of puppies ...

5. What's your opinion on the frustration-aggression hypothesis as it pertains to canine aggression?

   I am only superficially familiar with this theory so don't feel right commenting.

6. Are dogs sometimes aggressive due to imitation of people or other dogs?

   There is no good evidence of this.

7. What are some physical problems might contribute to aggressive canine behavior?

   I am aware that certain types of seizures, tumors as well as any medical problem resulting in acute or chronic pain can cause or facilitate aggression.

8. Do you have any great articles, reprints, or sources on this subject that I might quote from?

I have published two books (Culture Clash and Dogs Are From Neptune) and you have permission to quote from either.

9. Any other thoughts, opinions, or theories about aggressive behavior in dogs?

    Overclassification and presumption of motive are common in this field but not helpful, in my experience. If a dog bites when his nails are clipped, we know he doesn't like having his nails clipped. What we don't know is whether this has anything whatsoever to do with his self-perception of his "status" or "dominance" in the "pack."

Finally, may I have the following so I might cite you and your work correctly:

Name: *Jean Donaldson*

Degree/Profession: *Owner of Renaissance Training, Writer*

Affiliations: *Member of various trainer organizations*

Town, State, Country: *Montreal, Canada*

Other identifiers you would like used (email/website, etc.): *www.lasardogs.com*

Also, if you would like a reprint of the article when published, please provide a snail-mail address.

Thanks so much for considering my request!

—Terry L. Stawar, EdD

Terry L. Stawar, EdD, is a psychologist and writer from Georgetown, Indiana. His most recent book is *How to be a Responsible Father: A Workbook for Offenders* (American Correctional Association, 2006). He writes a weekly newspaper column in southern Indiana and is a frequent contributor to *Funny Times* and other publications.

This article first appeared as "The E-View: Five Steps to Successful Email Interviews for the Nonfiction Writer," in the online newsletter *Absolute Write* (www.absolutewrite.com).

Show, Don't Tell:
Before and After

by Barbara O'Connor

I TEACH writing workshops for elementary school students. One of the most difficult parts of the writing process to teach children is revision. I've learned that the best way to keep children from being overwhelmed by the process is to focus on specific elements of their writing. My favorite (and one that children grasp quickly and easily) is the element of "show, don't tell."

I've also learned that, when it comes time to revise, one of the best ways to help kids understand specific writing techniques is to present them with examples of *before* and *after* revision.

Check out these "before and after" examples from biographies of parents and grandparents written by fifth graders:

> *Before*: Bob wasn't happy when his father told him they were moving.
> *After*: Bob's father came in and announced, "We're moving." Bob groaned when he heard the news.

> *Before*: John loved to play baseball with the kids in the neighborhood.
> *After*: As soon as John got home from school, he dashed back to his room to grab his baseball mitt, then hurried to meet his friends in the vacant lot next door.

> *Before*: She was good at swimming.
> *After*: Swimming medals covered her bedroom wall.

> *Before*: Sam loved to go to the Cape every summer with his family.
> *After*: Sam counted the days until his family would load the

beach chairs and boogie boards into the car and head for the Cape.

Before: He hated doing chores, like vacuuming, washing dishes or raking.
After: He groaned when he had to vacuum. He whined when he had to wash dishes. He grumbled when he had to rake.

Before: His favorite subject was geography.
After: He loved it when the teacher whacked her pointer on the map, pointing out countries and rivers.

Before: Melissa lived in an apartment building in a big city. She loved to read.
After: Melissa didn't even notice the constant sound of traffic outside. She sat curled up in her favorite chair, reading. Every now and then she glanced out the window to the sidewalk below. It was crowded with people hurrying off to nearby offices and stores.

For any kid who didn't quite "get" Show, Don't Tell, hearing these usually lights the old proverbial light bulb for them.

Barbara O'Connor is the author of 14 novels and biographies for children. Titles include *How to Steal a Dog, Moonpie and Ivy* and *Fame and Glory in Freedom, Georgia*. Drawing on her Carolina roots, Barbara's novels have a distinctly Southern voice. Her books have received many awards, including the Massachusetts Books Award and Parents Choice Award, and are on reading award lists in 17 states. Her most recent novel is *Greetings from Nowhere* (Farrar, Straus & Giroux/Frances Foster).

Her website is www.barboconnor.com. This piece is drawn from a blog entry that appeared November 2007 on her blog, www.greetings-from-nowhere.blogspot.com.

Writing Humor

by Penney Kome

I DON'T MEAN to write humor. Honest. But people are always telling me that I'm funny. Guess it's a result of a misspent youth, immersed in joke books and Mark Twain.

Most of my recent writing has been for presentations. Presentation delivery offers obvious advantages for humor, such as timing and inflection. And sometimes, when I share the script afterwards, the humor comes across on the page, too.

In describing the origins of Chinese New Year, I said, "The word *nian* means *year*, but Nian is also the name of this legendary monster, who is often named as the reason for the biggest New Year tradition. Nian used to come out once a year and eat up villagers. Eventually, the villagers discovered that Nian was afraid of firecrackers and fireworks. They've been setting off firecrackers every year to scare Nian away. And it works! He hasn't been seen in centuries."

In a presentation about gratitude, I said, "Eckhart von Hochheim, also known as Meister Eckhart, was a 13th-century Dominican priest. He said that: 'If the only prayer you ever say in your entire life is *thank you*, it will be enough.' Of course, the Catholic church has changed its policies since then."

Well, maybe you had to be there.

I find that humor often appears in what I think of as the "bridges," the transition points between one train of thought and the next. A little incongruity in juxtaposition often produces a laugh.

Public relations expert Fred Garcia has written that—whether we know it or not—reporters are always looking for the five Cs as well as the five Ws. The five Cs are: Conflict, Controversy, Contradiction in terms, Colorful language, and Cast of characters.

The last three Cs lend themselves to humor. As an editor, I often coin headlines using contradiction, such as "Hurry up: slow down to save the world" for a story about climate change.

Gerald Durrell used colorful language expertly. I used to study his books, such as *My Family and Other Animals*, trying to figure out how he could spin out such long elliptical sentences that ended with a crack of laughter.

Here's a sample from Durrell, from *Two in the Bush*, which happens to be the closest at hand. Note the foreshadowing, which amounts to setting up the joke:

> We had meant to creep unobtrusively into New Zealand, film and see what we wanted to, and then creep unobtrusively out again. But when the ship docked at Auckland, we found that the Wildlife Department—having been appraised of our arrival—had unrolled a red carpet of embarrassing dimensions for us ...
>
> ... He handed me a sheaf of typewritten documents that looked like a cross between the plans for a Royal State Visit and some gigantic army maneuvers. It was full of fascinating suggestions and orders, such as "June five, 0500 hours, see Royal Albatross, Taiaroa Head." Had the Albatross, I wondered dazedly, been issued with a similar itinerary and, if so, would they fly past in formation and dip their wings in salute?

Durrell glories in exaggerations, but it's his pacing that fascinates me. Timing really is essential in humor, and usually that means a long lead-up sentence followed by a short contradiction. Or not.

Besides his convoluted sentences, Durrell also employs the colorful cast of characters, without falling back on stereotypes. Of course, he was blessed to have vivid characters in his family life. I'm reminded of another writer's response after a nonfiction reading where I shared a couple of pages about the drama and tragedy that marred my childhood from age six to twelve. "Lucky you!" she enthused, "to have such wonderful material in your family!"

Humor is often built on embarrassment or involves using a scapegoat. E.g., "My mistake," said the hedgehog, who had tried to mount a hairbrush. As a rule, I strenuously try to avoid making anybody the butt of a joke in my writing. (Umm, apart from the occasional politician, whom I quote. It's the deadliest thing you can do.) Irony actually works better in prose than it does in spoken word, in my opinion.

Sometimes humor comes in highly stylized writing. Clipped sentences. Dialec'. But hey, we're not all Damon Runyon. In fact, very few of us are. Mark Twain succeeded with dialect, but many more (e.g., Mencken, Thurber, Wodehouse) succeeded with very formal, even sometimes stilted writing. Normal good writing practices apply in humor too: complete sentences, variation in tone and rhythm, precise language.

Well, maybe not precise language. Puns and double entendres can be a lot of fun.

As editor of *Straight Goods*, an online Canadian newsmagazine, I'm required to find a new joke for each weekly issue. So I still read joke books and joke websites fairly often. Unfortunately, the great majority of jokes on joke websites tend to be about topics that apparently still make people squirm, such as sex or religion. That kind of humor doesn't really make readers feel better, in my view, and usually I don't find it funny.

Give me silliness, playfulness, leaps of logic, non-sequiturs, irony, flashes of insight and illumination, goofiness, something that goes completely against conventional wisdom. Give me dry, deadpan, droll wit. People will respond to echoes of a classic joke even if they don't think they've heard the joke before.

Humor is like any other kind of writing—immerse yourself in what you admire or enjoy, and you're likely to start replicating it, consciously or not.

Penney Kome is a Canadian author and journalist, editor of *Straight Goods,* Canada's leading independent online newsmagazine. She has published six nonfiction books on issues of women's history, peace and political action, including *Somebody Has To Do It: Whose Work Is Housework?* (McClelland & Stewart, 1982); *Women of Influence: Canadian Women and Politics* (Doubleday Canada, 1985); *Peace: a Dream Unfolding* (with Patrick Crean; U.S. edition by Sierra Club Books, Canadian edition by Lester & Orpen, Dennys, 1986); and *Every Voice Counts: A Canadian Woman's Guide to Initiating Political Action* (Canadian Advisory Council on the Status of Women, 1989).

She is also the former National Chair of the Writers Union of Canada (2003–2004). Awards include the Toronto Women of Distinction Award and the Robertine Barry Prize for Feminist Journalism.

This piece first appeared as a March 2008 post to WriterL (www.writerl.com), a listserv for nonfiction writers.

The Serious Nature of Comic Fiction

by Brian Yansky

WHEN IT COMES to comic fiction, some readers automatically assume that it will be less powerful emotionally because it's funny, but a lot of comic fiction has a serious aspect to it. Just as serious fiction can be enriched by comedy so comic fiction can be made emotionally powerful by balancing the humor in the work with serious intent. It's a tough job, joining comedy and tragedy, humor and sorrow, in such a way that a reader is both moved and amused, but successful manipulation of these two seemingly opposite ends of the emotional spectrum can give a necessary weight to a comic novel or story.

To achieve this, the work needs, beneath its comedic tone (whether it's the extravagant one of books like *The World According to Garp* and *Catch-22*, the slightly more subdued and lyrical one of a Lorrie Moore story, or the sort that exists in the bleak world of Denis Johnson and Flannery O'Connor), an origin in sadness or tragedy that affects the novel both scene by scene and as a whole, that seeps into style, structure, story and characters.

For some books it's something large and overwhelming that burdens the whole environment of a novel. In *Catch-22* it's World War II and war's attendant miseries. In *Huck Finn* it's the catastrophe of slavery. In Flannery O'Connor's stories it's the burden of original sin.

Sometimes the tragic is in the events that occur in the novel or story, as in *The World According to Garp*, a wildly comic novel in which tragedy frequently occurs: Garp's father dies of a war wound, his mother is murdered, his son dies, his other son loses an eye, and Garp himself, finally, is assassinated.

In Lorrie Moore's collection *Birds of America* there is a story that begins with the main character doing the unthinkable, dropping a baby and the baby dying; in another, a close friend of the narrator's has a terminal illness—terrible events that appear nevertheless in stories that move with typical Lorrie Moore breeziness and that deftly combine these tragedies with comedy.

In Anne Tyler's Pulitzer Prize–winning novel, *The Accidental Tourist*, it is the random murder of the narrator's son by a man who steps into a fast food restaurant and starts shooting and the fallout of this loss that destroys his marriage. But again, terrible as this tragedy is, the novel is primarily a comic one.

Sometimes the sadness that pervades a novel or story is not from tragic attitudes or terrible events; it may be much more mundane and everyday. In *Straight Man*, Richard Russo's wonderful novel, it's a man slipping ungracefully into the thick of middle-age. In another Anne Tyler novel, *Ladder of Years*, it's a woman whose children are grown or nearly grown and no longer need her in the way they once did.

These stories and novels are all very funny, but they're more than just funny because they've bravely pushed into the uncomfortable Darth Vader dark side.

Milan Kundera wrote, "There is a thin line between the horrible and the comic." Mark Twain said, "The source of all humor is sadness, not laughter."

Think of comic works you love and see if most of them don't have some source in sadness, or walk the thin line between the horrible and comic, and/or allow, in the work, tragedy and comedy to exist side by side. You can fill in the blank here for your own list but a few that come to mind for me are *The Tin Drum, Goodbye Columbus, Huckleberry Finn, Henderson the Rain King, The Unbearable Lightness of Being, A Confederacy of Dunces, A Prayer for Owen Meany.* These writers successfully create worlds where the writing skillfully slips back and forth between comedy and tragedy. That they are funny and serious to very different degrees, that sometimes the humor is so dark it hurts to laugh, is just fine by me.

How do writers give their comic writing a seriousness? Here are two specific examples of different kinds of comic writing: *Catch-22*, and a story included in *Best American Short Stories 2001* by Peter Orner titled "The Raft."

Catch-22

The novel *Catch-22* by Joseph Heller takes place on a mythical island eight miles south of Elba and in Rome, Italy, during World War II.

There is death everywhere in this novel, deceit everywhere, terror everywhere, injury, sadness, and there is also comedy. Heller ridicules human values that become twisted in war and maybe in life in general. He targets business ethics through Milo Minderbinder, religion through the ineffectual chaplain, and above all, the way men follow orders they know are idiotic or stupid and that will lead to their own destruction. The wordplay, the jokes, the absurdist situations all make the novel funny but what makes it deeply serious are the constant reminders of death and war and man's inability to escape his own destructive tendencies.

Captain Yossarian, our hero or anti-hero, believes that *they* are trying to kill him and he has no wish to be the victim of *them*. The fact is the enemy is trying to kill him along with everyone else on his side, so it's logical that he should fear them. At the same time it's absurd that he takes it so personally. Or is it? Yossarian's response strikes us as funny but at the same time the many deaths we'll witness in the war make it seem true as well. This is humor with a serious undertow.

One death that particularly affects Yossarian is that of a fellow solider, Snowden, whose blood and entrails splash on Yossarian as Snowden dies, an event that is alluded to often in the novel and described in detail eventually. This is a central event in Yossarian's war experience. He watches the boy die slowly and in great pain.

When Snowden is killed, Yossarian's uniform is stained with the boy's blood. Yossarian's response is to stop wearing clothes. This is funny. It creates humorous situations. For example, it causes some problems when Yossarian wins a Distinguished Flying Cross and there's a ceremony and Yossarian steps up to receive the medal completely naked. General Dreedle can't find a place to pin the medal on him.

It's an absurd scene. A comic one. At the same time we know he's quit wearing clothes because his uniform was stained with Snowden's blood.

Comedy and tragedy. We sympathize with Yossarian's reaction. We can see it as a psychological response to the horror of witnessing a boy die and of all the death around him. So as the scene between General

Dreedle and Yossarian plays out and we laugh, we're also aware of the connection between what causes the comic in the scene (the naked Yossarian) and what has caused the situation in the first place (the staining of his uniform as Snowden dies). This is walking the fine line between the comic and horrible.

"The Raft"

My second example is one of my favorite stories from *Best American Short Stories 2001*, "The Raft," by Peter Orner, a short short story that weighs in at a little over three pages. Maybe because of its brevity, it's forced to be sneaky.

Like many comic stories, it uses the absurd and ridiculous for a laugh. In this case the character of the grandfather and his mental problems.

From the first line we're lured into this situation. "My grandfather, who lost his short-term memory sometime during the first Eisenhower administration, calls me into his study because he wants to tell me the story he's never told anybody before, again."

Of course, it's the "story he's never told anybody before, again" that is contrary to reason and so absurd. It's funny because the voice of our narrator, a twelve-year-boy, is clearly letting us in on the joke right away. And, of course, the sarcasm of the voice seems appropriate to an adolescent boy, so we're expecting this situation to bear laughs.

As the old man tells his story we're made aware that the boy has heard the story many times because he prompts the old man when he wanders. We're also aware that his wife's heard the story because her reaction when he calls his grandson into the room is, "'Oh, for God's sake, Seymour. We're meeting the Dewoskins at Twin Orchards at seven-thirty. Must you go back to the South Pacific?'"

We get all this in the first paragraph. We get the grandfather's cranky, military voice in the next paragraph.

> "There's something I want to tell you, son," he says. "Something I've never told anybody. You think you're ready? You think you've got the gumption?"
>
> "I think so."
>
> "Think so?"
>
> "I know so, sir. I know I've got the gumption."
>
> ... "Well then, stand up, sailor."

Back to Mark Twain, "The source of all humor is sadness, not laughter." An old man with no short-term memory who retells a story again and again isn't funny when stated this way. His seeing his grandson as a soldier from World War II isn't funny either. Except that it is in the context of the story. However, what will eventually provide depth is the source of this humor, the tragic moment that is at its heart.

As the story moves on the grandfather takes his grandson and we readers back to the South Pacific when the grandfather, captain of a destroyer during World War II, is awakened in the middle of the night by two knocks on the door.

The boy humors the old man as he narrates the events of that night, but when the grandfather asks him if he understands a warning he's gotten about kamikaze flotillas and the boy answers, "Basically, it hits the side of your boat, and whango," the tone is changed by the grandfather's response which is: "You being smart with me? You think this isn't life and death we're talking about here?"

Up to this point we've been smiling at the situation, at the old man's treating his twelve-year-old grandson like a soldier, at the quirky things he says, but this line hints that maybe, in fact, all this is leading somewhere more serious than the tone thus far has led us to believe. The stakes are raised. Life and death. What could be more important?

Ultimately, in these two examples, the writers succeed in making their comic fiction both funny and serious by refusing to ignore the sorrow and tragedy in their fictional worlds.

My Top Nine List

Here are nine ways to combine humor and seriousness.

1. The more extravagant the comedy is, the more it has to be anchored in the central problem of a novel. Comedy, rather than excusing focus, demands it. Knowing the sad or tragic origin behind the comedy will give you an anchor and force the comedy to serve the novel's movement rather than float off into easy jokes.

2. From the very beginning, mixed in with the comic situations, characters, themes, there should be mention—in as direct a way as possible without sacrificing plot considerations—of this deeper source. It has to be there so that the reader feels the undertow beneath the comedy in the first few pages. This will help you find the tone and

the reader will be subconsciously expecting something more than just laughter as they read on.

3. Try to load a comic scene with humor that has, directly, a source in sadness like the scene in *Catch-22* when Yossarian accepts his medal naked because one of his uniforms has been stained by the blood of a fellow soldier.

4. Create a character with a character flaw that might be played for humor in places, but that also gives a seriousness to the character's troubles.

5. Set your novel against a background that is tragic, like Mark Twain does in *Huckleberry Finn* or like Milan Kundera in *The Unbearable Lightness of Being*.

6. Like John Irving in *The World According to Garp*, make tragic events central to story. Allow the events to be described with humor, gentleness, irony, but don't shy away from tragedy just because you are writing comic fiction.

7. Recognize that comedy and tragedy aren't opposites. Take Irving's declaration that while people might be sad, their problems are often funny. A blending of the two is not as foreign as it might at first seem.

8. (This might work for stories better than novels.) Be sneaky, like Peter Orner. Give clues that there is a darker side to the story, but withhold the tragic event so that when the story does drop its comic mask it seems transformed and the contrast between light comedy and comedy with an anchor in seriousness is exposed.

9. Follow Anne Tyler in *Ladder of Years* and Richard Russo in *Straight Man*—pick a subtle sorrow like growing old. A common sorrow most of us are forced to endure can be a powerful way to add weight to a comic novel.

Brian Yansky's stories have been published in literary journals such as *Crescent Review* and *Nebraska Review*. He is also the author of two young-adult novels, *My Road Trip to the Pretty Girl Capital of the World* (Cricket, 2003), and *Wonders of the World* (Flux, 2007). This piece is drawn from an article that appears on his website, www.brianyansky.com.

The Matrix of Multi-Character Development

by David Poyer

I OFTEN GET ASKED, "Where do your characters come from?"

I don't limit myself to sea novels, but since they're a significant part of my work I'll derive my example from them. When I have to introduce a navy captain, I can think about captains I've served under, captains I've known, captains I've heard stories about, and captains I've read about.

This mass of experience forms what Saul Bellow calls an arcanum: a known world within which one can set any type of story one wishes. Conflicts of duty and honor, career and personal loyalty, man and woman, youth and age, belief and disbelief—I can set any of these in a milieu I know intimately.

But though some minor details of my characters may be Frankensteined, I believe deep characterization stems from motivation. The question *What does this person want?* is far more important to me than what the beginning writer generally obsesses about, which is, How tall is he, what's his name, what designer does she wear, what color are his/her eyes or hair or skin.

The character sketch, then, should concentrate on the subject's background and motivation. It need not be long. If you feel comfortable with the character, a paragraph's enough. But try to include the central dilemma.

Preliminary Character Sketches

Here, for example, are my preliminary character sketches for *As the Wolf Loves Winter*:

> W.T. "Red" Halvorsen: An old outdoorsman and retired oilfield worker, HALVORSEN lives deep in the woods in the basement of his

burned-out house, alone except for a puppy. Once a noted hunter, he gave up both hunting and drinking after his wife died in the fire he caused.

> Ainslee Thunner: President and chief executive officer of the Thunder Group. Can she hold the line at Thunder against a trio of outside investors determined to force her out? It looks like she can—until she's stabbed in the back by one of her own executives.

> Becky Benning: Thirteen, thin and introspective, a vegetarian, her biggest concerns are her Barbie collection and her little brother, who's dying of AIDS. Her life takes a sudden turn when she refuses to dissect a frog in biology class.

> Jammy Benning: Five years old and he knows he's dying. But he wonders if the Wolf Prince can help him, "like in the story."

> Rudolf Weyandy: Thunner's executive secretary and admirer. Ainslee senses he's in love with her. It's true, he admires her. But Rudy has more important plans: after 20 years of waiting, to finally gain the presidency of Thunder for himself.

> The Silver Wolf: Old and wary, he's survived hundreds of traps and ambushes. He doesn't quite understand how he got to this strange new land. But now it's his, and he'll defend his pack against anything and anyone.

> Rod Eisen: Halvorsen had to fire him once, when he was a kid and the men caught him stealing tools. Now he's grown, a lantern-jawed, competent man whose only flaw is that he's willing to do whatever he's told, for pay.

> Minor Characters: J.M. Zias, engineer and electronics hobbyist who is cornered by wolves; Leah Friedman, town doctor; Alma Sweet, Halvorsen's daughter; Halvorsen's beer-soaked cronies, Charlie Prouper, Mase Wilson, and Len DeSantis; Jerry Olen, Eisen's second in command at the Floyd Hollow lease; old Dan Thunner, long-retired founder of Thunder Oil Corporation; Lark Jones, the Thunner bodyguard.

Remember: During the course of your work the characters will *change*. Major protagonists you started with may lose steam. Minor characters will morph and steal the show. Don't be bound by what you've written the first time!

Character Analysis

George Witte, my long-time editor at St. Martin's Press, gave me a simple but powerful tool years ago for analyzing (taking apart) novels. For each major character, we ask:

> What does the character want?
> What does he/she do to get it?
> What's the result?
> Why should the reader care?
> How does character conflict or braid with others?
> How is it resolved at the end?

In a book with a single major or point of view character, a single narrative line, we can quickly outline the entire action proper of the book by answering these questions. For a multiple-character novel, we add more rows. As we add characters we also lay in points of interaction among them.

This multiple-character chart begins to resemble something familiar to students of economics and matrix algebra. It's an *array*. If you change any one element in an array, such as a spreadsheet, all the other elements will change too.

In the same way, if the novel's carefully put together, each change in the narrative line of one character will affect the others; maybe not in action proper, but if for no other reason, for juxtaposition and contrast.

The narrative lines can't proceed independently. Why not? Because then you have separate novels that just happen to be under the same cover. The reader would wonder why these people are in the same book. Fortunately editors know this, and they may be kind enough to point it out—in your rejection letter.

What one character wants, and does, and tries, should conflict with what the other characters want. This not only heightens tension, it gives a flavor of real life. Not that all the characters need to know all the others. Character No. 1 may know 3 and 4, but not 2 and 5.

Even if you don't want to work with a complete outline, the character analysis will clarify the underlying structure of the book for you.

Narrative Streams

Looking at the character analysis, and disciplining the jumble of ideas, scenes, research, and life experiences in my head, I sketch out each narrative stream. Following only one character, this starts with her introduction and proceeds to her involvement in her individual and/ or general climax and resolution. I set it out in a series of linked boxes, each box representing a chapter.

The book's built just like a wooden sailing ship. First we lay the keel: the primary narrative line, that of the character who'll witness and comprehend the largest part of the action.

Next we add the "strakes," the narrative lines of the other major characters. If split off, each would form a nearly complete novella.

At each point where the characters meet and interact, we add the stringers. These tie the strakes together, giving ship and novel unity, coherence, and strength.

These points of interaction need not be long or intimate. They can be as simple as two characters seeing each other on the street. But they can also be very powerful.

For example, one of the most effective scenes in *The Med* occurs after Private Willard S. Givens dies trying to execute flawed orders. His squaddies are carrying him to the medevac chopper. Commodore Sundstrom, whose vacillation and careerism helped kill Givens, sees the litter going by and calls the sergeant in charge over. Sergeant Cutford, who has persecuted Givens throughout the book, says to Sundstrom, "He was my best man."

To Sundstrom the body's just a marker in his campaign to make admiral. But the reader knows "Oreo" Givens. He knows how hard it was for him to find courage, and how wrong it was for him to die. The juxtaposition conveys the irony and waste of war far more powerfully than any intrusive authorial homily ever could.

Braiding the Narrative Streams

Near the end of a braided narrative, the reader expects the till-then separate narrative streams to gradually converge, then merge in a single climax or series of climaxes that lead not only to the resolution of each character's dilemma, but also illumine the theme of the work as a whole.

Remember our matrix? Each character has been trying, throughout the book, often in conflict with the other characters, to achieve a solution of his or her central problem or dilemma, along with the other obstacles we place in his path along the way. The resolution must address whether or not he finds one, and how he changes as a result.

Note I didn't say "how he *succeeds*." In my experience, simply having a character finally "win," achieve his original goal and live happily ever after, does not resemble life as we know it and is a pretty unsatisfactory resolution in anything purporting to resemble serious fiction. Some alternate resolutions could be:

> Realizing the original goal was impossible and settling for less
> Realizing it (or he) was wrong and changing sides in the crunch
> Getting what he wanted and just starting to regret it
> Getting it but paying such a huge price it's useless
> Not getting it but coming close enough to achieve something resembling happiness
> Not getting it but preventing any of the other characters from doing so either
> Watching as one of the other characters succeeds in his place.

David Poyer is the author of 29 books, including bestselling novels of the modern navy: *The Med*, *The Gulf*, *The Circle*, *The Passage*, *Tomahawk*, *China Sea*, *Black Storm*, *The Comman*; and *The Threat*, *Fire on the Waters*, *A Country of Our Own* and *That Anvil of Our Souls*, about the Civil War at sea; and other literary novels. His latest is *Korea Strait* (St. Martin's, 2007). His work is required reading in the US Naval Academy's "Literature of the Sea" course, along with that of Joseph Conrad and Herman Melville. A founding editor of the *New Virginia Review*, Poyer currently teaches in the Creative Writing program at Wilkes University in Wilkes-Barre, Pennsylvania.

First Person or Third Person?

by Nathan Bransford

First person or third person? Ah, the great debate that begins before a writer types their first "Once upon a time." Thousands of virtual trees have been felled for all of the pages and pages of debates on Internet writing message boards about this very topic. So which should you choose to write that novel?

Only you can answer that. Ha! You probably thought this was going to be easy. Twenty pushups, on your knuckles.

Nevertheless, I do have some thoughts that you might keep in mind as you're both making this decision and then putting it into practice.

First Person

The absolute most important thing to keep in mind as you're crafting a first-person narrative is that everything that occurs has to be filtered through your narrator's perspective. Everything the reader sees is therefore infused with the narrator's personality and pathos. Things don't just happen *in* a first-person narrative, they happen *through* the narrator's perspective.

The really compelling first-person narrators are the ones where a unique character is giving you their take on something that is happening, and yet it's clear to the reader that it's not the whole story. You're getting a biased look at the world, which is central to the appeal of the first-person narrative.

Think about it like this:

reality (the world of the book) >>>>>> || *prism* || >>>>>> *the narrator's perspective and thoughts*

One of the great tensions in a first-person narrative, then, is between what the narrator is saying and what the reader senses is *really* happening beyond the narrator's perspective. This doesn't necessarily have to mean that the narrator is unreliable, it just means that we're seeing the world through a very unique character's eyes—and *only* through that character's eyes. A protagonist might really convince herself, for instance, that she isn't sad that her mother died, but the reader senses that there's more to the story. Not necessarily unreliable, but it's also not the whole picture.

The other great essential element of a first-person narrative is that the narrator has to be compelling and likeable. I may get a lot of grief for the "likeable" part, but hear me out. Nothing will kill a first-person narrative quicker than an annoying narrator. Now, this doesn't mean the narrator has to be a good person, and hopefully the narrator is well-rounded enough to be a complex character. But the narrator has to pass the "stuck in an elevator" test. Would you want to be stuck in a room with this person for six hours? Would you want to listen to this person give a speech for six hours? If the answer is no, then you might want to reconsider.

Third Person

There are many different ways to craft a third-person narrative, and perhaps the hardest part is deciding how far you want to get inside your characters' heads. Do you want to use that god-like ability to really show the reader every single thought? Or do you want to keep their thoughts slightly hidden?

I tend to believe that the most interesting third-person narratives leave some distance between what is happening on the outside and what the characters are thinking. This way, to take the example of a character's mother dying, rather than knowing exactly what the character is thinking, the reader does the work to try and empathize with what the character is feeling in that moment and based upon a character's actions.

Think about it this way. The diagram for first person is reversed for third person:

what the reader sees (reality) >>>>>> || *prism* || >>>>>> *what the characters are thinking*

The tension, then, is still between what's really happening and what the reader gets to see, but in this case we're using our reading ability and natural empathy to deduce the character's motivations and feelings based on the god-like narration of what's really happening in the world of the book. In other words, we see the outside world, but the inside is slightly hidden.

One of the very most common mistakes writers make in third-person narration is doing too much work for the reader—using the omniscient perspective to tell the reader what the characters are thinking and how they're reacting, rather than trusting the readers to do that job. "Show not tell" is the cardinal rule of third person: show the characters acting upon their emotions rather than telling us how they feel. This keeps up that really fascinating barrier between what we're reading and what we sense is happening behind the prism.

So, to boil all this down:

The tension in first person is between a character's unique perspective and what is actually happening in the outside world.

The tension in third person is between what is happening on the outside world and what is happening from the characters' perspectives.

Nathan Bransford is a literary agent with the San Francisco office of Curtis Brown Ltd., a New York–based agency representing writers since 1914. His interests include literary fiction, mysteries and suspense, historical fiction, narrative nonfiction, business, history, sports, politics, current events, young adult fiction and science fiction.

This post appeared July 2007 on his blog (http://nathanbransford.blogspot.com).

Dialogue:
Say What?

by Meghan Miller

> "Say something witty."
> There was a long pause.
> "That wasn't witty."
> "What's it for, your article?"
> "Maybe."
> "Why are you writing our dialogue? Oh! Because you're doing dialogue tags."
> "Yup."
> "You're a jerk."
> "No, I'm researching."
> "You're not researching, you're chatting!"

Guess how many people were involved in that conversation. If you guessed two, you're wrong. Try it again.

> "Say something witty," she said.
> There was a long pause.
> "That wasn't witty," came a voice over the cubicle.
> "What's it for, your article?" he asked.
> "Maybe," she said.
> "Why are you writing our dialogue?" he said. "Oh! Because you're doing dialogue tags."
> "Yup." She didn't look up from her typing.
> "You're a jerk," he said.
> "No," she replied, "I'm researching."
> "You're not researching," said the voice from the next cube, "you're chatting!"

Now how many people? Without the dialogue tags, you don't even know how many people are involved in the conversation, let alone who's saying what.

Some people dislike dialogue tags—they feel they disrupt the flow of the conversation, or that the tags tend to be too repetitive. And, to be fair to those people, sometimes tags are disruptive or repetitive, but it's usually not for the reasons that people think. When they're done *right*, dialogue tags add to your writing, making it easier and more enjoyable to read. Done wrong, they're not only repetitive and disruptive, but sometimes downright confusing and silly.

Going back to our example (which is, in fact, an actual conversation that occurred in the office while I was gearing up to write this), let's talk about how to do it wrong. Obviously the first way, with no tags at all, is confusing. But what about something like this?

> "Say something witty," she announced.
>
> There was a long pause.
>
> "That wasn't witty," informed the woman in the next cubicle.
>
> "What's it for," he retorted, "your article?"
>
> "Maybe," she prevaricated.
>
> "Why are you writing our dialogue? Oh! Because you're doing dialogue tags," he presumed.
>
> "Yup." She kept typing.
>
> "You're a jerk," he interjected.
>
> "No, I'm researching," she decreed.
>
> "You're not researching, you're chatting!" shrilled the woman in the next cube.

In that example, it's still clear who's saying what, but it's much more awkward to read. We have announced, informed, retorted, prevaricated, presumed, interjected, decreed, and shrilled. They're all good, but used in a row the way they are here, they interrupt the flow of the conversation and fail to add anything—other than, maybe, the sense that the author really, really likes her thesaurus.

The other weird thing about the conversation above is that at no point did I use the word "said." But, you're saying, *said* is boring! *Said* is repetitive! *Said* is a meaningless filler word that doesn't add anything to the conversation—at least not unless you add adjectives to it.

To all of that, I say this: *Said* is one of those magical words that most readers will never even notice. With rare exceptions, authors want to be invisible to their readers. You want your reader to be wondering what your characters will do next, not wondering what clever writing technique or phrase you'll use next. The problem, then, is that the dialogue belongs to your characters, but the dialogue *tags* belong to you. *Said*—no adjectives needed—is easy. It's unobtrusive. *Said* is simply assigning words to someone, and most readers will barely notice that it's being used. The more complicated your dialogue tags are, though, the more *you* are showing in your book—and if people are paying attention to you, they're paying that much less attention to your characters or your plot.

So let's say, then, that you agree *said* is largely invisible, that *said* is unobtrusive, that *said* is useful. In the last paragraph I said that *said* was easy, and for the most part, I believe that's true—it's an easy way to convey who's saying what without getting caught up in seventeen ways to say *said*.

But I lied a little bit, because *said* is hard, too. Like I said, it's just assigning words to someone; it doesn't assign an emotional value to the words. Using *said* means that your dialogue has to be strong enough to stand on its own. The reader will need to be able to look at the character's dialogue and body language and understand that the character is angry or sad or delighted—and they'll need to understand without being told that she was exclaiming gleefully.

"Creative" dialogue tags are often an excuse for the author to tell rather than show. What the character is saying no longer matters as much as how the author tells us that they're saying it.

Let your dialogue speak for itself.

Meghan Miller is an editor with Ellora's Cave Publishing, Inc. Based in Akron, Ohio, the independent press focuses on genre fiction: romance, erotica, women's fiction, mystery/suspense, horror, science fiction and fantasy/paranormal. This piece appeared February 2008 on the publisher's blog, Redlines and Deadlines (www.redlinesanddeadlines.blogspot.com).

Developing a Sense of Place

by Philip Martin

"Every story *would be another story, and unrecognized ... if it took up its characters and plot and happened somewhere else.*"
—Eudora Welty

What do great stories do? They take you to another place.

Place obviously is where everything in a story happens: characters, plots, suspense, turning points, and such. But it is more than just a platform for stage action.

For emerging writers, the role of place may be almost invisible, as water to a fish. But place influences stories far more than many realize. Before I became an editor, I was a folklorist, doing field documentary projects, writing several books on regional culture, and running a small museum of traditional folklife. I saw the truth in what a great writer, Wendell Berry, said: that if you don't know *where* you are ... you don't know *who* you are.

Place is not just where stories happen. It creates character. It patterns our actions. It becomes a desire: to be home, to achieve a sense of belonging, to save home from intruders. Consider the role of the southern plantation, Tara, to Scarlett O'Hara in *Gone with the Wind.*

Think of the great novels you know and love. If you have any doubts, go to your bookshelf. Pull out half a dozen favorite books, and see how they start. As I'm sitting here, I'm looking at *The Yearling,* by Marjorie Rawlings, a touching story set in the Florida backwoods; the Navajo mysteries by Tony Hillerman (Native sheepherders and deep canyonlands); the gothic novel *Rebecca,* by Daphne du Maurier, with its eerie mansion Manderley; and any number of classic works of literary fiction such as the novels of Ernest Hemingway, Sinclair Lewis, John Steinbeck, and others.

Consider the role of Hogwarts in the Harry Potter series. From the first volumes, Hogwarts played a tremendous role in the story, gathering the young protagonists—Harry and his friends—into its curious and often-changing halls. It became the place where magic was learned and friendships formed. It stood for what must be saved: the ideals of the Hogwartian school, where magical powers were taught for the sake of good. It provided the thread for the multi-book series, each installment following Harry and friends through another year.

If Hogwarts had not been so unique—if you removed that creative element—the fantasy story, despite its endearing characters and complex plot, would nonetheless have been more commonplace. In many ways, Hogwarts was the core of Rowling's new vision. We journey with Harry in each book from the ordinary world to this enchanting castle in the mist ... and are thrilled to be transported to a fantastic but somehow believable place.

Place also plays a key role in nonfiction stories. As the setting of any newsworthy event, Where is one of the essential questions, the Five Ws of journalism (Who, What, Where, When, Why?). These elements are intricately linked. Consider how Place, the Where of the story, can play an active role in defining the elements of Who, What, even Why.

Stories that lack a "sense of place" are ordinary (and seldom advance from the depths of the slush pile). The settings are generic ... the same as those found in every other (unpublished) story. In a word, they are McSettings. (Note to McDonald's corporate lawyers: before suing me, consider I'm using the reference here to indicate uniformity, a lack of surprise ... a good thing perhaps in fast food, a bad thing in creative fiction or nonfiction.)

Stories with a strong sense of place, on the other hand, come alive. They fulfill that desire of the reader to be transported, for short time, to someplace else.

Let's look at some techniques for creating Place in your stories, starting with the basic task of introducing a place to readers.

Introducing a Place

TECHNIQUE #1: DESCRIBE A PLACE AS AN INSIDER KNOWS IT.
Think of your own home. What stands out most when you know a place very, very well?

Charlotte's Web is a wonderful fantasy in a rural setting, delivered in the beautifully simple prose of journalist and essayist E.B. White. In the book, most conversations between Wilbur the pig and Charlotte the spider take place in a barn.

This barn, introduced in a chapter of the same name, is described with a lyrical passage. Note how it is written from the point of view of someone who knows the barn intimately, through all seasons and over time.

> *The barn was very large. It was very old. It smelled of hay and it smelled of manure. It smelled of the perspiration of tired horses and the wonderful sweet breath of patient cows. It often had a sort of peaceful smell—as though nothing bad could happen ever again in the world. It smelled of grain and of harness dressing and of axle grease and of rubber boots and of new rope. And whenever the cat was given a fish-head to eat, the barn would smell of fish. But mostly it smelled of hay, for there was always hay in the great loft up overhead. And there was always hay being pitched down to the cows and the horses and the sheep.*
>
> *The barn was pleasantly warm in winter when the animals spent most of their time indoors, and it was pleasantly cool in summer when the big doors stood wide open to the breeze. The barn had stalls on the main floor for the work horses, tie-ups on the main floor for the cows, a sheepfold down below for the sheep, a pigpen down below for Wilbur, and it was full of all sorts of things that you find in barns: ladders, grindstones, pitchforks, monkey wrenches, scythes, lawn mowers, snow shovels, ax handles, milk pails, water buckets, empty grain sacks, and rusty rat traps. It was the kind of barn that swallows like to build their nests in. It was the kind of barn that children like to play in. And the whole thing was owned by Fern's uncle, Mr. Homer L. Zuckerman.*

Note how the passage is crafted with clear, effective language. White starts with short sentences. Then he builds slowly, introducing the sense of tired, sweet patience. We encounter the diverse scents, as we begin to image the place fully. We learn who shares the space: cat, cows, horses, sheep.

There is almost no visual description until the second paragraph, when the big doors are thrown open. Then we see some details: the repetitious organization of the stalls, the clutter of objects here and there. Finally, it is summed up as a warm place where animals and children can find a cozy place to spend time.

What does a person see and feel when he or she arrives somewhere as a newcomer, to see a place for the first time?

Here is the beginning of a story, *Skellig* (Delacorte, 1999), by British author David Almond. The cataloged summary reads: "Unhappy about his baby sister's illness and the chaos of moving into a dilapidated house, Michael retreats to the garage and finds a mysterious stranger who is something like a bird and something like an angel."

As the story begins, we approach the family's new home through the eyes of the young protagonist, Michael, as he recalls how a real estate agent had given a tour, letting them peek first in the cluttered garage, then leading them through the rundown house itself.

> We called it the garage because that's what the real estate agent, Mr. Stone, called it. It was more like a demolition site or a rubbish dump or like one of those ancient warehouses they keep pulling down at the wharf. Stone led us down the garden, tugged the door open, and shined his little flashlight into the gloom. We shoved our heads in at the doorway with him.
>
> "You have to see it with your mind's eye," he said. "See it cleaned, with new doors and the roof repaired. See it as a wonderful two-car garage." He looked at me with a stupid grin on his face. "Or something for you, lad—a hideaway for you and your pals. What about that, eh?"
>
> I looked away. I didn't want anything to do with him. All the way round the house it had been the same. Just see it in your mind's eye. Just imagine what could be done. All the way round I kept thinking of the old man, Ernie Myers, that had lived here on his own for years. He'd been dead nearly a week before they found him under the table in the kitchen. That's what I saw when Stone told us about seeing with the mind's eye. He even said it when we got to the dining room and there was an old cracked toilet sitting there in the corner behind a plywood screen. I just wanted him to shut up, but he whispered that toward the end Ernie couldn't manage the stairs. His bed was brought in here and a toilet was put in so everything was easy for him. Stone looked at me like he didn't think I should know about such things.

Notice how few details are given. The garage (described more fully in the next chapter as Michael explores it on his own) is described only by comparison: rubbish dump, etc. The house is seen only through the pathetic story of the man who died there.

The initial imagery, with its focus on emotions and lack of visual details, is true to a boy's perspective, which is unlikely to note architectural features like a Victorian gingerbread cornice or what type of hardwood the floor is made of.

The place is seen therefore only in Michael's reaction to it. This sets up the story to follow, as Michael explores the garage and discovers an odd creature, barely alive, a creature that strangely connects to the story of Michael's infant sister in the hospital.

TECHNIQUE #3: BE SELECTIVE IN DETAILS.

Know what to leave out. Both of the two master passages above use a controlled selection of details. As Jane Yolen wrote in her instructional guide, *Writing Books for Children*: "Remember, too, what you don't put down can be as important as what you do. Lao-Tse in his *Tao Te Ching* wrote that in a vessel of clay, it is the emptiness inside that makes it useful."

As with character, the fewer things that are pinned down, the more readers are free to flesh out the picture themselves. This can result in a fuller picture, paradoxically, than a detailed description delivered by the author.

Also, when fewer initial details are given, the reader realizes that those being given are significant, chosen by the author for a purpose. This is one of the core tricks of good storytelling, one that quickly engages the reader's interest.

I've often used the following passage to discuss good writing. Notice how Tolkien's *The Hobbit* begins with a description of place. Tolkien, a master of the art of story, starts with three simple points: a hobbit hole is not a wet hole nor a dry hole, but a comfy one. His limited choice of details, as he leads us into the well-appointed hole, presents the character of the inhabitant long before we meet Bilbo Baggins.

> In a hole in the ground there lived a hobbit. Not a nasty, dirty, wet hole, filled with the ends of worms and an oozy smell, nor yet a dry, bare, sandy hole with nothing in it to sit down on or to eat: it was a hobbit-hole, and that means comfort.
>
> It had a perfectly round door like a porthole, painted green, with a shiny yellow brass knob in the exact middle. The door opened on to a

tube-shaped hall like a tunnel: a very comfortable tunnel without smoke, with panelled walls, and floors tiled and carpeted, provided with polished chairs, and lots and lots of pegs for hats and coats—the hobbit was fond of visitors.

TECHNIQUE #4: PAN IN FROM A DISTANT SHOT TO A CLOSER PERSPEC-
TIVE.

In describing a place, it helps to create a sense of motion, to help read-ers enter the space, as Tolkien has in the example above. A good tech-nique is to move from a general or distant view (the hobbit hole) to a closer examination of some feature of interest (the round green door with a brass knob in the middle).

Here's a dramatic example by the great Jack London, from the beginning of his novel *White Fang*. It begins cinematically with a dis-tant, fly-over shot, then it catches a bit of motion in the scene, and zooms in to examine that curious item in more detail:

Dark spruce forest frowned on either side the frozen waterway. The trees had been stripped by a recent wind of their white covering of frost, and they seemed to lean toward each other, black and ominous, in the fading light. A vast silence reigned over the land. The land itself was a desola-tion, lifeless, without movement, so lone and cold that the spirit of it was not even that of sadness. There was a hint in it of laughter, but of a laugh-ter more terrible than any sadness ... It was the Wild, the savage, frozen-hearted Northland Wild.

But there was life, abroad in the land and defiant. Down the frozen waterway toiled a string of wolfish dogs. Their bristly fur was rimed with frost. Their breath froze in the air as it left their mouths, spouting forth in spumes of vapor that settled upon the hair of their bodies and formed into crystals of frost. Leather harness was on the dogs, and leather traces attached them to a sled which dragged along behind. The sled was with-out runners. It was made of stout birch-bark, and its full surface rested on the snow. The front end of the sled was turned up, like a scroll, in order to force down and under the bore of soft snow that surged like a wave before it. On the sled, securely lashed, was a long and narrow oblong box. There were other things on the sled—blankets, an axe, and a coffee-pot and fry-ing-pan; but prominent, occupying most of the space, was the long and narrow oblong box.

TECHNIQUE #5: USE A VARIETY OF SENSES.

I'll just refer you here to the above passages. Notice how often they use more senses, including a sixth sense of intuition, besides just that of vision. Like the best memories, they are based as much on a sense of space, of mood, of smells and sounds, of things missing or curious.

TECHNIQUE #6: BE ORIGINAL, BE SURPRISING.

This of course is good advice, and frustratingly hard to explain how to accomplish. How do you create details that are fresh, original in combination, surprising? I can only point to good examples to set the standard. Here is an achingly beautiful beginning to a wonderful novel, *The Piano Tuner*, by Daniel Mason (Knopf, 2002). Note how he builds this impressionistic first glimpse of the place where the story will take place, focusing on the sun and heat, and ending this prologue with an astonishing image.

> In the fleeting seconds of final memory, the image that will become Burma is the sun and a woman's parasol. He has wondered which visions would remain—the Salween's coursing coffee flow after a storm, the predawn palisades of fishing nets, the glow of ground turmeric, the weep of jungle vines. (…)
>
> Yet above these visions, the sun rises searing, pouring over them like a gleaming white paint. [Those] who interpret dreams in shaded, scented corners of the markets, told him a tale that the sun that rose in Burma was different from the sun that rose in the rest of the world. He only needed to look at the sky to know this. To see how it washed the roads, filling the cracks and shadows, destroying perspective and texture. To see how it burned, flickered, flamed, the edge of the horizon like a daguerreotype on fire, overexposed and edges curling. How it turned liquid the sky, the banyan tree, the thick air, his breath, throat, and his blood. (…)
>
> Now this sun hangs above a dry road. Beneath it, a lone woman walks under a parasol, her thin cotton dress trembling in the breeze, her bare feet carrying her away … He watches her, how she approaches the sun, alone. He thinks of calling out to her, but he cannot speak.
>
> The woman walks into a mirage, into the ghost reflection of light and water that the Burmese call than hlat. Around her, the air wavers, splitting her body, separating, spinning. And then she too disappears. Now only the sun and the parasol remain.

I hope these techniques will help you think of ways to introduce the Place in your story. I'll end with a few words by one of the great writers about place today, Barry Lopez, winner of the National Book Award. He summed up some essence of what we wish to feel about a place when he wrote: "Many of us, I think, long to become the companion of a place, not its owner."

Is Scarlett O'Hara simply the owner of Tara, or is she in a more complex relationship with her home? In all the examples above, place is far more than just a physical space to be inhabited, let along owned. It is something that we interact with on a deep emotional level.

To be a better writer, in all your note-taking, imagination, outline, research, drafts, and revisions, look for ways to develop a sense of place. Think of how to make the place someplace that a reader would want to visit and linger in, to enjoy having become an invited companion, for a while, of that special place that anchors your story.

Philip Martin is editor of *The New Writer's Handbook* and previously was acquisitions editor for The Writer Books, where he produced guides for writers on many topics. He is also author of a book on fantasy fiction, *The Writer's Guide to Fantasy Literature*, along with several other books on regional music and folklore. He lives in Milwaukee and is director of Great Lakes Literary (www.greatlakeslit.com), which offers editorial and professional development services for writers.

This article first appeared September 2007 in his free newsletter of advice for writers, found at his website.

Common Faults in Short Stories

by Stephen Moran

SOME PEOPLE have expressed interest in knowing why entries in the *Willesden Herald* short story competition are eliminated or advanced, so I offer the following notes on why all but the last few are eliminated.

Writers need to realize that writing is like music: there is no getting away with bum notes. Think of the judging process as a series of auditions—*The X-Factor, American Idol, Young Musician of the Year,* if you like. Now think of the hopeless cases. Out of tune: Next! Inept: Next! Hopelessly feeble: Next. Ego tripper: Next. An open competition is by definition a talent contest, and the entries can be imagined in the same way. But what are the bum notes, gaffes, misconceptions, delusions, ineptitudes in writing that are analogous to the failings of talent show entrants? Here are a few, not rearranged, but simply as they come to mind.

1. Failure to observe the rules. Let's get this most boring reason for rejection of entries out of the way. In this year's *Willesden* competition, the rule most breached was the one that specifies no author's name on the manuscript. Not double-spaced or single-sided also featured, as well as missing or incomplete entry forms. Last, in both senses, were entries received after the closing date. Something approaching one in ten was eliminated for not complying with the rules. It is likely that some people took incomplete information from third party sites, so I recommend that you get the official rules and entry form from the competition website. Then follow the rules exactly, not approximately. Any entry that is not in compliance with the rules will be binned, unread.

2. Overcrowded with characters. Seán Ó Faoláin said a short story is to a novel as a hot air balloon is to a passenger jet. Like a jet the novel

takes a long time to get off the ground, carries a lot of people and takes them a long way from where it started. On the other hand, the short story takes off vertically, rises directly to a great height, usually carries only one or two people, and lands not very far from where it took off. So when three, four, five and sometimes even more names are mentioned in the first two pages, it is inevitable that readers will be turned off. They will always suffer from the following problem as well.

3. Undifferentiated characters. A name is not a character. Pinky said this, Perky said that, Blinky said something similar and Pisky said the same, as the old wartime song might have gone. Each character should be a complete person, with their own C.V. if you like, their own history, temperament, habits, weaknesses, plans, objectives etc., though these need not and should not be explicitly listed as such.

4. Solipsism. One miserable person being miserable. This was the most common and depressing failing. Unrelenting monotony of one single, invariably miserable and oppressive viewpoint. No sign of concern or even mention of any other character, nothing other than one person's dreary moaning. If you are not interested in other characters, at least make it funny.

5. Well-enough written, but I just don't like it. This is the uncongenial protagonist or narrator, arrogant, cruel-minded, usually petty, often attempting gross-out effects, and usually going round in ever-diminishing circles before vanishing in a puff of studied triviality. It leaves a bad taste and invariably evokes the response that it's well-enough written, but I just don't like it. There is no gun to the reader's head. People do not read to be grossed out, or to join in somebody else's squalor or misery. There has to be an element of transcendence, transmutation of the base material into the gold of fiction.

6. Throwaway endings. The story has been going along fairly well, showing signs of life and suddenly the writer must have thought, "Oh I can't be bothered, I'm just going to put a twist here and finish it." It's literally almost impossible to believe sometimes why anybody would ever think of sending in something that is clearly truncated and given up on—what a waste of postage, etc.

7. Over-elaborated endings. All has been going well, we're hoping this

might be a contender, we come to an excellent sign-off line, then woe, woe, thrice or four or five times woe for every extra sentence or paragraph that follows after that, telling us what should be left for us to decide for ourselves. So frustrating to hit one of these after reading all the way.

8. Throat-clearing openings. A build-up to the fact that we are about to hear a story, what it's not about, what it is about, the fact that it starts here, the fact that it starts with something, the fact that it's of a particular kind, the fact that you're going to tell it. Cut, cut, cut. Then we come to the line where it really starts, but by then it's too late: for something to get on a short list, it has to be virtually flawless and you've just started with a whopping great flaw.

9. Boring. "Middle of page three and I am totally bored." "Well-enough written, but what is the point?" "I'm losing the will to live." Again, I keep repeating, the reader does not have a gun to his or her head. We have lives of our own. We don't need to substitute somebody else's dreary domestic arrangements in our minds for our own. To us, yours are far less interesting—and ours were not that interesting to start with. Who cares if somebody listened to a news story on the radio, went shopping, bought a packet of corn flakes. Yawn, yawn, yawn.

10. Banal. Commonplace, dull, the sort of thing you hear every day. This is really a continuation of "boring." A lot of stories about elderly people living in squalor. A particularly English phenomenon. A lot of stories about dying relatives. Okay, but they better be good. It's important to write about these things, but when you do you need to realise that there will be ten other people writing about the same thing, so you'd better make it very good. Life can be banal, but we turn to fiction to find—again—transcendence.

11. Mush. Mom and Pop and kiddie all having breakfast mush and school mush and boy and girl friend mush, car and scenery mush and all starting and ending up in a nostalgic sunset mush. I've given you English kitchen squalor, now I give you American kitchen mush. Both equally nauseating. I might as well add princess and frog fairytales in here.

12. Failed experiment. It's fine and admirable to try an experimental format, but it's not an excuse for slightness, skimpiness, overwriting, repetitiveness, underwriting, forced or boring content, or as

often as not for semi-disguised or decorated solipsism, or any of the other failings listed here.

13. Unconvincing. Clunky or melodramatic. I just don't buy it. This is fake, phoney baloney, unbelievable but presented as supposedly realistic. Often forced and plot-driven. Corny ending likely. Let's add in here "routine police procedurals," where hard-bitten Captain Craggy trades inscrutable comments on cases with eager tyro, etc.

14. Weak premise. The triviality of some themes submitted is hard to believe. When you get a story that is 30 pages all about a minor ailment that has no apparent effects or significance, what are you to make of it? The writer is talking to himself, like one of those poor souls you can see on the high street any day. A sort of sub-category here is the "clever-sounding" element, that is like a lump of gristle in the apple pie of the story. Some people have a compulsion to mention things they have some specialist expertise about or simply know the names of, in a certain way that makes me think, "Go away."

15. Not a short story. We don't tell you what a short story is, you're supposed to know. If you don't know, tough. You need to go away and find out. I can tell you it's not something over 220 pages long, as one entrant must have thought. Neither is it an essay. I presume people send in essays, thinking "Well it's a longshot." No it's not a longshot, it's a dud. Regardless of length a short story is not a mini-novel—a real tyro failing. The simplest advice is to read as many good short stories as you can and yours should be at home in their company—if you aspire to that. And if you don't then why do you bother writing?

16. Full of errors. Slapdash spelling and grammatical errors are like bum notes in a musical audition. Even if you are a shining genius (as you all think you are) it is unlikely you will get away even with one. More than one and you're stone dead. A lot of people who do not speak English seem to think they can find success in a short story competition with texts that contain errors in every sentence. Very rarely, there may be a story that is otherwise compelling but frustratingly riddled with errors.

17. Transparent attempt to pander to the judges. Every year we've had one or two (usually impossible) journeys in London, invariably

ending up in Kilburn or Willesden. Try to see it from my point of view; imagine I open a guide book and try and write something about your city, where I've never lived—imagine the phoniness of the result. I would suggest you do not attempt to write to order for a competition. You can if you insist, but I can spot it a mile off and it is really off-putting. It just suggests that you have no real hinterland of your own.

18. Poor dialogue. Exposition of the story in dialogue is a common failing. "We must be very careful, as it is raining now and visibility is low." "Yes, and it is cold. Ooh, look at the traffic there," said Pinky. "Yes, there is a lot of it, isn't there," said Perky. "Look out! Elegant variation dead ahead," muttered Pinky and exclaimed Perky simultaneously. Maybe you've heard somewhere that there has to be dialogue. What they didn't add was, "not at any price." If there is dialogue, it should be something that people really might say. Do not make your characters into ventriloquists' dummies to tell your story through. There can be long passages without dialogue or there can be lots or a little dialogue. What there must not be is phony dialogue. Another thing, if your characters are well enough defined, you should find that hardly any attribution is needed.

19. Unevenness. This includes unevenness of tone, pace, style and theme: parts of the story that are not in keeping with the rest, which should have been edited out or replaced. A story that starts out in one tone, maybe as a serious and really compelling story, then halfway through turns into a facetious spoof. A digression from the main theme that makes the reader think, "What is that doing here?" I think there was one entry we received that seemed to be three short shorts stuck together. More slapdashery. Remember: it's like music—you can't "get away" with anything. With most competitions it should be safe to assume you are writing for/playing your music for people who can say in all modesty that they are not tone deaf.

20. Summation. "All in the past" syndrome. This is a problem sometimes characterised as "undepicted action" or "telling instead of showing." Most writers seem to have a grasp of the need to get attention at the beginning, but an astonishing number by the middle of page two have started to tell us all about some ancient family history. All sense of immediacy and story is lost and instead we're

having summaries of complex events that happened, one sentence each, like a dry and tedious history book.

21. Underwriting and overwriting. Too sketchy or too longwinded. I get the impression that the longwinded are probably more pleased with themselves, but they're no more popular with readers than the skimpers—rather the reverse. Cut out as much as you can, without cutting into the quick, and you'll find that your text will improve. Isaac Babel said that our writing becomes stronger not when we can add no more but when we can take nothing more away. The skimpy efforts are just rushed, undercooked, choose your own metaphor. I'm sure we know when we have underwritten (I include myself), so why do we waste postage sending underwritten pieces out?

22. Unicorns and elves, chick lit, police procedurals and bodice rippers. These should only be submitted to specialist competitions for their specific genres. The *Willesden* is for so-called literary stories. It's not a pleasing term, so I would rather say non-generic stories. (I think Joyce once said that the word "literature" was used as a term of abuse.) Readers will not get beyond the first line of—and they are invariably labelled thus—the Prologue: "Nervelda gazed on the mistfields of Thuriber. Her green eyes glinted in the slanting sun, as the tribes of Godnomore straggled over the barren land." Lord and Lady Farquahar and their servants will journey in vain to quaint villages full of worthy and unworthy peasants. I think I've already mentioned Inspector Craggy (promoted in the sequel) and his eager sidekicks. As for chick lit: in reading as well as in life, we may be partial to a bit of office romance, but about ten or twenty of them later and they begin to pall.

23. Faux jollity. Particularly faux jollity centered around pubs, and particularly around pubs in Ireland. Industrially extruded quantities of guff about distant histories in small town life. Standing jokes that should have been left where they toppled. Weird spastic prose as if the task of writing the story had been given by a writer with a good idea to the former class dunce, now barman. I think humor only ever exists in something that sets out to be serious. Anything that sets out to be humorous is doomed.

24. Ankles. Particularly ankles in Asia. But I don't want to be overly negative and turn critique into a despicable blood sport, because

there have been many charming, fascinating and amusing entries from the sub-continent as well as from Africa and other (to me) strange places. As a matter of fact, I'm not at all sure that Ankles in Asia, though it sounds worryingly now like a rare disease, is not in fact a virtue. Let a thousand professors dream of butterfly kisses with a thousand feisty young neighbor girls. And please do try us again with wonderful tales of African village life and politics.

25. Clumsiness. Proliferation of unnecessary commas. Awkward mis-edited clauses, unintentional rhymes, pedestrian, dull prose, infantile expressions, over-formality ("Mr. Smith had a reputation as bit of a disciplinarian. Miss Elma Furblong often thought that, while thinking about what to get to ease the hunger pangs in her tummy.") Stuffiness generally. Let's save a few more categories and add here out-of-date literary sensibilities and pretensions, the aphoristic, portentous, pompous, didactic and polemical. If I think of any more I'll most likely add them into this catch-all category.

26. Clichéd. I'm thinking mostly of clichéd expressions. If I said I'm thinking "by and large" of clichéd expressions, that would be an example in itself. It's usually little clumps of words that always seem to go together, but also whole concepts that go unquestioned. Cities are always bustling, sunsets always golden, looks always stern etc. The Irish poet Jean O'Brien said (in a workshop I attended) "Beware of the bits that seem to write themselves." In avoiding clichés it is the underlying assumptions that have to be dispelled. A "translated cliché" would still be a cliché.

27. Unspeakable. "Actors call some lines pills to swallow, for they cannot be made to sound genuine" is an example of this syndrome. Maybe it's just me, but I find the use of the word "for" instead of "because" archaic and labored. I tend to think that if I wouldn't use the word in speech then I shouldn't in writing. I wouldn't say "I think it's very cold today for the pond is frozen" so why write it? Anything that would sound labored if read out has to go. You probably recognize the dismal effect when somebody says something and "it sounds like they're reading it out." If I write: "The solution to this problem is to read everything aloud first" that in itself contains an example of the problem. If I say that sentence, it sounds like I'm reading it out. Maybe it's acceptable in an after-dinner speech, but it's death to a story. It breaks the spell.

28. Pastiche. There can be cases where the whole story is a cliché, if you see what I mean, which is usually to say that it is derivative in the extreme. If it's not a simple case of writing to a formula, this is more seriously a lack of a genuine "voice." What I usually say about pastiche is that I'm very impressed by people who can emulate other writers to a tee, because I find it difficult enough just to write like myself. Here's a little story: When I was a kid I used to sing myself to sleep at night. One Sunday I went to see *The Jolson Story* (I think I saw parts one and two) at the Casino cinema in Finglas and memorized some of the songs. That night I began to sing them in bed, and trying to sound like Al Jolson. Lying back in the dark, after a while I asked my Grandad, who slept on the other side of the room, if he liked my new voice. I'll always remember his answer because it said so much. He said, "I prefer your own voice."

In summary, when there are hundreds of entries to a short story competition, only a story that is near as dammit technically flawless has a chance of reaching the short list. As you know, there are still more qualities beyond technical perfection that are then required. I remember hearing a conductor say that when he conducted a good orchestra he relied on the fact that every musician in it was technically perfect, which left him free to work on interpretation and expressivity. With stories I suppose it's subtle resonances and other quasi-poetic elements in the layering of words, a sense of adventure, newness etc.—another list for another day.

I've just added another three categories of fault, a couple of days after posting the first draft of this, and a list of books stopping short of literary theory, philosophy of language, and suchlike. In the Willesden short story competition we're not asking for high philosophy, but we are looking for something technically perfect, original, vivid and compelling in serious or humorous non-generic stories. How or why these come into existence may always remain a mystery but—like life itself—they do.

P.S. I should add that every single entry was a valiant effort. It's a labor of love to read them as it must have been to write them, when most of us have full working days and only the tired few hours remaining to devote to our art. I only wrote the list of points above to be helpful and to open my own thoughts and prejudices to constructive criticism. Speaking only for myself, I think and always think every year, that all of the writers who entered showed talent and potential, and that among the stories there were many "near misses."

Some books about writing:

The First Five Pages (Noah Lukeman, Prentice Hall)
On Writing (Stephen King, New English Library)
Bird by Bird (Anne Lamott, Anchor Books)

About the short story:
The Lonely Voice (Frank O'Connor, Melville House)

A few interesting online resources:
Belief and Technique for Modern Prose (Jack Kerouac)
www.writing.upenn.edu/~afilreis/88/kerouac-technique.html

A Short History of the Short Story (William Boyd)
www.theshortstory.org.uk/downloads/boyd.pdf

Principles of a Story (Raymond Carver)
www.theshortstory.org.uk/downloads/Essay-Carver-3.pdf

Stephen Moran has published a volume of short stories, *The London Silence* (Pretend Genius Press, 2004), and has contributed to anthologies and magazines. He is responsible for the annual *Willesden Herald* international short story competition (www.willesdenherald.com), which began in 2005. He also edits the New Short Stories series (http://newshortstories.homestead.com), which includes the winning entries from the competition. This post appeared February 2008 on the *Willesden Herald*'s blog.

Moran was born in Dublin, Ireland, and now lives in London. His own website can be found at www.stephenmoran.net.

Two of a Writer's Best (and Least Known) Friends

by Tom Chandler

TODAY, A WRITER'S ABILITY to quickly connect with readers is critical. What allies do you have in your fight to engage readers? (Stick around and I'll show you.)

Meet Left and Right: the Parentheses Twins

My English teacher said parentheses were the tools of lazy writers. Wikipedia says, "In most writing, overuse of parentheses is usually a sign of a badly structured text."

All true. But irrelevant.

In skilled hands, a parenthetical statement enclosed in parentheses will help bridge the gap between writer and reader, puncturing the invisible barrier between the two. (See what I mean?)

They give you the ability to step out of the copy and into the reader's space. You can even share what feels like a private joke (just don't tell anyone else!), transforming your reader from skeptic to confidant.

Here are a few ways you can put them to work.

The Reinforcer

"More than 2,000 people have already taken me up on this offer (they're making money as we speak). Isn't it time you joined them?

Create an Action Picture

"Execs at technology-driven companies tend to frown and spit when you mention marketing. It falls below cleaning the restrooms and filing payroll taxes on the desirability food chain. Pitch a marketing plan (frown, spit) to these companies, and you'd better bring a spittoon."

The Humorous Aside

"In the last six months he's been on the receiving end of so many fly rod orders that if you tried to order a rod in the parking lot before we fished, you'd wait 1.5 years to get it (actually, you'd probably get punched for coming between Jim and a rising trout, but I'm making a point here)."

Personal Call to Action

"*The Elements of Style* should be on every writer's bookshelf (if it's not on yours, stop reading and visit Amazon.com immediately), and owning two copies is more insurance policy than overkill."

Emphasis

"It has to rank as the worst (the *absolute* worst) Father's Day gift I've ever received."

Parentheses are not a tool for formal writing. But the rise of blogs and Engagement Marketing is driving the conversation away from the formal and towards the informal.

In fact, write blog entries for engagement purposes, and your goal isn't to sell—it's to step out of the screen and connect with your reader.

Careful use of parentheses will help.

Still, my English teacher was right about one thing—the utility of parentheses fades with overuse. So insert them sparingly.

Use them to project intimacy and personality. Use them to step off the screen and make friends with your reader. Use them to share a joke.

Use them, and watch your connection to your readers grow (see, I told you it was worth the wait).

Tom Chandler has written copy and consulted on marketing issues for more than 20 years for companies big and small. He currently focuses on engagement marketing, helping clients develop a clear messaging platform and sound marketing plan. A photojournalist by training, he also writes three blogs (one on fly fishing) and lives at the base of a 14,000-foot inactive volcano in the mountains of northern California, giving him a chance to enjoy the great outdoors.

This article first appeared 2006 on his blog, The Copywriter Underground (http://copywriterunderground.com).

PITCHING YOUR WORK

Querying

by Rebecca Skloot

WHEN I FIRST started freelancing, I was constantly trying to expand my client base, so I sent out a lot of blind queries. Aside from the obvious (the ability to write and a story idea), I think the most important requirements for writing successful queries are persistence, thick skin, pre-query research, more thick skin, and more persistence.

Developing the idea and writing the query sounds like more work than it actually is. I got my queries down to a kind of formula, which includes a basic paragraph about who I am and why I should write the story. I cut and paste that, then tinker to fit the publication and story. I often write on related topics, so background information and basics of the story can work via cut-and-paste too.

I used to spend hours and hours doing pre-query research and writing the letter, but after doing that a few times and having the query flop, I decided it was best to not go overboard. I do enough to make sure there's a story there, then if an editor replies with interest, I go back and do more research.

Querying Tips

> Don't try to break into every magazine at once. It's a lot more effective to pick one and do a good job with it. Editors know when you're blanket pitching—it's obvious.

> Know the publication so that in your query you can show them that you've done your homework and are right for them. Don't pitch a profile to a magazine that doesn't do profiles; don't pitch a news story to a magazine that does mostly literary or historical stuff.

> Make your blind pitch as far from blind as possible (see "the query letter/email" section, below).

> Pitch to an associate, assistant or senior editor instead of the editor-in-chief, executive editor, or managing editor, who truly are too

busy to read queries from new writers and aren't always as on-the-lookout for new talent.

> Try to have at least two queries in circulation at all times.
> Never let a query sit on your desk for more than a day—once it's been rejected or ignored, pitch it somewhere else, so you always have something out there.
> Don't feel like you *have* to live in New York if you're going to be a writer. Non–New York writers are actually very desirable. Editors depend on them to tell readers what's going on in the rest of the world.
> One way to make connections with editors no matter where you live is to volunteer to organize and moderate panels. Then you get to hand-pick who you want to meet.
> Loyalty really means something to editors. Keep coming back, let them know you're pitching just to them. The fact that you actually know something about the magazine and care about it is important.
> If I'm interviewing somebody, I always let them go off on tangents. New stories often come from digressions in stories I'm already writing.

Pre-query Research

I recommend never calling an editor. They're busy and fielding phone calls from countless writers and PR people wanting their attention. And, if you call to pitch a story, the only answer they can give you is, Write a pitch and send it—they can't tell whether you can write over the phone. Pitching over the phone makes you appear inexperienced and runs the risk of annoying an editor to the point where he/she won't read your ideas once you send them. If you want to get in touch with an editor you don't know, call the reception desk at the magazine and ask for his or her email address.

I use Internet searches and databases (like Lexis Nexis) to read what's been written on any subject I'm hoping to write about. And I make quadruply sure no one has already written the story I'm pitching (I learned this lesson the hard way after pitching a story to a big national magazine days after the exact story ran in their competitor's magazine, which made me look like an idiot). I do this by reading at least the table of contents and leads from zillions of magazines on a regular basis so I can keep up on what's being covered by which publications. I also ask friends who follow the media, because they'll often know whether my story—or something like it—has been done recently.

I always do a preliminary interview (these are usually very short) to make sure I have access to the story I'm pitching, and to get quotes and character details I can use in the query to (a) show my access and (b) give the pitch some life. Since I often get story ideas while doing interviews for other stories, when anything grabs my attention, I'll ask enough questions to find out if there's a story there, which serves as my preliminary interview if I pitch the story in the future. That makes the whole process easier, and much more efficient.

The Query Letter (or Email)

To make your queries as far from blind as possible, I suggest a three-part approach. First, plant your name in their heads in a short email introducing yourself, saying who you've written for and something about how you know them (either "so-and-so recommended I contact you," or "I saw you speak at Blank Conference, and was struck by what you said about blah, which inspired me to contact you," or "I read this piece you wrote or edited in *Blah Magazine*, which inspired me to contact you" … or something along those lines). From my experience as an editor, and from talking with editors, I say this can help you get in the door without landing in the slush pile.

Second, after introducing yourself and making it clear you've done your homework about the editor and/or the magazine, explain that you have a story idea you think they'd be interested in, and ask how they prefer to receive queries: email, fax, snail mail, etc. In my experience, editors usually respond to this preliminary email within a day or so, because it's easy for them to fire off the information. This is good for several reasons: you don't end up sending a query by email to someone who despises email queries, and most importantly, *you've planted your name in their brains.* Chances are they'll then open your query when you send it. (I can only think of one time an editor didn't respond to say email queries were fine.)

Third, write your actual query. Keep in mind that queries aren't just about showing that you have a good idea; they're about making yourself stand out by showing that you can write. Try to keep your actual queries to one page, and structure them as you would structure a story: make sure to have a lead, a nutgraph, and an overall structure to the whole thing (like coming back to the lead in the end, or something like that) to show them you know how to put a story together. The hardest part of the whole thing is usually finding the lead.

It's good to throw at least one line in the query to indicate that you know their magazine and/or audience, like: "Since readers of *Blah Magazine* are primarily women of blah age, this story would appeal to them because of blah," or "Like the story you did last month on blah, this story will do blah for your readers ..." or something like that.

At the end of my queries, I say if they'd like to see samples of my writing they can do so on my website, which I provide a link to (they often don't look for it in the sig line so I give it in the text of the email). Then I say if they'd like hard copies of clips I'd be happy to send them if they provide me with a mailing address. I've only had one editor reply and ask for hard copies of clips.

Following Up

The kind of follow-up I do depends on the timeliness of the story. If I'm pitching a story that needs to be acted on quickly, I say so in my query and end with something like, "Given the timely nature of this story, I hope to hear from you soon so I can market it elsewhere if you're not interested." I've found this to be effective, partially because editors are people too and it's good to remind them that you're trying to make a living, and also (I think) because it gives a hint of competition, like if they don't grab it someone else will, but that may just be in my head.

On a timely story, if I haven't heard back in a week (or a few days, depending on the story), I'll send an email saying I wanted to check to see if they got it, and I'll paste my original email at the bottom so they don't have to go digging for it. (The more you can do to show an editor you understand and respect how busy they are, the better.)

If I don't hear after a week (maybe less, depending on the story), then I'll call. If I call and get no reply, then I move on to another publication and don't waste my time with that editor any more.

If it's a less pressing story, I'll give them several weeks to reply (this is usually about four weeks—my rule of thumb is, resist the temptation to nag an editor until you can't stand it any more, then wait another week). Then I follow a similar path (email, call, move on).

Usually the follow-up email gets some response, even if it's a simple "We're not interested." Don't follow up on these to try to find out why they weren't interested, just send it to someone else.

Use the Buddy System

It's very important to have a network of writers you can depend on. My friends and I send each other stuff all the time. I know what they like to write about, and vice versa. We help each other keep up with the reading ("Oh my God, did you see the piece on blah? You've got to read this!").

One of my best friends is a wonderful writer I met in grad school—he and I read every one of our big magazine stories out loud to each other over the phone as we write them (we've been known to talk more than 12 times in a day, sometimes calling to read each section of a story as we write it if we need feedback). We also read every finished piece before we submit them to our editors. This is invaluable. It's also good to just get together and whine, because writing is hard. You help each other through it. Both psychologically and financially.

The freelance mantra: Never turn down work because you never know how long you'll have to go between assignments, but if something comes your way that you can't possibly do, you pass it on to a friend whose writing you know and trust, and they'll do the same for you.

Organize

For people interested in science writing, I suggest getting involved with the National Association of Science Writers (www.nasw.org). There's a job board page on there (I don't think you need to be a member to peruse it), and there's also a link to NASW's freelance site, which is full of helpful information.

Among other things, they have several email listservs that are amazing resources (for members and nonmembers). NASW-freelance and NASW-talk are great ways to network and meet other science writers (both established and beginners), and editors, who often pass work on to each other.

Make sure to look at all the online tips for beginning science writers, and peruse the list archives before diving in and asking the list, "How do I become a science writer?" since that question has been answered at length on NASW's site. You can find a lot of helpful information in the list archives.

Another list, NASW-jobs, is essentially a job board that sends out announcements of magazines needing employees and/or freelancers, and places looking to make staff hires.

If you're interested in something other than science writing, there are plenty of other similar organizations you'll find helpful, such as the National Writers Union (www.nwu.org). The American Society of Journalists and Authors (www.asja.org), my personal favorite, has a wonderful online community, which is great for meeting other writers and editors, and they do one of the best annual conferences (it's in NYC every year in April, full of great editors and writers). The National Book Critics Circle (www.bookcritics.org) has a similar community.

Rebecca Skloot is a contributing editor at *Popular Science* magazine, an occasional correspondent for NPR's RadioLab, author of a monthly Pets column for *Prevention* magazine and a vice president of the National Book Critics Circle. She writes feature stories, essays and reviews for the *New York Times*, *O: The Oprah Magazine*, *Discover*, *New York Magazine* and others. She specializes in writing about science and medicine but has been known to cover topics ranging from food politics to goldfish surgery. Her work has appeared in the *Best Creative Nonfiction* and *Best Food Writing* anthologies, among others.

Her first book, *The Immortal Life of Henrietta Lacks*, is forthcoming from Crown/Random House. She recently joined the faculty at the University of Memphis where she teaches creative nonfiction in the graduate writing program.

Her website is www.rebeccaskloot.com.

This article is drawn, with the help of Elaine Vitone, from materials Skloot developed for *The Creative Nonfiction Student's Playbook*, a guide to building a portfolio of published work from the Creative Nonfiction Writers' Professional Development Society, University of Pittsburgh, where Skloot received her MFA.

Ten Ways To Land
a First Assignment

by Jean Reidy

ASSIGNING ARTICLES to unfamiliar writers is risky business for an editor. "There's no way to know if a new writer can really deliver a great, polished draft. They may turn out to be an awful writer, or a lazy researcher, or they might just miss the point of the assignment," says Debra Immergut, senior editor at *FamilyFun.*

So, if you're not in a magazine's freelance "stable," how do you get editors to take a chance on you? You can start by understanding the fears that editors face with unfamiliar writers, and then minimize those factors you can control.

What are the editor's risks?

> Unusable articles that leave large editorial spaces to be filled.
> Pieces containing incorrect information from unreliable sources.
> Missed deadlines that cause last-minute scrambles for content.
> Articles that don't match the publication's tone.
> Excessive expenses for writers who are on assignment.
> Stale or overworked article angles and ideas.
> Lazy or uncooperative writers.

Successful freelancers use these strategies to dismantle editorial apprehension when breaking into new markets:

Know the publication.
While many writers can pound out professional letters, queries should demonstrate knowledge of a publication. For example, a preachy query will be filed in the trash bin at *CosmoGIRL!* Put in the time up front to study the magazine.

Sascha Zuger, who writes for publications *Gourmet* and *Good House-*

keeping, treats magazines like characters in fiction novels. They all have their own voices, Zuger says, and she works hard to stay in character. Zuger also pays close attention to reader demographics when styling her queries.

Sara Fujimura, a freelancer from Gilbert, Arizona, subscribes to several writing e-zines and scours their updates of magazine markets. Her research allows her to tailor a pitch to fit a magazine's needs. So when *FamilyFun* needed short, science-based articles for its Try This Now department, Fujimura sold an oil, water, and food-coloring experiment that she angled as "Make your own fireworks in a glass" for the July/August 2007 issue.

Study the publication's types of articles, topics, and story construction, says Jim Morrison, former president for the American Society of Journalists and Authors, who writes for magazines such as *Smithsonian* and *National Wildlife*. Then make sure your style fits, and use the right voice in your query.

Propose a short piece.

Magazines buy hundreds of short articles. They can be written and revised quickly, and often command the same per-word fee as feature articles. In addition, they can lead to longer assignments. Jennifer Nelson, who has written hundreds of articles for magazines such as *Better Homes and Gardens* and *Self*, broke into *Woman's Day*—and national publication—with a health short.

She refers to short pieces as "one source" articles. Low word count plus one source equals minimal risk for editors. When a short piece doesn't work out, editors only need to fill a small space. "It's a great strategy to prove yourself," Nelson says.

Zuger proved herself to *Cookie* with a short roundup of outdoor sculpture parks, and that piece opened a lucrative door. She now regularly writes road-trip features for the magazine.

When proposing a short piece, embed most of your article in your query, allowing an editor to essentially see it on spec.

Submit on spec.

Shannon Caster, a frequent contributor to the *Christian Science Monitor*, favors submitting on spec. Editors can judge immediately if they like your topic and your writing. Caster boosts her chances for a sale by targeting her submissions carefully. She follows guidelines, researches theme lists, reads back issues, and writes to word count.

Many magazines and newspapers carry essay departments, which bypass the query process because queries can't capture the nuances of personal essays. If a publication permits full manuscript submissions, give it a try. Regardless of your writing history and experience, an editor will see up front what might go to print long before deadline.

Pitch a personal story.

Pitch the story only *you* can tell, freelancer David Axe suggests. Axe, who "embedded" with combat units in Iraq, used his first-hand experience to sell war-related articles to *Popular Science* and *Salon*.

Editors will take a chance on new writers who are privy to compelling personal experience or human-interest stories. That's why *East West* couldn't pass up Fujimura's "Waving the White Flag," an article about raising bicultural children. *East West* had previously covered inter-Asian dating and interfaith unions, but Fujimura's tale added another viewpoint. As a white woman married to an Asian man, Fujimura put a unique and personal spin on the story.

Editors may suggest partnering with a respected co-writer to further minimize the risk associated with you—the unknown. Agreeing to such a relationship shows cooperation and flexibility.

Pitch your hometown or family vacation.

Travel pieces tied to your family vacations or featuring your local destinations and attractions allow magazines to cover the globe with minimal expense. Just make sure the spot you pick and the spin you put on it are fresh. For *FamilyFun* travel pieces, Immergut wants to see in-depth, insider knowledge of the place. Consequently, she'll take a chance on a local, albeit less-experienced, writer.

The market for travel writing is huge. After taking a day trip with her family to Multnomah Falls in Oregon, Caster researched the site and discovered a unique angle: undercutting—the process of waterfall erosion. She sold "Water is mightier than rock" to the *Christian Science Monitor*. Caster also brings her camera wherever she goes for photos to accompany her article ideas.

Query well in advance.

Pitching an idea to the right place at the right time may seem serendipitous. But successful freelancers leave nothing to chance. They have ideas on editors' desks when they're needed. Six months in advance may be too late for some national magazines, Immergut says. She advises writers to query early.

Nancy Viau, a freelancer from Mullica Hill, New Jersey, pitched a Halloween piece to *FamilyFun* in the fall of 2005. The article was accepted in July 2006 and appeared in the October 2006 issue.

Review guidelines and editorial calendars, then call publications to verify their submission deadlines.

Send your best clips.

Published articles are your best marketing tool. Clips may win your pitch a closer look, Nelson says. If you have them, send them, even when querying for short pieces. Solid clips from reputable magazines signal to editors that you can work within the structure of a publication and meet deadlines. Clips from national publications assure editors that you're open to multiple reviews, revisions, and fact-checking.

And if querying by email, include links to your online clips. Alison Formento, who's written for *Parenting* and the *New York Times,* always links her electronic queries to her blog, where she has several of her articles posted.

Conduct a preliminary interview.

Quoting respected authorities in your query lets editors know that 1) you have access to the experts, and 2) you know how to interview. Morrison uses preliminary interviews to flesh out his ideas and make them more compelling. That certainly worked when he interviewed Tree Climbers International founder Peter "Treeman" Jenkins for a pitch about the organization that he sent to *Smithsonian.*

Remind interviewees that you'll conduct a more extensive, follow-up interview should the assignment get the go-ahead.

Be persistent.

Carmella Van Vleet, a freelancer from Lewis Center, Ohio, landed her first national byline with *Woman's Day* during a phone call from an editor rejecting a previous submission. After receiving the bad news, Van

Vleet pitched an unfinished humor essay, and the editor loved it. Van Vleet garnered first-rate editorial direction and a terrific clip. Good thing she stayed on the phone.

"Freelancers underestimate the work necessary to break into a good market and give up too easily," Morrison says. He's been flown all over the world and has sold more than a hundred stories to *American Way*, American Airlines' in-flight magazine, and its sister magazine, Southwest Airlines' *Spirit*. After his first sale to *American Way*, his next 11 ideas were rejected.

"I've often wondered what I'd be doing now if I hadn't sent that 12th idea," Morrison says. And after 10 ideas and 18 months, he netted his first sale to *Smithsonian*. "You have to stay in there swinging," he says, "or you'll never get a hit."

Give them more.
No doubt, a new writer has to work harder to get noticed. Van Vleet offers more experts and sidebars. Caster supplies photos. Viau perfects hook-worthy quotes for her queries. All go the extra mile.

For his *Smithsonian* story on tree climbers, Morrison even offered to spend a night "high in the limbs" with the "modern-day Tarzans." He sums up the solution for success perfectly. "Be more persistent, have better clips, know more insider information, and be more perceptive than your competitors."

Your query is your audition, Morrison says, so "make your writing sing."

Whether you're new to a publication or new to freelance writing, use one or more of these strategies in your submissions to minimize editorial risk and increase your chances of landing that elusive initial assignment.

Jean Reidy is an award-winning writer and children's author. Her articles and essays have appeared in more than 50 publications including *FamilyFun* and the *Christian Science Monitor*. Her website is www.jeanreidy.com.

This article first appeared in *The Writer* magazine, March 2008.

Describing Your Book's Benefits

by Rick Frishman and Robyn Freedman Spizman

To CLEARLY DESCRIBE your book, you must know what it's about and whom it targets. What it's about will be what you're selling, and whom it targets identifies the audience to whom you hope to sell it.

Agents and editors tell us that a surprisingly large number of writers can't clearly explain what their books are about.

These authors usually can detail their motivation, philosophies, and their personal dreams, but they can't describe the specific benefits their books will give their readers. For example, they don't say that it will teach novices to hook up computer networks, to bake mouthwatering lemon squares, or to design stylish children's sweaters.

When authors can't clearly describe their books, agents and editors usually conclude—with good reason—that they can't write a salable book. And if writers can't describe their own books, how can they expect agents or publishers to sell them?

Instead of describing their books, many authors tend to litter their descriptions with unverified—and often unbelievable—superlatives. They might say, "This is the best, the most informative, the most up-to-date, or the only book on ..." Or they will claim that it will become a runaway bestseller, an all-time classic, or a great TV series. In describing your book, forget the hype and stick to the facts. Simply state what it will do.

To create an effective publicity campaign, understand your niche. Since the public has so many options and listens so selectively, your first big hurdle, which can be huge, is to get their attention!

To make them stop and listen, you must know:

> What your book is about
> Exactly for whom it was written

Clarify who your audience is—identify the specific group or groups that will be most likely to buy your book and why they would buy it. If you believe that your book has a broad or universal appeal, name the demographic groups that would be most interested in it, according to their size. Don't fool yourself into thinking that it will appeal to everyone, because it probably won't, and it will distort who your audience actually is.

Authors tend to mistakenly believe that it's better to appeal to wider, broader-based audiences than smaller, more defined groups. They don't want to overlook any potential buyers, thinking that if they pitch to larger groups, more people will buy their books.

However, publishing experts tell us that the opposite is true: The shotgun approach seldom attracts as many readers as tightly targeted methods do.

Know your niche. Identify the principal audience that will most likely read your book, and then focus your publicity campaign on it. Then, if you believe that your book will appeal to additional audiences, decide what resources, if any, you will commit to reaching those additional groups.

Your Book's Benefits

Readers buy books because of the benefits they hope to receive. They may want news and information, mental stimulation, or just to escape. Often, they may want to learn how to solve particular problems such as putting up a website, making electrical repairs, or preparing holiday dinners.

When you're competing in such a crowded market, tell potential buyers the precise benefits they will get from your book. Explain specific problems your book will solve, new information it will provide, or hidden secrets it will reveal. Draw up lists of the important facts contained in your book, and clearly identify material that is controversial, shocking, or groundbreaking. Be prepared to rattle off a dozen specific issues that your book addresses.

Don't fall into the trap of generalizing or being vague when you can be precise, even if you think it could attract more readers. In reality, readers whom you address specifically are usually the only ones who listen to your words. So, be specific, exact, and leave no room for doubt. Enumerate the concrete benefits your book will provide.

Rick Frishman is the founder of Planned Television Arts, based in New York City, and has been one of the country's leading book publicists for over thirty years. He has worked with many bestselling authors, including Mitch Albom, Bill Moyers, Stephen King, Mark Victor Hansen, John Grisham, Jack Canfield and Harvey Mackay. He is the co-author of eight books, including bestsellers *Guerilla Publicity* and *Networking Magic,* along with the popular four-book Author 101 series. His new book, *Where's Your Wow?* (with co-author Robyn Spizman), was released by McGraw Hill in March 2008.

Robyn Freedman Spizman lives in Atlanta and is a popular consumer advocate and prolific author whose books and ideas have been featured on countless television and radio programs nationwide. She is co-author of the Author 101 book series with Rick Frishman on writing books and getting published. As a speaker, she offers presentations on gift giving, consumer topics, women's issues, inspirational themes and promoting yourself.

This is an excerpt from *Author 101: Bestselling Secrets from Top Agents.* For more, visit the website, www.author101.com.

Seven Ways to Get an Agent's Attention

by Penelope Trunk

I LOVE MY LITERARY AGENT, Susan Rabiner, because she just sold my second book proposal to the same editor who bought Barack Obama's book. Susan also represents Debby Applegate, the author who just won the Pulitzer Prize for biography for her book, *The Most Famous Man in America* (about 19th-century preacher Henry Ward Beecher). So you can be certain that following Susan's advice is a good idea if you want to sell a book.

Here's her list of seven things to do to improve your chances of getting an agent's attention for our book proposal:

1. Think in terms of genre.

To you, it's a novel. To an agent, it's a thriller, a mystery, chick lit, woman's commercial fiction, or a literary novel.

The same is true for nonfiction. You'd be surprised how often I read a cover letter that gives me no clue as to whether you are pitching a memoir or a self-help book on the topic.

Why do agents think in terms of genre? First, because most of us specialize. More important, the rules change as genres change, and we can't make any decision until we know what standards to apply.

So before you go on and on about what's in your book, either identify its genre, or tell us who you are writing this book for, or modestly suggest the title of a recently published successful book that you'd like your book to sit next to in the bookstore. Nothing makes a would-be author seem more like a rube than going on and on about a book that is ill-defined.

2. Tell me who you are.

I want to know something about you in the first paragraph. Why? To eliminate you if I don't think there is a good enough match between you and the book you want to write. If you are a lawyer who tells me you have always wanted to write about quantum physics, you are heading for the reject pile. There are certain topics where credentials are all important and physics is one of them. But you don't necessarily have to be a Harvard-trained historian to write a book about a historical event, or a psychiatrist to write about the experience of depression, provided there is some other meaningful connection between the book you want to write and you as the author.

So what to do if you have no tight connection to the topic? Don't go for a book proposal quite yet. Start a blog on the topic. Prove that you can attract a devoted readership with your commentary. Interview known experts on the topic. They'll come in handy as outside validation later on. If you really have something to say, your blog will get buzz and then agents will find you and ask you if you might have a book in you.

3. Show outside validation.

The key to self-praise is to have others say it for you. So, for instance, if someone else has called you a gifted writer and that someone is not your wife or your mother, do tell us. Outside recognition could be that your blog gets a gazillion hits a day or was just cited in *Time* magazine. This is what we want to hear. There's an art to bragging and it involves finding someone else who will do it for you.

4. Have a story to tell.

Good proposals don't just communicate facts. They tell the story of how you found this topic and why you became convinced that with all we know about this topic, the most important questions have still not been addressed; the story of how you came to realize the deeper meaning of an experience, the story of an idea that has changed as we as humans have changed. The best proposals read like good mysteries, then they throw out tantalizing tidbits as partial answers so we salivate for more.

5. Check your competition.

Agents can Google. So can editors. If either of us finds most of what you are saying by spending five minutes on the Web, we know that we are working with an aggregator, not an author. Especially today the question editors ask is: What value does this author add?

6. Tell me why I should care.

Why will readers find what you have written irresistible? How will reading this book change them for the better? Will it make them happier, richer, more at peace with themselves? Will it give them insight into a topic of great interest? Will it teach them about something they have already been curious about but could never quite master?

Remember these words: Agents and editors are advocates for the reader, not the author. Impress upon them the payoff for the reader and they will be interested.

7. Answer the question, Why now?

The typical publishing contract gives the author 12 to 18 months to write the book and gives the publisher 8 to 12 months to publish the book. So how do you, as an author, answer the question: Why now, when now is likely to be two to three years from today? By telling agents and editors why the topic is not going to go away and exactly what you will say that will be of interest to people two or three years from today.

So, take and use these seven tips to guide you as you write your proposal. And then send it out. How do you know if your idea is good or bad? By the responses. If you haven't heard back from an agent in 30 days, consider it a no and move on. If you do get a response, take a look at that letter. Agents will only spend time writing something specific when they were truly impressed with what you wrote and want to acknowledge that fact.

If all you are getting are form rejections, there is a message in those one-sentence letters: Time to rethink that proposal.

Penelope Trunk is author of the book *Brazen Careerist: The New Rules for Success* (Warner Books, 2007). She is a columnist at Yahoo Finance and the *Boston Globe*, and her syndicated column runs in more than 200 publications worldwide. Trunk spent ten years as a marketing executive in the software industry, then founded three companies of her own. Prior to that she was a professional beach volleyball player.

She is dedicated to helping people find success at the intersection of work and life. This post appeared on her Brazen Careerist blog (http://blog.penelopetrunk.com) in April 2007, where she posts daily tips for "making work life and personal life one happy, synchronized adventure."

Susan Rabiner is a New York literary agent who founded the Susan Rabiner Literary Agency in 1997 with her husband Alfred Fortunato. The two are also authors of the book *Thinking Like Your Editor: How to Write Great Serious Nonfiction and Get it Published*. Their agency focuses on serious nonfiction written by public intellectuals, scholars and journalists. Before beginning the agency, Rabiner was editorial director of Basic Books, and previously a senior editor at Oxford University Press, St. Martin's Press and Pantheon Books.

Multiple Queries:
Playing the Waiting Game
by A.C. Crispin

TRYING TO GET PUBLISHED can be a frustrating endeavor. I think the waiting is probably the hardest thing. Compared to glaciers, an alarming number of publishers are usually quite leisurely in how fast they move to acquire books, publish them, and (especially) issue checks.

This slow pace is extremely frustrating for writers who are querying, or waiting for a publisher to read a partial or a manuscript they've asked to see, or biting their nails, wondering whether the "editorial and marketing team" will decide whether their book will be acquired.

I used to think writers had short fingernails because they typed all the time. *Hah!* I finally figured it out ... it's the *waiting*.

So what's a first-time aspiring author to do? How long should you wait?

Well, in the first place, if you're at the beginning stage of querying agents or editors, *don't wait*. Multiple queries are not the same thing as multiple submissions, and nobody expects you to send in one query, then wait until the recipient replies before sending in another.

If you can genuinely target 100 agents or editors that your manuscript would be appropriate for, then you're free to send off 100 queries. I usually suggest to my students that they do it in batches of 10–20 at a time, and that they keep a record of it, in a notebook or, if they're computer-savvy, in a database.

So ... query your little hearts out, my friends, as long as you've *targeted* your book properly, and *researched* the agent or publisher. (Remember, the time to do your research is *before* that query or submission goes out!)

Okay, let's assume that your query letter is terrific, a real whiz-bang showstopper, and you get responses from agents or editors asking to see the work.

[So how long is it going to take? And how many will reply? Worst-case scenario … a long time, and not many. From what I've heard recently, a 50 percent (and I include both rejections and requests to read) response rate is doing pretty well. Also, some agents, not to mention editors, are incredibly s-l-o-w. I've heard stories from SFWA members who reported finally receiving a rejection back on a query … six months after they'd sold the book to a publisher!]

If you get a response back asking to see the full manuscript (as opposed to a request for a "partial"—usually the first three chapters and synopsis, also often called an "outline")—*don't stop querying*.

The only exception to this is if the agent or editor asks for an "exclusive" on the work. That means you agree to send the manuscript only to that person exclusively for a given period of time.

Note: *Never* send work out as an open-ended exclusive. This way lies madness. Most agents or editors will tell you how long they need, but 60 to 90 days is pretty typical. If the agent or editor doesn't specify the duration of the exclusive, you should. You would say something to the effect of "(Title) is being submitted on an exclusive basis, and will remain exclusive for 60 days, until (date)"—and put that into your cover letter that accompanies the manuscript.

If, at the end of the 60 days (plus ten days, say, as a "cushion") you haven't heard anything back from the agent/editor, it's proper to drop them a polite note via email or snail mail, asking them if they've had a chance to read the work. If you get no reply, then go back to querying, and chalk it up as a rejection. Agents/editors are usually quick to communicate with a writer when they want a work. Waiting months and months on tenterhooks, without a word, figuring "no news is good news" is probably a flawed strategy. Go back to querying. Then if the agent or editor comes back at a later date with a positive response, you'll be pleasantly surprised, not a raving lunatic.

What if you've submitted your work to a publishing house, unagented? Unsolicited? In the first place, lots of publishers won't read unagented, unsolicited manuscripts these days. But there are still some that will. If you send off a manuscript "over the transom" like this, expect to wait. And wait. And wait. And wait some more.

Many publishers admit it will take them six months to a year to read the submission. So submit the work, and then keep querying or submitting. Don't drive yourself crazy running to the mailbox each day. (Actually, many agents and editors call when they like a ms., as opposed to writing back.)

What should you do while you're doing all this waiting?

Write!

Write some short stories and get them published, so you can include those credentials in your query letters. Start a new novel. Write a nonfiction book you've always wanted to write.

Starting work on a new project will help you through those months of waiting.

I submitted my first book, a Star Trek novel titled *Yesterday's Son*, to Pocket Books in February of 1979 when I was about two months pregnant with my son. By the time the editor called me to make an offer on the book, in the summer of 1982, my son was almost three years old.

Admittedly, I had been in touch with the Pocket Books editors during that time, and had received the reassuring news that the book had been approved for publication by Paramount. So I knew my chances were better than average. Still, that was a *long* three years.

Ann Crispin is the author of more than 20 fantasy and science fiction novels, including seven *New York Times* bestsellers. She is also Chair of Writer Beware (www.writerbeware. com), an industry watchdog group sponsored by the Science Fiction and Fantasy Writers of America to warn writers of literary scams, schemes and pitfalls, from questionable contests to con artists posing as literary agents on the Internet.

This piece was posted April 2007 on the Writer Beware blog (http://accrispin.blogspot. com). Her own website is www.accrispin.com.

Status Queries

by Cynthea Liu

So things haven't gone as you'd hoped. Your manuscript went off months ago, and your phone didn't ring off the hook with five editors or agents vying for your awesome book.

You find yourself wondering—*what are they doing with my manuscript?*

Did it get lost in the mail?

Did my dog Rufus eat my rejection letter?

Did I even include my manuscript in the submission?!

Status queries is a touchy subject where people will have different opinions. Especially about 1) *when* to query for status, and 2) *how* to query for status.

I'll give you my take on status queries.

I don't status query. (See below for one exception.)

Q: *Gasp!* Why?

A: I view status queries as a waste of time for both you and the editor or agent. You can also be an annoyance if:

1. You've status-queried *too* soon from the editor's or agent's point of view.
2. You've somehow given the editor or agent the impression that you can't trust her to get to it when she gets to it.

You will never be able to control how an editor or agent will interpret your status query. While it is doubtful that editor or agent will reject your submission simply because you queried for status, it's not exactly a positive interaction to have with him or her. At best, it is a neutral or a negative one. But more importantly, this is about you and your anxiety over something that is beyond your control.

Trust the system.

Q: But how do you get your questions about the status of your manuscript answered?

A: I make logical assumptions.

1. If my book had sold or if the agent had wanted to rep me, he would find a way to reach me via email or phone. (The magazine market is a bit different though. I'm only going to speak to the fiction book market.) Therefore, if the person had responded by mail, and I didn't get it somehow, it was probably a rejection one way or another.

2. If I *never* hear from them, no biggie. There are plenty of agents or editors in the sea. And there is nothing that precludes me from sending a different book to them—into the black hole—if I so wish. Getting no response has only happened to me *once*. I learned from Blue Board (Children's Writers & Illustrators Chat Board, http://www.verlakay.com/boards/index.php) that other people never heard from this editor either.

3. This brings me to a relevant point: there is a trend with many publishing houses and literary agencies where editors and agents will not respond unless they are interested.

4. Finally, there's one more conclusion I can draw. *The editor or agent hasn't gotten to it yet.* Bingo!

Please note: If you simply must, must, must have closure, do what you need to do. Sometimes things *do* get lost in the shuffle, but always make sure you check the publisher's guidelines and wait beyond the expected response time before querying.

There is *one* case when I do a status query:

The editor or agent has specified that she would like me to do so if a certain amount of time has passed (not too common). She *wants* me to nudge. I will perform the status query as the editor or agent requests, either by phone (yes, they sometimes ask for a call), by email, or by letter.

Q: But what if my manuscript is on an exclusive and they've had it forever?

A: Perhaps you haven't read this post on my website: "Exclusive Submission or Simultaneous Submission?" If you had, you would have known to set an expiration date on your exclusive. This date either matches what the submission guidelines were for the recipient. Or it was a date established by you if there were no guidelines *and* you had to grant an exclusive because of certain circumstances.

Setting an expiration date eliminates the need to let the editor know that the exclusive no longer applies. There is also no need to nudge or status query.

If you did give an exclusive and you'd like to set an expiration date with the editor or agent, then you need to give the person a status *update.* Read my related post on my website: "Status Updates: When and How to Do It." This article covers the cases in which you *should* contact the editor or agent post-submission.

Cynthea Liu left a career as a technology consultant to become a full-fledged children's book writer, proving that anyone, no matter how inexperienced, can write for children if one has the drive and the patience to learn. She obtained a literary agent within her first year and sold three novels soon after to the Penguin Group. She is represented by the Andrea Brown Literary Agency.

Her middle-grade novel *Paris Pan Takes the Dare* (G.P. Putnam's Sons) and her young adult novel *The Great Call of China* (Puffin/Speak) are forthcoming in Spring and Summer 2009. A third novel will be released in 2010.

Liu is also the author of *Writing for Children and Teens: A Crash Course* (how to write, revise, and publish your kid's or teen book with children's book publishers), now available in paperback.

Her website Writing for Children and Teens can be found at www.writingforchildren-andteens.com. This article appeared there June 2006.

A Word on Pitching a Novel

by Jessica Faust

PITCHES ARE AS IMPORTANT as your manuscript, especially if you are an unpublished author.

Pitches, like writing a book, a query letter, or, really, any other aspect of this business, is not an exact science. So often I hear desperation from authors who are looking for that magic answer. They want me to tell them exactly what they should and should not be doing. Trust me, if I could tell you that I would be living in a nice penthouse overlooking the Hudson River right now. I'm not (just in case you were wondering).

In an online challenge, I encouraged readers to try to give a pitch in one sentence, or at least limited to 100 words. Why? Because you are forced to be as concise as possible. It is possible to pitch your book in one sentence, although it also depends on how big of a concept you have and the genre the book is in. I've sold books on basically that, one sentence. A cozy mystery series featuring a Bible study group. A thrilling romantic adventure series featuring heroes who are hotshots, elite firefighters often considered the Navy SEALS of the firefighting world.

Both of those books would need more of a description, but when asked what their books are, the authors can describe them in one concise sentence. Do such ultra-short pitches give you the plot, the characters, and the conflict? No, not in so many words, but they do hook an editor in (at least one who might be looking for these types of books).

I get a lot of questions from readers wanting to know how long a pitch should be and how long is too long. For those of you who need numbers, I would say one to five sentences. The truth, though, is that a pitch is too long when an agent stops reading. You aren't writing a synopsis, you are simply trying to hook someone in. If we want more, we'll start reading the book.

I also know that many of you are looking for a format or formula that you can simply drop your own storyline into. The truth is that no one format works for all persons or all books. For some the conflict is going to have to come from the characters, for others the plot. The trick is that you need to figure out what really makes your book stand out from every single other book in your genre. Is it the unique situation the characters find themselves in or is it the characters themselves?

It will also depend on your readers. Cozy readers often pick up a new series simply based on the crafty, cozy hook; romance readers often look for a unique hero or heroine; and fantasy readers will want a world they haven't been in yet. Of course that's oversimplifying, but I think you might know what I mean. Knowing your reader and what she looks for can help you define your pitch.

Here's an example of a pitch that grabbed me:

Caroline Hayes installs gutters on a house that sees only two inches of rain a year, bubble-wraps her CDs so they won't get scratched, and scotch-guards her car seats religiously every six months, but the one thing she values most she can't protect. When a drunk driver careens around a curve on California's coastal highway, Caroline's life as she knew it is ripped apart. The secret she's kept from her husband about that night tear at the seams of their relationship, and she finds herself turning to a stranger who is keeping secrets of his own. Little does she know how deeply her life is intertwined with the drunken woman who died beside her, who left her with scars that would not heal, and a gift beyond anything she could fathom. My novel Ocean Deep *delves into the murky waters of secrets, lies, and the ties that bind people together.*

I love this! What a great pitch. I see who Caroline is and I clearly see her conflict. It also has a great title, and even the very vague last line works. Why? Because the author had very specific opening sentences prior to that. I would definitely request to see more based on this. In fact, this pitch is so strong it has the potential to get requests for the full manuscript right off the bat. This type of pitch gets editors and agents at conferences talking.

And last, it's important to remember that a pitch is different from a query letter. A pitch is that enticing paragraph that grabs the reader and only talks about the book. The query letter, in addition, will include title, word count, series potential, genre, etc.

Jessica Faust is a literary agent and cofounder of BookEnds, LLC (www.bookends-inc. com). She looks for unique fiction with a strong hook, with a focus on historical, contemporary, fantasy, paranormal and erotic romance; erotica; women's fiction; mysteries; suspense and thrillers. In nonfiction, she looks for creative ideas and large author platforms in business, finance, career, parenting, psychology, women's issues, self-help, health, sex and general nonfiction. Faust began her career in 1994 as an acquisitions editor at Berkley Publishing, Macmillan, and Wiley, acquiring and editing both fiction and nonfiction.

This piece is based on a February 2008 post on her agency's blog (http://bookends-litagency.blogspot.com). It appears at the conclusion of several online critiques of writers' pitches. The novel mentioned, *Ocean Deep*, by Heidi Willis, is currently under review.

First Page Test

by Scott Westerfeld

When buying books, I usually avoid the back cover (spoilers!) and go straight for the first-page test. Judging an 80,000-word document on the basis of one page may seem cruel and unusual, but I've found that most books reveal a lot about themselves in that first minute. At least, they reveal more than real-live human beings when you first meet them. A human, after all, might just be having a bad day.

So here's a quick First Page Test for your delectation.

Chain Mail, by Hiroshi Ishikazi (Tokyopop)

> *I stood in front of the mailbox and cried. Snow fell around me, frosting my hair and shoes, slowly blotting out the words of the test results I held in my hands. Out of over twenty-five thousand test-takers, I had placed first in Japanese, Mathematics, Science, Basic Studies, and General Studies. I had finally made it.*
>
> *But it was too late. My mother was gone, and she wasn't coming back. If I had only studied harder, if I had only gotten these results a month earlier, maybe it would have made a difference.*
>
> *Melting snow slid down my back. I shivered, remembering the sound of flesh striking flesh …*

Things that brought me in

1. "I stood in front of the mailbox and cried" is a lovely first sentence. We are somewhere specific, and something specific is happening.
2. I like "frosting" a lot, because it's being used in a slightly unusual way, and is strong visually. And there's something perfect about the snow alighting specifically on the character's "hair and shoes." Hair, because it reveals that she's not wearing a hat—she just stepped out to grab the eagerly awaited mail. And shoes, because

she's looking *down* at the letter, and also because she's crying—staring at your shoes is not usually a sign of happiness. (I'm assuming the protag's a girl because of the cover, by the way.)

3. Wait, she's crying because the test results are *perfect*? Brain was ready for the opposite. Unexpected is good.

4. The second paragraph sets off a wave of micro-mysteries for the reader. How did her test results make her mother go away? And is her mother dead, or something else?

5. "Melting snow slid down my back. I shivered, remembering ..." is a cool way to physicalize the bad memory. And "flesh striking flesh" is definitely bad, bad, bad.

Things that kicked me out

1. The construction "test-takers" is clunky to me. Like, why not say "students"? I mean, we *know* this is about testing. You could just say "Out of twenty-five thousand, I had placed first" and it would make sense. Still, the term is probably just a literal move from the more elegant Japanese. Translations get a few extra free passes, because I like the odd feel of an occasional literalness.

2. Maybe we're going a little *too* quickly into the explanation of this little micro-mystery? I'm not a fan of flashbacks that start before we're fully in a scene, which always seems stagey.

These are minor quibbles, though. I'd definitely keep going.

Scott Westerfeld is author of novels for adults and for young adults. His YA books include the popular series Midnighters (five teenagers born at midnight, for whom time freezes every night, revealing a hidden world), and Uglies (set in a future where cosmetic surgery is compulsory when you turn 16; the series includes *Uglies, Pretties, Specials* and *Extras*).

His other YA works include three stand-alone novels set in contemporary New York. His books have been named as *New York Times* Notable Books of the Year and American Library Association Best Books for Young Adults.

This piece was posted June 2007, on his website's blog (http://scottwesterfeld.com/blog).

Chain Mail: Addicted to You, by Hiroshi Ishizaki (TokyoPop, 2007), is a YA novel about four Tokyo teenagers drawn together by a mysterious chain-mail message sent to their cell phones, a tale that blurs the boundaries between reality and fantasy.

Resonance in Titles

by Barry Eisler

THE MOST IMPORTANT QUALITY of a title is resonance: that is, "the ability to evoke or suggest images, memories, and emotions." Resonance matters because resonance makes things stick. Without it, a title produces no emotion—it stands for nothing and is instantly (and rightly) forgotten. The resonant title, by contrast, beckons you, it insidiously hooks you, it provides the first step in a seduction that culminates in the pleasure of the book itself.

There are two kinds of resonance: automatic and acquired. They're not mutually exclusive. Let's examine both.

Automatic Resonance

Automatic resonance exists in a title that moves you before you've read, or even heard anything about, the book. The title taps into something that already exists in your mind: an experience, an archetype, a memory, a famous phrase or line of poetry. The title stirs that preexisting thing to life, and in doing so makes you feel you know something important and appealing about the underlying work.

One way of checking whether a title has automatic resonance is to ask someone who has never heard of the book, "What do you think it's about?" If the person has a sense, a feeling, if the person can grasp the broad emotional contours of the story, the title has automatic resonance. If you get a giant "huh?" in response, something is wrong.

Recently I heard of a book called *Cemetery of the Nameless*. I'd never even heard of the book, but the title alone gave me a shiver. I couldn't tell you the plot, but my guess is, emotionally we're talking about something having to do with death, being forgotten, masses of anonymous people ... perhaps, ultimately, loneliness and despair. *Motherless Brooklyn*, by Jonathan Lethem, was another one that hit me instantly. Presumably the story takes place in Brooklyn, but an unmoored Brooklyn, a Brooklyn that grew up fending for itself, a Brooklyn of the disen-franchised and the dispossessed. *The Blade Itself,* by Marcus Sakey, was another: a story about violence, and violence's allure. David Morrell's last two titles, each consisting of a single word, have been right on the money. *Creepers* and *Scavenger.* Think they're love stories? Coming of age? Or stories driven by fear and suspense?

Automatic resonance requires hitting a sweet spot, a note that lies somewhere between the hopelessly vague and the embarrassingly literal. Vague doesn't work because it tells the potential reader too little. For example, *Rain Fall* was a bad title for my first book (I didn't know better at the time). The phrase is too common, and the phenomenon it describes too ordinary, to offer any automatic resonance. Certainly it fails the "What do you think the book is about?" test (even if it passes, it's misleading—rain fall has gentle connotations, while assassin John Rain is anything but). But be careful not to go too far in the other direction: one of the titles my publisher favored for a more recent install-ment in my series was *The Quiet Assassin.* Something as literal (and redundant) as that can't give you an emotional sense of the story. It's really no different from *Novel About An Assassin*—which is exactly the response you'd get, no more, no less, from someone in response to the "What do you think it's about?" test.

Like everyone else, Hollywood makes mistakes, but when they're on, oh, man, do they nail automatic resonance in movie taglines. One of the best ever was *Alien:* "In space, no one can hear you scream." Pause for a moment. Pretend you never saw the movie; you're hear-ing about it now for the first time. What do you think it's about? "Mor-tal terror alone in space, probably with a monster" would be my guess. But then why not just call the movie something like that? *Mortal Terror Alone in Space: Stalked by a Predatory Alien ...*

We intuitively understand the problem with being too literal (although the intuition doesn't always prevent mistakes). Getting too literal is obvious; obvious feels silly; silly feels like parody. It's not a coincidence that *Airplane, Scary Movie, Date Movie,* etc. are all comedies. And *Snakes on a Plane* was a giant wink at the audience.

Alternatively, the *Alien* producers could have gone for something vaguer: *Space Danger* as a title; "Fear" as a tagline. Pause again: why was what the producers chose infinitely better than a more literal or a vaguer approach? The principles you tease out will apply to titles, too.

Of course, titles are part of the overall book packaging, and the impact of a title will change when it's combined with artwork. But ideally, the title will have automatic resonance on its own. If it doesn't, your susceptibility to word-of-mouth advertising will be reduced, because someone hearing about a book for the first time from a friend can't see, and therefore isn't affected by, the artwork on the cover.

Acquired Resonance

Whereas automatic resonance occurs because of a connection between the title and something in your mind or experience, acquired resonance has to do with a connection between the title and the contents of the book itself. The reason I call it "acquired" is because it doesn't adhere until after you've read the book—that is, the book acquires resonance from being read.

Choosing a place name as a title is usually a bid for acquired resonance. If you haven't read the story, the place name doesn't mean much, but if the story is memorable enough, it imbues that otherwise neutral place name with tremendous power. *Empire Falls, Lonesome Dove, Mystic River, Watership Down* ... these are such overwhelmingly powerful stories that they breath life into their own titles. Titles with stories like these behind them function as a form of shorthand, a place keeper, a vessel that carries forward the emotional weight of the story. A body for the story's spirit to animate and inhabit.

Note that the titles above aren't devoid of automatic resonance. Words like lonesome, dove, mystic, and empire have inherent connotations that lead to an unavoidable degree of automatic resonance. But if all these titles had going for them were the automatic resonance, they would be weak. What makes them work is that acquired effect, what trademark lawyers call "secondary meaning."

Let's talk about the concept of secondary meaning for a moment. Some of the world's most powerful trademarks (and the brands they stand for) derive their market power almost entirely from consumer associations that have little or nothing to do with the marks themselves. Think McDonald's, for example, or Harley Davidson, or bmw. These titles have come to stand as shorthand in the minds of consumers for the products the companies make. Without experience with those products, consumers would have no emotional association with the trademarks. All are therefore good examples of the potential power of acquired resonance.

[Contrast these marks with a company name like Yahoo!, which has automatic (as well as acquired) resonance. Yahoo! couldn't possibly be the name of a stuffy financial services company. It has to be something fun, exciting, and free.]

When evaluating a possible title, publishers tend to lean toward automatic resonance. There are several reasons for this tendency. First, automatic resonance is reassuring. If you have it, the book just sounds good right off the bat. The title will goose sales up front, when the publisher and the rest of the world is paying the closest attention. Acquired resonance, by contrast, is scary. What if the book doesn't work? The title will seem silly then. And even if it does work, it might take a long time, because acquired resonance only derives its power when people have read and are talking about the book.

The second reason is institutional. To have an opinion about whether a title has acquired resonance, you have to have read the book. Yet many of the people behind the title decision will not have done so. So whether they realize it or not, their only means of evaluating the title's impact is along automatic resonance lines.

The third reason publishers tend not to focus on acquired resonance is that an acquired resonance title takes more thought and skill to discover. It requires a keen understanding of the heart of the story, along with an instinct for what word or phrase is best calculated to make that heart beat loudly enough for the reader to hear it long after she's finished the book.

A few other titles, in addition to the ones above, that for me carry tremendous acquired resonance: *The Godfather, Going After Cacciato, The Kite Runner, The Prince of Tides, Snow Falling on Cedars, Sophie's Choice.* All these titles are connected to something at the heart of their stories, or otherwise able to encapsulate that heart. All are powerful titles, but none began with that power. Instead, the power of the title is a function, an outgrowth, of the power of the story.

If you had to favor one type of resonance over the other, how would you make the decision? There are at least two factors at work here. The first involves the kind of market you're trying to reach. The second has to do with timing.

Market. The more your audience is focused on a genre, the safer you'll be in favoring automatic resonance. A genre audience has tastes and expectations that are relatively easy to understand. Choosing a title that immediately signals to this audience "this is just what you're looking for" is a smart way to make sure you sell an adequate number of books (and of course, that message should be an explicit part of other aspects of the packaging, too). So a romance gets a title like *Unchained Desire,* a western might be *High Plains Drifter,* horror is *The Howling,* science fiction is *The Terminal Experiment,* etc.

A non-genre audience, by contrast, has much vaguer expectations. They're looking more for an emotional experience than they are for the traditional indicia of a specific genre. It's therefore more difficult to signal to a non-genre audience that "It's just what you think it is," and more sensible to make a play for acquired resonance, instead. Think *The Kite Runner,* or *Shantaram,* or *The Road,* etc.

Timing. Here, the question is, where is the author is in his career? I haven't read Dennis Lehane's first few books, but I love the automatic resonance of the titles: *Gone, Baby, Gone* (loss, mourning, and a certain hip attitude). *A Drink Before the War* (a reprieve, the calm before the storm, a moment of peace before the unavoidable violence to come). *Darkness, Take My Hand* (seduction, surrender, an embrace of the forbidden). And then Lehane wrote *Mystic River,* which I consider to be a masterpiece—a perfect blend, a perfect weaving together, of people, place, and plot. At that point, Lehane's audience was large enough to guarantee a certain level of sales even without the strong automatic resonance of his previous titles. And the new story was so powerful, and the title so perfect a vessel for that power, that all the people who bought the book more on Lehane's name than on the title were enabled and motivated to spread the word about the book. Had the same book been Lehane's debut, entitling it *Mystic River* would have been much more of a risk.

Simply put: automatic resonance tends to help a book gain momentum; acquired resonance is what sustains it. For genre, or for any book that isn't expected to have that long a shelf life, automatic resonance will probably suffice. But if you're selling something you hope will go the distance, an attempt at acquired resonance will certainly help.

Ideally, of course, your title will have both.

Barry Eisler lives in the San Francisco Bay Area and travels frequently to Japan and other parts of Asia. He is the bestselling author of a series of thrillers featuring the half-Japanese, half-American hired assassin John Rain. Titles include *Rain Fall, Hard Rain, Rain Storm* (which won the Mystery Ink Gumshoe Award for Best Thriller of 2006), *The Last Assassin* and *Requiem for an Assassin* (*Wall Street Journal*: "a literary page turner"). The books have been translated into nearly 20 languages. Eisler is, according to *January Magazine*, "writing the best thrillers available today." He has a black belt in judo and worked for three years with the CIA.

His website is www.barryeisler.com. This article appeared in two parts in March 2007 on M.J. Rose's blog of marketing advice for writers, Buzz, Balls, and Hype.

Competitive Titles

by Chip MacGregor

THE HARDEST PART of a book proposal for many authors is the "competitive analysis" section. Here are some tips.

Think about the purpose of that section. Publishers basically sell in "lines"—that is, if they are currently selling a lot of fitness and health titles, they're going to want to publish *more* fitness and health titles in the future, since they know how to market and sell those. (One of the things that drives publishers crazy is seeing a proposal that screams, "You've never seen anything like this!" Or an agent that says, "You're not currently doing any books in this genre, so I thought I'd send this to you." Huh? If a publisher isn't doing any books in one area, they're probably not going to know what to do with that project. An easy rejection.)

So the "competitive analysis" section of your proposal serves as an advance organizer. It tells the publishing team, "*This* book is similar to *that* book. If you could get excited about *that* title, you're sure to like *this* title." Make sense?

What most authors do is to head over to Amazon.com and spend a little time doing research. Search by title. Look at key words. If you find an author who has done a book similar to yours, check out his or her other titles (authors have a tendency to maintain an interest in a topic, just like publishers). What you are looking for is a handful of titles (about three to seven) that are similar to your proposed book.

In your proposal, list the title, author, publisher, and release date. You need to give some indication of what the sales were (that will take a bit of research). You want to explain very briefly how that book is similar to your own. And, in many cases, you want to offer a short explanation of how your proposed book is different.

Some traps to avoid:

1. *Don't* pick a book that has sold more than 250,000 copies. If you've writing a book for young readers and compare it to Harry Potter, you're going to look stupid ("Rowling sold a bazillion copies, so I can too!"). Anything that has sold that many copies isn't a competitor, it's a conqueror. Ignore it and use something else.

2. *Don't* pick a book that has sold twelve copies. That suggests to the editor that "nobody cares about this topic." Hey, the writing of books is endless. If there has never been a successful book on the United States Parrot Importation Act, there's probably a reason.

3. *Don't* ignore the obvious successes. If you're doing a military historical novel on the Battle of Gettysburg, it would be pretty dumb to leave off Michael Shaara's *Killer Angels.* That sends the message to the editor that you don't really know your field.

4. *Don't* make snarky comments about each book. I often see that, and it's annoying to have some unpublished wannabe send me something that says, "*This* book was successful, but it's not nearly as good as mine" and "*This* book sold 100,000 copies, but the author made mistakes in his chronology." A comparative analysis section isn't a review of everything on the market—it's simply a vehicle for helping the editor know how to position your particular title.

5. *Don't* guess if you use one of the publisher's own books. In other words, if you're going to send something to Little, Brown, and you want to use Elizabeth Kostova's *The Historian* as a comparable title, make sure you have all your facts correct. Because you'll look like a bonehead if you state the book came out in 2002, the author's name was "Kosovo," and sales were about 50,000. (All of those facts are wrong.)

6. *Do* use a publisher's own titles. If you have a Jane Austen-like novel that you're trying to sell to Harvest House, by all means reference their Debra White Smith titles. (She wrote modern updates of the Austen novels, and they did well for Harvest House.) It will immediately help them understand the audience for your project.

Again, the goal here is to help a publisher get a frame of reference for your book. It's a way of stating, "My book is similar to these five titles that have all seen success in the marketplace. There is clearly interest in this type of book, and your house has done well with this genre in the past."

You're basically making the editor's job easy for him or her. It won't be the deciding factor in whether or not they publish your book (for that I suggest you come up with a good story and some great writing), but it helps move your proposal along. One less reason for them to say no.

Chip MacGregor runs MacGregor Literary, placing books with all of the major publishers in the Christian and general book trade. Agency writers have hit the *New York Times* bestseller list and won many awards. He has also worked as an acquisitions editor and book developer, and written more than two dozen titles himself. He strives to support books that make a difference.

A popular conference speaker, he maintains a blog of writing advice at his website, www.chipmacgregor.com, where this article appeared February 2007.

A Day in the Life of a Literary Agent

by Michael Bourret

PEOPLE ALWAYS ASK ME what my day is like. I often respond by saying that it's nothing but email and phone, which is only somewhat true. It's a long, tiring, very rewarding day, and I hope this provides some insight.

6:30 A.M.: Wake up. Feed cat. Shower, shave, dress. (Pray to get the order right at early hour.)

7:22 A.M.: Leave house to catch 7:30 C train (no, subways don't technically run on schedules, but the C train only comes once every 10 minutes during rush hour, and it happens to come on the 30-minute mark).

8:00 A.M.: Arrive at Starbucks. Purchase "Grande" mild coffee (iced during the summer).

8:10 A.M.: Arrive at work. Log into computer, remove reading from previous evening and sort into "reject," "request more," "offer representation," "get another read," or "do editorial letter" piles. Check news.

8:10–8:30 A.M.: Read the news. Look for stories that would make great book ideas, either fiction or nonfiction.

8:30–9:00 A.M.: Morning meeting. The whole staff gets together each morning to go over business. We discuss where we are on projects (Do you need a writer? Is money due? Did the editor get back to you about bound galleys?), ask Jane and each other for advice, generate book ideas, and discuss news items.

9:00–10:00 A.M.: Respond to all the emails I received the previous night. There are often many from the West Coast, as they're still going when we leave for the day. Also, since writing isn't the primary employment for most authors, it's the only time they have to correspond. And, many writers don't seem to sleep. Really, guys, sleep is good!

10:00–10:30 A.M.: Take care of any other author correspondence: contracts, amendments, agency agreements, editorial letters, royalty statements, and more.

10:30–11:30 A.M.: Return phone calls and make follow-up calls on proposals and manuscripts on submission. This is when we find out that someone is very interested in a project. Hopefully.

11:30 A.M.–12:30 P.M.: Put together and submit new material. Make any calls associated with the new submission that I didn't make earlier.

12:30–2:00 P.M.: Lunch with an editor. This is our chance to meet new editors and catch up with old friends. The agent lunch seems to mystify those who aren't in publishing, but I find it a necessary, important, and enjoyable part of the job. The book business, for all the analyzing of numbers that we do, is still very subjective, and it's often at these lunches that I get a real sense of someone's taste. It's when I learn that the editor who typically does political nonfiction also loves anything to do with cats and can acquire whatever he wants. Books are often sold to unlikely editors based on such information.

(When I don't have a lunch, I take this time to read through blogs looking for book ideas or gossip, or a recap of the *America's Next Top Model* episode that I missed.)

2:00–3:00 P.M.: Return the calls and emails from lunch time. Check Gawker and Galleycat to make sure no one was fired while I was out, which could change where I send that proposal I packaged in the morning.

3:00–4:00 P.M.: Open mail and review e-queries. There is a lot of mail coming in, and even more email these days. It takes this long to review all the material and request what looks interesting.

4:00–5:00 P.M.: Go back to checking client email and answering calls. This is *the* busiest time of day for phone calls, as everyone's looking for information before the close of business.

5:00–6:30-ish P.M.—Wrap up the day. Print out any reading for the evening, get together any material to review contracts, make last-minute and West Coast phone calls. Some nights, have a drink with an editor or author who's in town.

6:30–7:15 P.M.: Train ride home. This is when I get to read for pleasure! Right now I'm reading *Pop!* by Aury Wallington, which a client gave me. I also read magazines and newspapers during this time.

7:15–9:00 P.M.: Feed cat. Eat. Watch DVR'ed TV.

9:00 P.M.: Whenever necessary: Read and edit proposals and manuscripts. Vet contracts. Write and revise submission letters and create submission lists. Sometimes there's also email and phone calls.

Honestly, an agent's work is never done. It's difficult, frustrating, and can make for a very boring social life. It's a good thing that I love my job (and didn't have a social life to begin with).

Michael Bourret joined Dystel & Goderich Literary Management after studying film and television production at New York University's Tisch School of the Arts. An internship at the agency led to an unexpected career in publishing. Authors he represents include Sara Zarr, whose first novel *Story of a Girl* (Little, Brown, 2007) was finalist for 2007 National Book Award for Young People's Literature; Lisa McMann, whose debut novel *Wake* became a *New York Times* bestseller (Simon Pulse, 2008); Anne Rockwell, critically-acclaimed author of more than 100 picture books; Aaron Glantz, independent journalist and author of *How America Lost Iraq* (Tarcher, 2005); Jim Bell, author of the critically-acclaimed *Postcards from Mars*; and Doug Lansky, travel writer and author of the hilarious *Signspotting* and *Signspotting 2* (Lonely Planet, 2005 and 2007).

This post appeared in March 2007 on the Dystel & Goderich Literary Management blog (http://dglm.blogspot.com). The New York agency was founded in 1994 by Jane Dystel, a respected figure for more than 30 years in publishing as an editor, publisher and agent. The full-service agency has a roster of Pulitzer Prize–winning journalists, celebrated experts in nonfiction fields, and literary and commercial fiction writers.

INTERNET MARKETING SKILLS

Sling Your Web

by J.A. Konrath

LET'S TALK about traffic. Not rush hour bumper-to-bumper traffic, but the Internet kind.

Writing is part art, part craft. But publishing is a business. That means you have to earn money to survive. If you're an author, the secret to earning money is becoming a brand name—an automatic purchase.

Use the World Wide Web to help achieve this. According to www.internetworldstats.com, there are more than 1 billion people online, and almost 70 percent of Americans are surfing the net.

Five years ago, only a handful of authors had websites. Two years ago, very few people knew what a blog or a podcast was. And who could've predicted the amazing success of YouTube, MySpace, and Wikipedia?

No matter what type of writer you are—fiction, nonfiction, even unpublished—you must use the Internet to maximize your brand.

Your Home Page

All authors need a home page. Yet very few know what to include on it. Many people believe it's simply a 24-hour advertisement for your books, requiring no more than an image of your book's cover and a few jacket blurbs. Those people are wrong.

Here's the secret to a successful author website: It should be sticky. As the name implies, there should be enough content on your home page to make people stick around for a while. Content comes in two forms: information and entertainment.

My website, www.jakonrath.com, features more than 100 pages of content. Besides the standard book excerpts and reviews, I have free short stories, full e-book downloads, dozens of pages of writing tips for newbie authors, contests, a message board, a sign-up newsletter, videos, and funny pictures, along with an updated appearance schedule.

Your website—and everything you do on the net—isn't about what you have to sell. It's about what you have to offer.

Your Book Site

Taking a cue from the movie industry, authors and publishers have begun creating websites for individual book titles. David Morrell created a whole interactive Web experience for his bestseller *Creepers* at www.theparagonhotel.com, which features the setting from the book. You can also visit www.nextgencode.com, the fictional company Michael Crichton writes about in his novel *Next*. And my own more modest effort can be found online at www.thesegunsforhire.com, to coincide with the release of an anthology I've edited.

Your Blog

A blog is a way to directly communicate with people several times a week. Successful blogs focus on a specific topic and become forums for like-minded individuals to comment and exchange ideas. Thriller writer Barry Eisler's blog, www.barryeisler.com/blog.html, focuses on politics and language, while chick-lit (or more precisely, mommy-lit) author Melanie Lynne Hauser posts funny anecdotes about motherhood, www.melanielynnehauser.com/wordpress.

My own blog, A Newbie's Guide to Publishing, www.jakonrath.blogspot.com, features more than 300 essays about writing, marketing and promoting. Often other people—even bestselling authors—disagree with my opinions. This is great. There's no such thing as bad publicity, and controversy draws in readers.

Should you be blogging? Yes. But first you need to figure out what your blog is going to be about and if you can write on that topic three times a week forever. Check out www.blogger.com and www.wordpress.com. These sites are free and can help you get started.

Your MySpace

I've heard statistics that MySpace has four times more daily visitors than Google. It's easy to see why.

MySpace is all about you. Your favorite books, music, and movies. Your pictures. Your likes and dislikes. Your friends.

If you're a published author, chances are someone has already mentioned you on their MySpace profile. When you put up a MySpace page (which is free) people will come to you, wanting to be your online MySpace Friend. Once someone is your Friend, you can send them messages, post comments on their MySpace pages, or even send bulletins to all of your friends at once about your new book release, magazine sale, author signing or anything else regarding your work.

But it gets better. You can search for like-minded people, as well. I write thrillers similar to Harlan Coben, but they're funny like Christopher Moore. So you can bet I looked at Coben's and Moore's MySpace pages and invited their Friends to be my Friends.

Your Amazon

Amazon, the world largest online bookseller, encourages authors to add content to their site in a variety of ways:

Amazon.com Connect allows published authors to set up their own bio page and blog, which is linked to every book of yours they sell. It lets you stay in touch with readers who've bought your book through Amazon and alert them when your new titles are released.

Amazon.com Shorts allows people to download a short story of yours for 49 cents. It's great for fans who are anxiously awaiting your next book, and it's also a cheap way for a potential buyer to give your writing a try. Plus, you make money; every download earns you 20 cents—which is pretty good considering a paperback sale nets an author only roughly 55 cents.

You don't have to be a novelist to partake in this program, as long as you're published somewhere and Amazon sells that book. Humorous mystery writer Tom Schreck has three Shorts on Amazon, and his only prior publishing cred was a story in one of the Chicken Soup books. The success of his Amazon Shorts helped him find a publisher for his novel.

Amazon.com Listmania allows you to create a list of books that are similar to yours, which comes up as a sidebar when people do searches on those authors. Your recommendations can lead fans of other authors to your books.

Your Audio & Video

If you don't have an MP3 player yet, you're ignoring this technology at your own peril. People love to download audio content, either to their computer or to their iPods. And you have a couple of options as an author to deliver your readers content.

You can try an MP3 blog. It's an audio file posted to your home page, blog or MySpace page, which can be listened to online or down-loaded as a file and played on various equipment. You can also create a regularly updated podcast, which can be attached to an RSS feed, allow-ing syndication. The audio recording software is available for free (I use www.audacity.sourceforge.net). Then you can visit iTunes to make your recording into a podcast, also free.

Your audio blog or podcast can be as simple as you reading your work or doing an interview. Or you can create entire radio shows with music and commercials.

If video is your thing, then visit YouTube and upload your book trailer that you created using Flash or a video of you speaking at your last bookstore event. Once you're on YouTube, you can embed the clip in your website, blog, and MySpace.

The Real Secret to Internet Promotion

The simple fact is that anyone looking for you on the net can find you. While it's good to make your current fan base happy, most writers are looking for new fans. But how are people going to find you if they don't even know you exist?

You have to lead them to you.

Every time you send an email with your URL in your signature line, post on your blog, leave comments in a forum, exchange links with another author, join a Yahoo Group, make a MySpace Friend, upload a YouTube video or add content to your website, you're building roads. These roads can last for years, and they always lead back to you. The search engines find them. Surfers find them. People looking for other things find you, instead.

Using www.statcounter.com, you can see where your site visitors come from, how long they stay and what search engine terms they used to find your site. I still get hits on blog entries I wrote three years ago, by people looking for "free e-books," "co-op money," "how to get published," and, of course, "Jack Daniels."

The bigger Web presence you have, the more links you have coming in, the more chances people have to discover you. And they will discover you.

You can spend a fortune hunting mice—mount expeditions, buy expensive mouse-hunting equipment, tour the world, and devote all of your time to tracking those little suckers down. Or you can toss some cheese in the corner and wait.

The choice is yours.

Getting People to Find You

SEARCH ENGINES

I don't recommend paying to be listed on a search engine, because all of the important ones will list you for free if you have a regularly updated site with a decent amount of information. There are plenty of services who offer to list your URL on 40,000 search engines for only $9.99. That seems like a bargain, but when was the last time you used maxpromo.com or wisenut.com to look something up? Save your money.

LINKS

Remember that old shampoo commercial, where the woman told two friends, and they told two friends, and so on, and so on? Links do the same thing for your website. The more people who link to you, the better off you are. The secret to attracting links is to have content that people want. Trading links also works. Just email a fellow writer and ask to trade. Search engines love links, and the more you have going in and coming out, the higher your placement will be.

NEWSGROUPS, LISTSERVS, YAHOO GROUPS, MESSAGE BOARDS

Or any public forum where like-minded individuals band together and exchange ideas. The key to successfully establishing a presence on these forums is to contribute intelligent points in a polite and logical manner, rather than yelling, "Buy my book!" every time you post. Your comments should always have a signature line that leads to your blog or website, but people will click on that because they want to know more about the clever person who said those smart things, not because you beg them to.

PAPER

I'm a firm believer that the more pieces of paper your name is on, the better you'll succeed in publishing. Because of this, I write a lot of short stories and articles, do a lot of mass mailings, and pass out a ridiculous number of coasters and business cards. Each of these lists my website URL. You should put your URL on everything. Mine is on the bumper of my car, on every ad and flier, and even on my checks. Every piece of mail I send out gets a JAKonrath.com rubber stamp on the back. I always mention my URL in newspaper and radio interviews, on panels, and while doing signings. Overkill? I get 1,000 unique hits a day, and I'm a midlist genre writer.

WIKIPEDIA

Chances are, if you Google something, Wikipedia will be one of the top responses. It's an online dictionary where the entries are written by the readers. If you're a published author, have a friend do a Wiki on you (you can't do one on yourself).

Coming Up with Content

For sites to be visited frequently, you have to keep up a steady supply of new content. That's the reason most blogs fail and why most author websites get updated only once a year. Coming up with new information and entertainment regularly makes most writers dizzy.

But don't worry; you can work around this dilemma. If you look closely at successful sites, you'll see there are some secrets to providing regular new content.

AGGREGATE THE CONTENT

The Web has become so overwhelmingly huge, you can't possibly look at everything you find interesting. Neither can anyone else. This is a good thing, though, because once you find something interesting, you can share it.

Providing links to interesting sites, excerpts from interesting sites or even media from interesting sites has become easier than ever. You can share things with your fans that you didn't have to create yourself, because it already exists on the net. This saves you time and can bring readers back day after day to see what you've compiled.

HELP FROM FRIENDS

No one said your site had to be a solo effort. The multi-author blog means fewer individual posts for you but higher overall traffic because each author has her own fan base. Killer Year (www.killeryear.word-press.com), First Offenders (www.firstoffenders.typepad.com), and The Good Girls Kill for Money Club (www.good-girls-kill.com) are all great examples of this.

You can also interview people, which creates content. Or have guest bloggers. When a guest is on your blog, she'll point people in your direction. Some of those people will like what they see and come back on their own.

LET THE SURFERS DO THE WORK

I set up a new blog called The Anonymous Publishing Vent Club (www.ventclub.blogspot.com), where industry pros can complain about this business without naming names. The visitors are the ones who write the posts, not me. All I do is make sure the queue keeps going, which is only a minute or two of work every day.

If you host a message board or a forum, you can keep people coming back to your site with minimal effort on your part. Plus, when people have input in something, they develop a sense of ownership and community, which accounts for longer surfing times and multiple daily visits.

BEING INNOVATIVE

Don't be afraid to try something new or different. Innovation is what spearheads Internet success, not copying what was done last week. Experiment. Get crazy. Analyze what works on you, then try to make that work for other people on your site. If it flops, you can always delete it with no residual effects. In this age of uber technology, you're limited only by your imagination. Think big.

J.A. Konrath is a fiction writer working in the mystery, thriller and horror genres. He spent years garnering close to 500 rejections for nine unpublished novels. His tenth, *Whiskey Sour*, was picked up by Hyperion in 2003. It was the first in a series, all named after mixed drinks, featuring Lt. Jacqueline "Jack" Daniels of the Chicago Police Department. The fifth, *Fuzzy Navel*, appeared in May 2008.

Konrath is also known for his advocacy of self-promotion. Konrath believes that writers must play a large part in marketing their own books, and his blog, A Newbie's Guide to Publishing (www.jakonrath.blogspot.com), focuses on this.

This article originally appeared in *Writer's Digest* magazine, October 2007. The author's website is www.jakonrath.com.

Better Writing Through Design

by Bronwyn Jones

GOOD WEB DESIGN has a signature style: It's approachable, it's easy to understand, and it packs enough punch to catch the roving eye of even the most mercurial user. Web designers know this doesn't happen by accident. It's the result of a finely honed process that asks—and answers—important questions about a site's intended audience. You might call it "visual language" or "design vernacular." Either way, what you find in a truly good design is a unique perspective. A point of view. A voice.

It's no accident that we use such language-based terms to describe effective design on the Web. The Web is all about communication—from the position of a navigation element to the size and shape of a button, every detail furthers the conversation. So how is it that the very foundation of the Web, written text, has taken a strategic back seat to design?

You do research. You devise tack-sharp strategy. You sweat the details. All to create a design that truly speaks to your user. Does your copy do the same? Apply a design process to your words as well as your images and you just may find your voice.

Say it, don't display it.

It's one thing to write copy that fits on a website. It's quite another to write copy that fits in with a website. You wouldn't try to force an incongruous visual element into a carefully considered design. Same goes for written content. Even if you've wisely designed a site around the content it delivers, written copy may fit neatly physically but still ring false to the intended audience.

Ideally, you should work with a writer from day one to design the voice of the copy in conjunction with the visual language of the site. And getting a writer involved early can help you solve lots of other problems—from content strategy issues to information architecture snags. Remember that writers are creatives too, and they are, in many cases, the keepers of the content your design ultimately serves.

If you simply don't have the resources to hire a writer, you'll have to keep an ear on the language yourself. This is where the user experience research you did way back in the design concept phase comes back into play. It helps you design your words.

Make personas more grata.

You remember those burning questions. The ones you ask yourself every time you kick off a new project. They probably go a little something like this:

> > Who's visiting this site?
> > What does she want to know?
> > What does he want to do?

If you've ever worked with them before, you know how invaluable user personas can be to answering these questions. Maybe they're not of the fake-name-and-glossy-headshot variety, but even the most rudimentary personas (i.e., "my mom" or "the skeptic") transform your audience into real human beings. Human beings with day jobs, complicated espresso beverage orders, and no time to waste looking for things instead of finding them.

In a sense, you create characters from these personas. Establish what your characters will respond well to, build in contingencies for second- and third-tier players, and you move closer to an effective design. Not coincidentally, effective storytelling works much the same way. It demonstrates how different characters respond in different ways to the same situation. The only thing missing from this analogy is a narrator. Time to write yourself into the story.

Call me Ishmael.

Ask people why they love the stories they do, and you often hear the same response: "I really identify with the characters." Create a persuasive voice for your website by giving your users someone to identify with: A first-person "narrator" with a distinct yet welcoming personality. Developing this personality shouldn't be too difficult. You did the heavy lifting when you created your original user personas. Now you just need to create one more.

First, try adding these to your list of questions:

> How do I want to make this user feel?
> How would I carry on a face-to-face conversation with him?

Then imagine your target persona's peer. Someone who shares her interests and speaks with her, not at her. A professional video editor. A fellow foodie. A sports car enthusiast. That's who you'll channel to find your voice during the next step in the design process: Brainstorming.

Sing in the rain.

Ah, that magical moment when Moleskines reach capacity, people pass out from dry-erase fumes, and there are no bad ideas (except for that one ...). The time-honored brainstorming session (even confined to one brain) helps you build design concepts around strategy. No reason your copy can't come along for the ride.

While you're sketching designs, jot down a quote or two. Collect tear sheets of words as well as images. Shoot rough video of someone you think would make the perfect spokesperson. Remember that by introducing your narrator persona, you're creating an expert peer your users will come back to for advice, information, and inspiration. That's worth spending some time on. It also makes the actual business of copywriting much easier. Learn the language, then tell your story—not the other way around.

Work on your dialogue.

Design a voice for your site and you do more than make words and images play nice. You engage your users in a discussion you both want to carry on. So if you find yourself laboring to craft the perfect written sentence, improvise. Speak what you want to say, then write it. Email it to a colleague. Chat it. Text it.

Great Web design reflects the way we interact, and the primary vehicle for that interaction remains text. We share, we chat, we comment, we tag, and we do it all via the written word. The Web is One Big Conversation. Let's talk.

⌐◡⌐

Bronwyn Jones is a web writer living in San Francisco, where she enjoys Britpop, agit-prop and cookies with butterscotch chips. This article first appeared July 2007 in the online magazine *A List Apart*.

Why I Blog

by Christopher "Chip" Scanlan

"A BOOK," according to the tormented writer Franz Kafka, "should be an ice-axe to break the frozen sea within us."

I know what he's talking about. A sea of ice—in the shape of a serious bout with depression—immobilized me as a writer and reader for much of last summer and fall.

Usually I read several books a week, sometimes devouring one in a one-day orgy of prose. But during this period I was lucky if I could get through a few paragraphs before losing interest or attention.

I also had the worst case of writer's block I'd ever experienced. Writing my weekly column, "Chip on Your Shoulder," felt like trying to break through that frozen sea with a teaspoon. Production ground to a halt. I blew deadlines for two major projects.

Eventually, a caring and knowledgeable doctor, a combination of therapy, a powerful daily pharmaceutical cocktail, and the love of friends, family, and understanding colleagues pulled me free from the darkness. I began reading again, and in January, I found myself itching to write.

But after three years and more than 180 columns, I looked down into the well of my experience and interests as a reporter, writer, and teacher and saw, or at least believed, it had gone bone-dry. I thought I had covered all the subjects that mattered to me and ones that readers had asked me to address. I needed to try something new. I wanted to blog.

Since the mid-1990s when the first blogs began to emerge, I had made several abortive attempts to create one of my own. I missed access to the printing press that a life in journalism had offered for two decades. But I always ran into the roadblocks put up by my lack of techno-savvy.

I needed help, so I told my editor, Julie Moos, an active blogger who has made it possible for many others to find their voice online, that I wanted to try again.

"Pull up a chair," she said.

Within minutes, using TypePad, a weblogging service that provides templates and an Internet hosting service, Julie had assembled a home for a title I'd been harboring ever since I heard Jacqui Banaszynski talk during a seminar about two helpers that every writer needs: a mechanic and a muse. Sitting there, I wrote down a book title, *The Mechanic & the Muse*, that would be a kind of owner's manual for writers. That was the name I told Julie I wanted for my blog.

The Mechanic & the Muse was born on January 17. As of this morning, I've written more than 20 items and posted half of them. Many are long enough to be columns, Julie points out, but I'd much rather be blogging. Here are seven reasons I joined the millions who communicate through a form that is part reverse diary, commonplace book, and soapbox.

1. Blog items respond to a rapidly changing media landscape.

I like the way blogging lets me tackle multiple topics in a day or through the week instead of focusing all my time and energy on one weekly column. It's the difference between being a beat specialist and a general assignment reporter. I can write on subjects that draw my attention. I've written about journalistic subjects and pointed readers to repositories of stories that represent best practices. But I've also written about fiction and memoir, two forms that are passions of mine. Like Cream, the '60s mega-group, sings, "I feel free."

2. When I blog, my standards are lowered.

This is always a key element in producing writing that can be revised, even after it's published. A blog, by its very nature, is more informal than a column and less freighted with the expectations that a metro or sports column can impose. Blogging hasn't made me indifferent to revision or accuracy; it just makes the process of generating words less susceptible to the inner critic.

In a recent radio interview (on NPR's *All Things Considered*, 2/7/06), former US Poet Laureate Billy Collins talked about his art, and it helped me understand why I like to blog.

"The real thrill is composition," Collins said. "To be kind of down on your hands and knees with the language at really close range in the midst of a poem that is carrying you in some direction that you can't foresee … It's that sense of ongoing discovery that makes composition really thrilling and that's the pleasure and that's why I write."

3. I'm my own editorial board.
As a newspaper reporter, I was trained to keep my opinions out of my stories. In a blog, I can be as opinionated as I want. Case in point: a post (1/31/06) with my no-holds-barred reaction to the James Frey/Oprah's Book Club fiasco. I feel free to have an opinion and share it.

4. Change is vital.
Wise editors realize that a reporter can burn out on a beat and so they switch their assignments, knowing that a fresh pair of eyes will bene-fit the writer and readers. They feel free.

5. Blogs are not new, but they're still on the leading edge of communication technology.
I've always been an early adopter and I don't want to be left behind. In a time when reporters and editors are blogging on their news organi-zations' websites, I feel free to be part of this experiment.

6. Let's face it, a blog can also be a great marketing device.
I've posted examples of my own writing, some published and others that have not yet appeared in print, along with books I've written or co-authored with links that make online purchasing a snap. Like most writers, I harbor the dream that an agent or publisher may see com-mercial possibilities in my work.

7. To paraphrase Kafka: my blog is the ice-axe that broke the frozen sea within me.
It has helped me find myself again as a reader and writer. It has set me free.

Blogging doesn't mean I won't write columns ever again. Sometimes that space is appropriate for interviews with writers. So I've continued the "Chip on Your Shoulder" column on Poyter Online.

I haven't moved really. Blogging is like having an office but also keeping a studio where you can experiment, take risks with your craft, and share your discoveries with others.

Some things won't change. I'll always and be grateful for comments, questions, story suggestions, and most of all, your companionship.

Chip Scanlan is Senior Faculty (Writing) and Director of the National Writer Workshops with the Poynter Institute of St. Petersburg, Florida. He produces "Chip on Your Shoulder," a writing advice column for Poynter Online. He spent two decades as an award-winning reporter and feature writer (*Providence Journal, St. Petersburg Times*, Knight Ridder Washington Bureau).

He is the author of *Reporting and Writing: Basics for the 21st Century* (Oxford University Press); co-editor of *America's Best Newspaper Writing* (Bedford/St. Martin's); and editor of *Best Newspaper Writing 1994–2000*.

With his wife, Katharine Fair, he wrote *The Holly Wreath Man*, a serial newspaper novel syndicated in 60 newspapers and then published in hardcover (2005). In 2006, the couple produced another Christmas serial, *Mystery @ Elf Camp*.

This article was posted February 2006 on his blog, The Mechanic & the Muse (http://poynter.blogs.com/the_mechanic_the_muse).

To Blog or Not To Blog

by Maryn McKenna

THERE ARE SO MANY angles to consider in the intersection of books and blogs. First, there's the blog as a venue for a writer who has no other regular "publication place" or is writing as a new voice in a crowded field. Just two recent examples of this—where publishers noticed the voice and recruited the blogger to do a book—are the blogs of food writer Clotilde Dusoulier and stripper/memoir/Oscar-winning screenwriter Diablo Cody.

Then there's the blog as a tool for an established author, which breaks down into two types: pre-pub and post-pub.

Post-pub is self-evident in purpose. You use your blog, which may or may not be housed within your book website or personal website but should at least be linked to it, to update your community of readers and fans about where you're appearing, what you're thinking about while on the road, where they can find the sound files of media appearances they missed, and so on. It's a simple, low-cost (in time and money) marketing tool that helps you engage your audience and sustain their interest.

I can't see why anyone who has a book coming out would not be doing this.

Pre-pub to me is more interesting, and more open to question. The idea here is that you "blog the book" as you are researching and writing it, in hopes of engaging an audience well in advance of the book's actually existing. This audience could be passive readers, or they could be people sufficiently interested in your topic that they will engage with you via blog comments, and in so doing can help you push your thinking further than it might otherwise have gone. Such a blog allows you to create a Web presence and following for a book long before there is enough of a book to justify a static website.

Several authors have tried this. Chris Anderson's "The Long Tail" blog (www.thelongtail.com/about.html) is the ur- and meta-example, since it was a blog and a book about the economics that permit blogging a book to make sense. David Shenk is trying it now for a book due out in 2009 (http://geniusblog.davidshenk.com), and does appear from the comments to have an ongoing readership.

The problem with pre-pub blogging is that, even though the blog is about the same topics that the book is about, the blog will devour time that you probably ought to be spending on the book manuscript instead. (This is the same ultimately beneficial, but near-term crazy-making, dynamic that makes writing freelance articles out of your book research so difficult.)

I am struggling with this myself. I have a personal website (www.MarynMcKenna.com), and a site devoted to my first book (www.BeatingBacktheDevil.com). But I also have started a blog (http://drugresistantstaph.blogspot.com) for my second book, *Superbug* (Free Press, 2009), and it is eating my life.

The problem is not the putting of posts on the blog, per se, but rather the reaching out to readers and posting on other blogs and all the other things that I have to do to drive traffic to my new blog. Those are very time-consuming—and yet necessary if a blog is going to fulfill its purpose of creating and sustaining an audience in advance of publication. Because if no one is reading it, you might as well not be doing it.

There are three important questions. First: does blogging actually make a difference in the long run to either book content or book sales? Second: do you give away so much of your research and/or arguments that you exhaust a portion of your audience's interest in advance of publication? These questions are likely to remain unanswered, because no one has data, only anecdotes.

The third question: do publishers want books to have sites, blogs, trailers, and other shiny new multimedia things? The answer to that one is definitely yes. But, sadly, not enough to pay for them.

Maryn McKenna is a journalist, author and a staff member at the Center for Infectious Disease Research and Policy. She lives in Minneapolis and Atlanta.

This piece is based on a January 2008 post to the nonfiction writers' discussion list-serv, WriterL (www.writerL.com).

Evaluating Blog Results:
Does Your Blog Suck or Succeed?

by Ron McDaniel

You may believe that your blog sucks if you set a specific goal and do not achieve it. But blogs are not an all-or-nothing tool. They increase the probability of things happening for you.

I recently presented to a group that I'd also presented to about eight months before. I spoke with four people that had started blogs based on my first presentation. Of the four, three reported fantastic results. The funny thing: all four were measuring different things that they considered success factors.

The one person that reported bad results was entirely focused on one thing: no one was commenting on her blog.

The three that were succeeding were all different.

1. Increased visibility, is now being paid to write for other sites, directly because of his blog.
2. Added three new clients that cited her blog as the reason they finally hired her.
3. Sold significant add-on products to existing customers and to the public.

All three have added to their income, but in entirely different ways.

Here is a list of things that are more likely to happen for you (or your organization) if you do a good job of blogging.

> **Write a book.** Eventually you get used to writing and have a lot of material to draw from, so writing a book becomes a no-brainer.
> **Sell products.** As you build an audience, it is easy to recommend products you know they will like, and earn a commission.
> **Speaking.** Before hiring a speaker, many event planners read the blog of a potential speaker to make sure they fit the need.

- > **Add clients.** No matter what you are doing, you can add clients via blogging because your blog increases search engine results and it increases relationships.
- > **Build community.** Depending on your topic, your blog can become the center of a community on a particular topic.
- > **Advertising income.** As a blog becomes a respected resource, you will get offers from people that want to advertise on the site.
- > **Interviews.** Your blogging increases your visibility, and you become an attractive person for interviews.
- > **Reviews.** Writing reviews means you will get free stuff—like books—sent to you regularly.
- > **Moral support.** Bloggers are great at helping each other out and offering moral support. It is a strong community of people that really care.
- > **Improved communication.** You may just want to become a better communicator, and blogging is a great way to organize your thoughts and improve your writing skills.

So what does blogging success look like for you? To decide if you are successful, pick the two to three goals that matter most to you and measure those.

Ron McDaniel has been a university professor and has worked in service, retail, technology and sales industries, for start-ups and Fortune 500 companies. He is the founder of Buzzoodle (www.buzzoodle.com), a firm that trains and empowers employees of client organizations to develop skills in marketing and buzz generation. He is the author of *Buzzoodle Buzz Marketing* and conducts training sessions over the Web and with companies around the country.

His personal website is www.ronmcdaniel.com. His piece is drawn from a September 2007 post on his Buzzoodle Blog site (http://blog.buzzoodle.com).

BUSINESS SAVVY

Marketing Your Freelance Writing Business

by Colin Galbraith

A CONSTANT PROBLEM in the life of every freelance writer is the require-ment to promote your writing services while allowing enough time to actually provide them. Time management is tricky enough when work-ing from home, and it's very easy to become swamped in marketing activities, thereby taking away valuable writing time from your busy schedule.

So how can you free up more writing time without letting your business disappear into obscurity? And is it possible to keep new busi-ness coming in, without infringing on the copy production line? This article illustrates five easy-to-implement marketing methods that will help you strike that all important balance.

1. Create Standard Templates.

It sounds rather obvious, but creating templates for frequently used documents can not only provide huge time savings, but also enhance your company's professional profile.

For example, press releases all contain the same basic information: who, what, where, why, and when. A template can have the "who" and "why" completed in advance, and sometimes even the "where," before you sit down to write the release.

Personal introduction letters also work well with templates. If you use strong sales techniques to promote yourself, include those in the letter, so you only have the recipient's personal details to complete before posting it.

And it doesn't stop there. This approach can be used for queries, marketing material, and even emails; all of which can be transformed into templates. Any document you need to send regularly can be trans-formed into a template to speed things up.

It may take you a little while to get the templates up and running, and you may eventually need variations on the same theme, but once you have them it takes only a small amount of work to adapt them as your business needs grow.

2. Look for People with Something to Offer You.

When was the last time you scanned your local or evening newspaper with your marketing hat on? Or read a copy of a trade magazine without knowing anything about it? By training your eye to spot opportunities from a variety of sources no matter where you are, you will start to see more and more places where the savvy freelance writer can generate work opportunities.

You might be sitting in the dentist's waiting room reading a magazine or newspaper, or maybe you are on a train, in a motorway service station, browsing the shops—anywhere there might be an advert or somebody with a story to tell is a potential opportunity.

Look for stories or adverts where local businesses are seen to be expanding, have won an award, or where a key member of staff has changed. New businesses to the area might have a feature story, or perhaps a local event is looking for input or sponsorship.

Take notes of names and addresses, then write short letters of introduction (from a template) that mention the story and how your services can benefit them. Throw in a couple of business cards and send it off. It's a method that might just generate the type of interest you are looking for, and will certainly go a long way to creating a memorable impression.

3. Team Up with Other Freelancers.

Networking with other writers is great for a freelancer's soul, but for maximizing business opportunities it helps to create a sub-network of people in other industries who are willing to work with you when the opportunity presents itself.

Hook up with local photographers and graphic designers, and use them when a project comes around that requires their skills. You will find you are able to take on more and varied types of work this way, and can complete jobs much quicker. By throwing work their way you are scratching their backs, and they will be inclined to forward job opportunities that require a talented freelance writer in return.

4. Join a Local Business Organization.

Join a local organization such as a marketing or business club. Meetup. com has loads of these types of groups, and there may also be local directories with this type of information for your area.

Face-to-face networking is one of the best ways to get the word out about your business, and if you can do it within social time, then that's even better. Always keep business cards in your pocket, and don't be stingy with them either—two at a time to prospects, at least.

Once you are part of an organization, get active within it and get people moving and motivated by your energy. Getting noticed by taking a visible role will put you at the top of people's minds, and you will find you are their first port of call when work opportunities present themselves.

5. Pitch Yourself—Short and Sweet.

Cold calling is not something I particularly enjoy, and there is a debate about whether it benefits a business or hinders it. But there are methods similar to cold-calling that have a much warmer feel to them and that are not as scary for the freelance writer to execute without feeling like an alien from outer space.

When you go out, take your business cards, prepared leaflets detailing your business services, and a small folder containing several of your best printed clips. Call into local businesses and shops you use frequently and build up a relationship with them. Chat to the staff about their business and get to know them. When they ask about your business, have a short informal pitch about the services you offer, and how you can benefit them.

Leave some of your material for them to look at later, and if they fancy getting together to chat some more, then it could be the start of a long and profitable relationship. A friendly face goes much further than an unsolicited phone call.

Colin Galbraith writes nonfiction articles, fiction and poetry. An editor for two magazines, he has published one novel, two chapbooks and several e-books. He lives in Edinburgh where he splits his time between his family, his freelance writing business and getting his next novel published. His website is http://freelance.colingalbraith.co.uk.

He also writes a weekly article for Daily Writing Tips (www.dailywritingtips.com), a blog focused on advice for writing skills, freelance writing and web content development.

Boost Your Personal Brand Online

by Philip Martin

> *"Earn a character first if you can, and if you can't, then assume one."*
> —Mark Twain (Samuel Clemens)

Let's take a quick look at your personal brand as a writer, especially your web presence. When someone looks for you on the Web, can they find you? And if so, do you present your brand well?

Samuel Clemens, writing as Mark Twain, was one of the first American writers to become a celebrity. He practiced many aspects of personal branding. He wrote in a distinctively sardonic, conversational style. His writings and talks presented a down-home persona, a homespun narrator full of folk wisdom and tall tales. He assumed the trappings of brand image: a white suit, a cigar, a distinctive mustache, tousled hair. He got out on the lecture circuit, testing and honing his best stuff. He developed a knack for the "sound bite," the short, quotable epigram (such as, "Man is the only animal that blushes—or needs to.").

In addition to his novels, he published many brief pieces: speeches, articles, short stories. And most notably, he adopted a pseudonym: Mark Twain, a wonderfully punchy, memorable, plausible name, imbued with a folksy, easily spoken resonance (taken from a Mississippi riverboat call).

Clemens/Twain knew the secrets of personal branding. Creating a brand involves, as he noted, both earning it and assuming it. You don't develop a brand without some active involvement in creating its form.

What is Your Personal Brand?

Your brand image is not how *you* see yourself, but how *others* perceive you—quickly, clearly, positively. What comes to mind when they think of you as a literary professional? Prompt? Reliable? Humorous? Thoughtful? Broad-ranging? Laser-focused?

Do you deliver the goods in a friendly or fun or factual manner? How do others describe you if they recommend you to another person?

Think of today's major writers with a brand image, from Dave Barry to Stephen King to Suze Orman—writers whose names appear in bigger letters than the titles of their books. All serve up products that are consistent and recognizable, in style and content, and strongly identified with their writing personalities.

In a smaller vein, when someone like you or me turns in a piece of writing, do editors and readers expect it to be a "Philip Martin" or [fill in your name here] product? Can they rely in advance on your work having valuable and unique attributes, with your own version of writing that is useful, entertaining, thorough, or in someway identifiable?

A brand, says branding guru Tom Peters, is "a promise of the value you'll receive." In other words, it is an expectation, in advance of the product itself.

You can and should develop your brand consciously. And by being consistent, others will begin to recognize it. (It's not a brand until it's recognized by others.)

Over the coming months, with a few easy steps, you can better define how others see you. To stand out from the crowd, take some time to strategically develop your brand.

Identify Your Attributes

Tom Peters suggests: "Start by identifying the qualities or characteristics that make you distinctive from your competitors—or your colleagues." Pinpoint what colleagues or customers say is your greatest, clearest strength. What is your most notable personal trait?

Take a few moments to write down a few attributes about your personal brand. Attributes need to be clear, quick, positive ... and true. Trueness or authenticity is essential. Brands are not invented willy-nilly, they are identified and reinforced. It won't work to pretend to be something you're not.

In my own case, as a person who helps others with writing, publishing, branding, and blogging, I focus on a few core concepts: I'm Midwestern (practical, down-to-earth), zen (calm, focused on steady practice), nurturing (like a gardener, looking for the right place and nutrients for your creative work), holistic (embracing the entirety of what is needed to succeed). It comes out in a phrase I like to use: the proof is in the pudding. (Or in the Midwest, maybe the proof is in the hotdish.)

But is that Midwestern practical sensibility how others see me? What can I do to build and reinforce that?

What are *your* chief attributes?

Creative Ideas

1. COMBINE TEXT AND VISUALS … WITH ATTITUDE.

Look again at your website or blog. Can you paint a quick picture (in words, images, and attitude) of who you are? Dave Barry's home page shows a photo of him with a sledge hammer looming over a toilet with the words: "If you leave this web site, I will kill this defenseless toilet." Suze Orman's home page immediately pitches her products, but uses not one but four pictures of her (two of them on product covers); all feature her distinctive hairstyle, smile, and in the largest one, the cocked finger of admonishment. If you look at her bio page, it gives her philosophy: "People first, then money, then things." That's memorable enough to remember a day later.

For many writers, the brand image is a literary one. Check the website of novelist Joshua Henkin (www.joshuahenkin.com) as a thorough example. Clean design, professional bio photo, artsy photos from a recent book cover, blog, contest, events, reading group guides, video interview, and quick links to booksellers.

Check the websites of topflight romance, mystery, or thiller novelists for themes, images, style, contents that relate to brand image. Look for unique aspects. If countless romance writers' websites all feature red roses as a typical motif … what can you do that's different (in a positive, memorable way)?

2. WHERE DO YOU LIVE?

As you may know, I'm a big proponent of developing a sense of place as a way to distinguish your writing. This can be true also for your personal brand. Stephen King is known as a writer from Maine, the setting for many of his stories. Sure enough, on his website, he includes a map (under Miscellany) showing the state of Maine with real towns (names in green) and fictional places from his stories (in blue).

Dave Barry is known as a newspaper columnist based in Miami, something he mentions often in his writing.

To distinguish yourself from others, a sense of where you live, without needing to be too specific, gives a flavor to your brand. Look for the positive connections. Yes, Wisconsin is known for overweight beer- and brandy-drinking cheeseheads. It's also the birthplace of John Muir, the home territory of conservationist Aldo Leopold and Earth Day founder Gaylord Nelson. Guess which way I went when looking for a quote?

3. YOUR NAME.

Suze Orman selected a variant of her first name, one that reflects her "girlfriend, let me give you some advice" brand.

Some writers naturally have memorable names: Agatha Christie and Daphne du Maurier come to mind, for some reason. But some of us have a name that's hard to remember, or for others, hard to spell. Others (like me) have a name that's incredibly common.

Consider ways to present your name. You can use initials (R.L. Stine) or a nickname (Bill Bryson, born William McGuire Bryson).

You can add a middle name or other identifier, or even choose a pseudonym. I started writing as Philip Martin before the Web was a key finding aid. Now, I need to consider how to be more distinctive, name-wise. I might want to use my middle name, Nevin (an old British Isles name, bestowed on me to honor some obscure relative). Never was that keen on it ... but I'm rethinking.

Many have gone with the middle-name solution, like Arthur Doyle. Who? You know him better, and unforgettably, as Arthur Conan Doyle.

4. BRAND AS VOICE.

In fiction or nonfiction, you seek to develop your voice; in marketing, your brand. The concept is similar. Look for what comes naturally to you (authenticity), while pushing forward what is different in your writing (a recognizable uniqueness).

Blog writers are savvy to this. Some blog names are descriptive (Problogger, etc.) while others go for cool, goofy names (Boing Boing)—like the strategy used by alternative rock bands with names like They Might be Giants or Barenaked Ladies. Or consider the books by marketing guru Seth Godin, author of *The Big Red Fez, Purple Cow, All*

Marketers are Liars, Free Prize Inside, and *Meatball Sundae*. The pattern of titles is intrinsic to his "think outside the box" brand.

It's harder to brand diversity, but some writers do it successfully. Linda Formichelli, author of many articles and several books for writers, including *The Renegade Writer*, leads her website with a fun photo and a friendly welcome: "Hi, I'm Linda." The next line: "I wear more hats than your old Aunt Millie."

Brand Worklist

1. Write out your key brand attributes. Name three to five things. Be sure they are clear, quick, positive, and honest.

2. Pick out the attributes that are most distinctive. How can you develop, refine, and describe those even more uniquely?

3. How clear is your brand identity *online*? Rank it one to ten for these criteria: clear, brief/quick, visible, specific, unique, positive, valuable (to your target customer), authentic.

4. Ask a couple of people to find you online and give specific feedback about the image you present. (Remember, it's not a brand until others can see it.) Start with a close friend who knows you well, then try someone who knows your work less well! Ask them to summarize what they see to be "your brand."

5. Create a short descriptive brand statement: My brand is ("I am different and valuable because ..."):

6. Experiment with a catchy tag-line. (Create more than one, and try them out on friends.) One key test: can someone remember it correctly a day later? Or do they forget or mangle it?

7. Look at your website. What simple changes can push your brand forward? (The answer is often to diminish or delete unnecessary or common things.) Think in terms of words, images, and attitude. The simpler, the better, for the first page or two. A brand does not pop easily off a page with a cluttered layout.

8. Add your "brand story" to your website or blog. For a writer, this is the journey that led you to write what and how you do. This can range from early influences to things that happened later in life. You're a writer. Tell your story, in a brief, engaging way. What's the promising opener? What's the complicating/transformational event? What's the great outcome? What's the theme (that mirrors your brand)?

9. Besides a search on Google and Yahoo, check your other online presences: encyclopedic listings at Wikipedia or your alumni directory. Do you have bios on Amazon (as a reviewer?) or as a member of a professional organization? Do you have a profile on LinkedIn or Facebook? Are you a guest contributor on other blogs, websites, e-zines? If you can, update those profiles. Add major credits, affiliations, achievements. Submit new articles, guest posts, current URLS.

Once you've developed your brand and its descriptive elements, do what you can to disseminate it across the Web. Try to build an online web presence to present your professional profile in a consistent, brand-conscious manner.

It's not hard. It takes only a few steps, a few moments now and then, to keep things shipshape. Establishing and getting your brand out there in visible places on the World Wide Web is an important part of your writing platform.

Remember, it's not a brand till it's visible to others. To make that happen, you have to assume the trappings. Earn it *and* assume it. You'll be in good company, with Mark Twain and all the other successful authors who knew how to create an image and don the white suit, cigar, and tousled hair of success.

Philip Martin is editor of *The New Writer's Handbook* and previously was acquisitions editor for The Writer Books, where he produced guides for writers on many topics. He is also author of a book on fantasy fiction, *The Writer's Guide to Fantasy Literature*, along with several other books on regional music and folklore. He lives in Milwaukee and is director of Great Lakes Literary (www.greatlakeslit.com), which offers editorial and professional development services for writers.

This article first appeared May 2008 in his free newsletter of advice for writers, found at his website.

Business Card as Offline Home Page

by Tony D. Clark

ALLOW ME to set a familiar scene.

You're in need of a certain service. You know what you want, and you hit Google to do a search. On the first page of results, there are four or five entries that seem to fit what you're looking for. You click on the link, and *based on the first five to ten seconds on the home page*, you decide whether or not that company gets your business.

Now, let's go to another familiar scene.

You're at a networking function, and have talked to twenty or thirty people. You are getting ready to leave, and take a quick look at the business cards you've collected during the evening. Some you can match with a person you remember talking to. Others are so generic—you can't help but feel that the person they represented must have been too. You can't remember a thing about them.

Online Rules in the Offline World

How much time do you spend optimizing your home page or landing page for your online business? Do you take that *same approach to your offline landing page?*

This can be the role of your business card. Often, it's all a prospective client has to work with. The goal is to make sure the card is memorable, informative, clean, and professional—just like a good website landing page.

Think about the last time someone handed you a business card. What was your first reaction?

Let's try an experiment. What is your initial gut response when you see a card?

If you're like most people, you judged the business—even just a little—based on what was on the card. We do judge books by their covers. Otherwise thousands of book designers and marketing experts would be out of a job.

Fortunately, most times you have more than a business card to work with. But there are other times when it's all we've got. Wouldn't it be nice if your card represented you well?

A well-optimized card can be (with links to further resources):

> A tool (for creative design; see the website of Jeni Mattson, with this amazing example:
www.jenimattson.com/index.php?id=melvin#identity)

> A canvas (for personal expression; see the work of Hugh McLeod, a cartoonist working on the backs of business cards:
www.gapingvoid.com)

> A tiny direct-marketing piece (see this idea from executive recruiter Harry Joiner:
www.mpdailyfix.com/2006/08/building_a_better_business_car.html)

> A reflection of your personal style (see www.moo.com)

> Good quality, yet reasonably priced

It can also be forgettable, or worse, make it on a list of annoyances (such as this list from Scott Ginsberg, "The Nametag Guy," from his blog: (http://hellomynameisscott.blogspot.com/2007/02/8-thoughts-on-bad-business-cards.html).

So, while you're tweaking your online presence, and following the rules of a well-optimized site, don't forget your offline landing page.

Otherwise, a potential client might just forget too.

Forgetting you in the process.

Tony D. Clark is an entrepreneur, artist, writer and designer. He is also co-founder of Teaching Sells (www.teachingsells.com), a regular contributor to lifehack.org (a productivity and personal development blog), and cartoonist for Implementing Scrum (www.implementingscrum.com), a site to help software teams with methodology.

This piece was posted March 2007 on his Succcess from the Nest blog (http://successfromthenest.com), with marketing and business advice for home-based entrepreneurs.

School Visits:
How Much To Charge?

by Alexis O'Neill

"How much do you charge?" the school visit coordinator asks.

You freeze. You think, "If I name fee that's too high, I'll lose the invitation. If my fee is too low, they may think I don't have much to offer."

Nothing causes authors and illustrators more anxiety than putting a price on their school visits. No, wait! What causes even *higher* anxiety is when a school *expects* you to appear for *free*.

If you're suffering fee-freeze with every invitation, it's time to grow up. Begin thinking of yourself as a professional instead of a professional volunteer. Writing is a business. In the world of children's books, your income generally comes from four sources: royalties, freelance work, speaking engagements, and teaching. If you are one of the lucky ten percent in the world who can live off royalties alone, you can stop reading this column now. Otherwise, listen up.

Why Charge?
You are professional (probably without health benefits or a 401K). But potential hosts often believe that you:
1. are a missionary for reading and writing, in service to a celestial power;
2. make enough money from the sale of your (expensive) books to buy multiple yachts; and
3. write as a hobby.

What hosts don't understand is that you:
1. need to earn a living to put bread on the table just like teachers, librarians, administrators and booksellers;
2. earn between 1.5 percent and 10 percent per book sold; and

3. worked a lifetime—and invested lots of time and money—to become an expert at your craft.

Bottom line: If you don't have the mindset of a professional, you will never be treated as one.

How Do I Determine My Fees?

Clarify your goal. What's your business plan? How much money do you want to gross in a year? How far are you willing to travel and how many days are you willing to devote to meet your goal? The answer will differ from author to author. For example, if you want to gross $25,000 from school visits and your fee is $1,000 a day, then you need to do 25 days within ten months (the typical school year).

Research local markets. Ask other authors and illustrators in your geographic region what they charge. Ask what their school visit "day" consists of in terms of type (assemblies, class visits, workshops) and number of presentations. (Start online at the Society of Children's Book Writers and Illustrators' website, www.scbwi.org, and then check out SCBWI regional websites. Many list speakers' bureaus and individuals' fees.)

Research national markets. Publishers' sites often have an "author visit" sections. Some list speaking fees. For example: www.simonsays. com/extras/pdfs/AuthorKit07.pdf. Others link to authors' and illustrators' websites, for example: http://teacher.scholastic.com/authorsand-books/visitkit/authorregion.htm.

Factor in your experience. How many books do you have published by trade book publishers? Have you received good reviews in *School Library Journal, Publishers Weekly, Horn Book, Booklist,* or other respected outlets? Have your books won any awards? Do you have any teaching background? While teaching experience isn't necessary, it can help establish credibility with hosts. So, factor that in when determining your fee.

Consider the program or service you are offering. Authors charge:
> based on time spent (e.g., per assembly, per day, or per half-day), and/or
> based on services rendered (e.g. student writing workshops, teacher in-service workshops, family night events, keynotes).

What About Expenses?

Travel, hotel, and food are often expensed to the host separately. Handouts are usually reproduced by the school from your templates. However some authors charge a higher fee and cover all expenses themselves.

What Are the Ranges in Fees?

For "practice" presentations, the fee can range from $0–$150. As you gain experience, rates can range from $500–$800 and upwards to $2,500 or more. For example, in an analysis of the 2006 fees for 115 Scholastic authors and illustrators representing 21 states, the median fee was $1,100 for all regions (eastern, central and western states). Half charged this fee or more, half charged this fee or less. Some charged $100–$500 above their base rate for out-of-state visits.

Should I Negotiate My Fee with Hosts?

Negotiating can prove worthwhile. Authors commonly offer discounts to schools if two or more schools in the same area book on consecutive days. (This also means that schools share in the cost of your transportation.) Some authors are willing to visit two schools in one day for their daily rate so that each school pays half.

Should I Ever Do Freebies?

Professionals often offer *pro bono* work for their favorite charities. How much you do is dependent on your business plan and income goals. For example, if you have a new book coming out, there is great benefit in participating in events that offer you an opportunity to sell books and make fans. Bookstore appearances, teacher and librarian conferences, author fairs, and large book fairs such as the Los Angeles Times Festival of Books are examples of no fee/low fee events that can kickstart book sales and advertise your availability as a speaker.

How Do I Turn Down a Freebie Request?

Say, "I'm so sorry, but I'm not available." Do not engage in the "whys." Then recommend them to a local scbwi speakers' list or to someone who is new and needs experience (with that author's approval, of course).

What If Schools Just Don't Have the Money to Hire Me?

People usually find ways to afford what they value. If schools are struggling—and certainly schools without active parent groups are at a disadvantage—there are still many ways for motivated hosts to find funding for programs that directly support and extend curriculum goals. Give this link to your hosts to get them started: www.leeandlow.com/p/administrators_grants.mhtml. Other sources include local reading councils, service groups and friends of the library organizations.

Remember—school visits are part of your business. Act professionally and you'll be paid accordingly.

Alexis O'Neill, PhD, has been an elementary school teacher, a teacher of teachers and a museum educator. Her books include *Loud Emily, The Worst Best Friend* and *The Recess Queen*, a bully book that appeared on the *Los Angeles Times* list of bestselling children's books. Her articles have appeared in *Cricket, Spider, Cobblestone, Calliope* and elsewhere.

She teaches writing for the UCLA Extension Writers' Program and is a popular presenter and school-visit expert. Her website is www.alexisoneill.com.

Back Up Those Files Now

by Kay B. Day

ONE MORNING a few years ago, I got up at 5:30 A.M. to get the jump on a busy day. Three deadlines for rush assignments glared from my calendar. I tapped the button on my keyboard and the computer began to hum. After a few seconds, the hum did not develop into that comforting whirr I'd always taken for granted. My screen was black as a moonless, starless night.

By that afternoon, I admitted to myself my hard drive had expired. I didn't know whether to bury the computer or my body. There was a small comfort: a drawer full of floppy disks I had used to copy most of my document files. My email was unrecoverable because I hadn't thought to back it up.

Since that time, my files have grown more complicated and floppy disks are now an antiquated option. For awhile, I simply copied files onto USB flash drives. I realized how expensive this could get, though. I have a lot of photo files, five book manuscripts, videos, and all sorts of other files—because when my former computer died I naturally got a computer with more storage.

So what do you do to avoid having to copy all those files onto CDs or flash drives?

Remote backup is an option. I opted for the unlimited version of Mozy. There's a lot of comfort in knowing if one of those Florida hurricanes aims itself at my house, my files are safe in another location. I opted for backup every seven days, and the program can run in the background while I work. This program is the one I'm most familiar with, and I believe it is the most reasonably priced because, for one thing, you can get 2 GB free. But it isn't the only option.

Bruce Miller, IT Manager for the American Society of Journalists and Authors, is responsible for the equivalent of oceans of data. So he has a more complex approach, starting with email. Miller says the primary

ASJA account email is also forwarded to other email accounts at places like Yahoo and Google. These other accounts, he says, "provide a backup for incoming email and a way to check on email from any Internet-connected computer." There's comfort in knowing those emails are duplicated elsewhere.

Miller says the program he uses for regular backup is Save-N-Sync Corporate edition from PeerSoftware.com. Because he works on several computers, Miller also uses Mozy to back up his desktop computer. And just to be safe, he also uses USB flash drives. "For further backup, I frequently replicate the data from the latest version on the external hard drive to a second laptop identical (brand and model) to the first laptop."

Miller's needs outweigh most of our needs; he's backing up an organization that serves more than 1,000 members. Information about annual dues, the conference, the membership forum, the organization's website, and tons of other documents must be protected. Every once and awhile he says he also burns a DVD or CD and takes the data to the bank to place in a safety deposit box.

When you opt for a backup program, it's important to consider your operating system and your own needs. The Mac OS X Leopard comes with its own backup system, Time Capsule. Windows Vista also comes with a backup system, but the version you'll have depends on the edition of Vista you purchased.

Steve Morrill, a journalist and webmaster, suggests asking yourself two questions. Are you actually making backups on a regular schedule? Is at least one backup off-site?

"I back up to a hard drive about ten feet from the computer and also onto a laptop beside my regular monitor," he says. "Making CD backups is like watching parking meters expire. I'd rather let my computer do it on its own at 2 A.M."

Morrill says Silverkeeper is a program that comes with some LaCie freestanding hard drives and he uses that to back up nightly. Websites like his WritersCollege.com site are backed up on the hosting company's server. Morrill says to be sure to check whether your backup activates when the computer goes into sleep mode if you have your settings on automatic.

Many different backup programs are available, and it's wise to do a little research up front. If you have questions, phone or email the company and get answers first. At the least, buy a big flash drive, copy your files, and store the flash drive off site in a location like a safe deposit box or a trusted friend or relative's home. You'll have to be disciplined enough to back up those files on a regular basis. But if a calamity occurs and your computer is damaged, you'll have your files intact.

Gary Berline, writing for *PC Magazine*, advises, "The question isn't if you're going to lose data—it's when."

Ideally, it's best to have remote backup. An added advantage: if you're traveling without your computer, you'll be able to retrieve information if a need pops up.

And an absolute blessing: if you're sitting in front of a blank screen, your blood pressure won't skyrocket, because somewhere, away from your home or office, there's a security blanket covering all those files.

For more information, visit these links.
Mozy (www.mozy.com)
Save-n-Sync (www.peersoftware.com)
Windows Operating Systems (www.microsoft.com)
Mac Operating Systems (www.apple.com)

Kay B. Day writes for a variety of media and wire services. She is author of a biweekly column on Internet topics, Web Savvy, for the website of *The Writer* magazine. Her blog Covering Florida is a popular website about life in the Sunshine State. She is the author of two books, a poetry collection and a memoir, and is completing a nonfiction book and a second poetry collection.

This article appeared February 2008 in her Web Savvy column in *The Writer* online.

Simple Stretches for Writers

by Kate Hanley

As WRITERS, the computer may save us time, but that benefit comes at a high physical cost. Repetitive stress injuries, sore neck and shoulder muscles, lower back pain, and chronically tight hips are all natural results of spending eight hours a day hunched over a keyboard. Multiply those eight hours a day over weeks, months, and years, and the physical toll our sedentary profession can take on our bodies—if we don't take any steps to remedy it, that is—is considerable. Luckily, it is possible to ward off the aches, pains, and injury associated with heavy computer use.

"The most important thing computer users can do to stay feeling good is to take regular stretching breaks," says Sandy Blaine, Bay Area yoga teacher and author of *Yoga for Computer Users: Healthy Necks, Shoulders, Wrists, and Hands in the Postmodern Age* (Rodmell Press, 2008). "For every position you hold for any length of time, you have to regularly perform a counter-move, or your neuromuscular patterns start to set in in a negative way."

I spoke to Blaine to get her guidance on how we can all stay supple and relaxed as we hammer away at our deadlines. Here are her suggestions for elemental moves everyone—no matter your age, fitness level, or workload—can do. Just remember that in order to be truly effective, you should incorporate them into your daily work routine. "To really make a noticeable difference in how you feel, the more stretching, the better," Blaine says.

Neck Stretch

Counteracts: Jutting chin and shortened neck muscles

How to do it: Sit up tall and let your spine rest on the back of your chair. Drop your right ear toward your right shoulder and hold for thirty seconds to one minute. Repeat to the left side, then drop your chin toward your chest. In each position, allow gravity and the weight of your head to gradually encourage your neck muscles to lengthen.

Keep in mind: "Let your sensation level be your guide on how far to lower your head and how long to hold it," Blaine advises. "Because the neck is delicate and has an extremely important job, you don't want to overdo it."

Wrist Rolls

Counteracts: Stagnation and fragility in the wrist joint

How to do it: Sit up tall in your chair and clasp your hands together to form one big fist. Bend your elbows so your hands are at chest height, then being rolling your wrists in a simple figure-eight shape. As you take your wrists through their entire range of motion, you're providing a great counter to all the typing you've been doing.

Keep in mind: For added benefit, reverse the direction your wrists are moving for several rotations. "Because the move isn't something you normally encounter in your everyday life, it will help create new pathways in your brain," Blaine says.

Chest Opener

Counteracts: Rounded shoulders and sunken chest

How to do it: Sit up straight on the edge of your chair seat and reach your arms behind your back to lay one forearm on top of the other and clasp opposite elbows.

Keep in mind: This move can also help you avoid the afternoon slump. "Because this position opens the lungs and deepens the breath, it's also subtly energizing," Blaine says.

Seated Forward Bend

Counteracts: Painfully tight hips

How to do it: Sit at the edge of the chair and plant your feet on the ground wider than your hips. Bend forward at your hips and try to bring your rib cage down between your legs. Take several deep breaths here.

Keep in mind: To come up without straining your back, bring your hands to your thighs and use your arms to push yourself back up to sitting. Let your head come up last.

Kate Hanley is a Brooklyn freelance journalist and certified yoga teacher who specializes in exploring the mind–body connection. She is a contributing editor for *Body + Soul* and a regular contributor to *Alternative Medicine* and *Delicious Living*. She describes herself as a seeker of "simple things we can all do to feel better in our minds and bodies, especially when life is moving a million miles an hour."

She is founder of the website www.msmindbody.com.

This article first appeared in the February 2008 issue of *ASJA Monthly*, the newsletter of the American Society of Journalists and Authors (www.asja.org).

Five-Minute Decluttering Tips

by Leo Babauta

I'VE WRITTEN A LOT about simplicity and decluttering, and I've noticed that a lot of readers share my ideal of having an uncluttered home or workplace, but don't know where to start.

When your home is filled with clutter, trying to tackle a mountain of stuff can be quite overwhelming.

So here's my advice: start with just five minutes.

Sure, five minutes won't barely make a dent in your mountain, but it's a start. Celebrate when you've made that start!

Then take another five minutes tomorrow. And another the next day. Before you know it, you'll have cleared a whole closet or a room and then half your house and then ... who knows? Maybe before long your house will be even more uncluttered than mine. We'll have a challenge!

For those who are overwhelmed by their clutter, here are some great ways to get started, five minutes at a time.

Designate a spot for incoming papers. Papers often account for a lot of our clutter. This is because we put them in different spots—on the counter, on the table, on our desk, in a drawer, on top of our dresser, in our car. No wonder we can't find anything! Designate an in-box tray or spot in your home (or at your office, for that matter) and don't put down papers anywhere but that spot. Got mail? Put it in the inbox. Got papers? In the inbox. Receipts, warranties, manuals, notices, flyers? In the inbox! This one little change can really transform your paperwork.

Start clearing a starting zone. What you want to do is clear one area. This is your no-clutter zone. It can be a counter, or your work table, or the three-foot perimeter around your desk. Wherever you start, make a rule: nothing can be placed there that's not actually in use. Everything must be put away. Once you have that clutter-free zone, keep it that way! Now, each day, slowly expand your no-clutter zone until it envelopes the whole room!

Clear off a counter. You want to get all flat spaces clear of clutter. Maybe they have a few basic items, but not a lot of clutter. So start with one counter or area of your desk. Clear off everything possible, except maybe one or two essential things. Clear off all papers and all the other junk you've been accumulating there.

Pick a shelf. Now that you've done a counter, try a shelf. It doesn't matter what shelf. If it's a bookshelf, don't tackle the whole thing— just one shelf. Clear all non-essential things and leave it looking neat and clutter-free.

Schedule a decluttering weekend. Maybe you don't feel like doing a huge decluttering session right now. But if you take the time to schedule it for later this month, you can clear your schedule. Get boxes and trash bags ready, and plan a trip to a charity to drop off donated items. You might not get the entire space decluttered during the weekend, but you'll probably make great progress.

Pick up five things, and find places for them. These should be things that you actually use, but that you just seem to put anywhere, because they don't have good places. If you don't know exactly where things belong, you have to designate a good spot. Take a minute to think it through—where would be a good spot? Then always put those things in those spots when you're done using them. Do this for everything in your space, a few things at a time.

Spend a few minutes visualizing the room. When I'm decluttering, I like to take a moment to take a look at a room, and think about how I want it to look. What are the most essential pieces of furniture? What doesn't belong in the room but has just gravitated there? What is on the floor (hint: only furniture and rugs belong there) and what is on the other flat surfaces? Once I've visualized how the room will look uncluttered, and figured out what is essential, I get rid of the rest.

Create a "maybe" box. Sometimes when you're going through a pile of stuff, you know exactly what to keep (the stuff you love and use) and what to trash or donate. But then there's the stuff you don't use, but think you might want it or need it someday. You can't bear to get rid of that stuff! So create a "maybe" box, and put this stuff there. Then store the box somewhere hidden, out of the way. Put a note on your calendar six months from now to look in the box. Then pull it out, six months later, and see if it's anything you really needed. Usually, you can just dump the whole box, because you never needed that stuff.

Set up some simple folders. Sometimes our papers pile up high because we don't have good places to put them. Create some simple folders with labels for your major bills and similar paperwork. Put them in one spot. Your system doesn't have to be complete, but keep some extra folders and labels in case you need to quickly create a new file.

Learn to file quickly. Once you've created your simple filing system, you just need to learn to use it regularly. Take a handful of papers from your pile, or your inbox, and go through them one at a time, starting from the top paper and working down. Make quick decisions: trash them, file them immediately, or make a note of the action required and put them in an "action" file. Don't put anything back on the pile, and don't put them anywhere but in a folder (and no cheating "to be filed" folders!) or in the trash/recycling bin.

Pull everything out of a drawer. Just take the drawer out and empty it on a table. Then sort the drawer into three piles: 1) stuff that really should go in the drawer; 2) stuff that belongs elsewhere; 3) stuff to get rid of. Clean the drawer out nice, then put the stuff in the first pile back neatly and orderly. Deal with the other piles immediately!

Learn to love the uncluttered look. Once you've gotten an area decluttered, you should take the time to enjoy that look. It's a lovely look. Make that your standard! Learn to hate clutter! Then catch clutter and kill it wherever it crops up.

Have a conversation with your significant other. Sometimes the problem isn't just with us, it's with the person or people we live with. An uncluttered home is the result of a shared philosophy of simplicity of all the people living in the house. If you take a few minutes to explain that you really want to have an uncluttered house, and that you could use their help, you can go a long way to getting to that point.

"Three Rules of Work: Out of clutter find simplicity; from discord find harmony; in the middle of difficulty lies opportunity." —Albert Einstein

Leo Babauta lives on Guam, where he authors the popular Zen Habits blog (http:// zenhabits.net) on achieving goals, productivity, being organized, motivation, simplifying and successfully implementing good habits. He is the author of the e-book, *Zen to Done: The Simple Productivity System.*

This article is drawn from a longer article posted April 2008 on his blog, "18 Five-Minute Decluttering Tips to Start Conquering Your Mess."

LAST WORDS & LITERARY THOUGHTS

My Left Tackle

by Rachel Toor

I am in the market for a left tackle.

I do not play football, nor do I watch. But recently I read Michael Lewis's new book, *The Blind Side,* which uses an SUV-sized young man as a vehicle to look at race, class, and football in the South. Along the way Lewis explains how left tackle became one of the most highly prized—and paid—positions in football.

Here, in my limited understanding, is what happened: Lawrence Taylor.

When that linebacker came on the scene, teams needed to protect their quarterbacks, lest LT and his ilk crush them like cigarette butts. Most quarterbacks are right-handed, so when they pull back, twisting and turning to make million-dollar passes, their left side becomes a broad-shouldered, wasp-waisted target. Keeping those expensive quarterbacks safe, Lewis argues, became an unsung, rarely noticed, but important and lucrative job.

Someone who allows you to do what you do best. Someone who protects you while you take risks. Someone who guards you from dangers you can't see.

Who wouldn't want a left tackle?

Those of us who write have more than one blind side. Our twists and turns of mind make us vulnerable to sacking. Our focus often narrows. Who protects us?

Editors, of course, and agents. The review process used by scholarly presses and journals can ferret out weaknesses in manuscripts before the permanence of publication. But what about when you're still practicing? Suited up, perhaps, but not ready for a big game?

Graduate students have coaches. The mentoring process, when it works, can be a series of drills and exercises to develop intellectual muscles. But what about after grad school, when you're out there on your own, in a job, in a new place, with people who you may or may not feel are on your side? Who will shield your academic flank?

The problem comes from the realities of daily academic life. There is never enough time to do the teaching, advising, and writing that is part of the job; finding energy to help a colleague often gets lost between the intention and the undertaking. Asking someone to read a paper, an article, or a book manuscript is, let's face it, an imposition. No one really wants to read unpublished work. And the effort that goes toward polishing someone else's work is often, even if asked for, underappreciated.

As I pointed out in a recent essay, most of us wouldn't show our work if we didn't think it was good. What we want, if we're being honest, is the correction of some typos and a pat on the head. Once someone notices problems, we have to fix them, which is hard work and not as much fun as scrubbing the toilet. But for most of us, once the initial sting of good and right criticism has passed, we put our heads down and get back to work. And we are thankful to the reader who has saved us from ourselves.

But what if we each had a bunch of readers? If we met regularly with people we respected, regardless of field? If sessions were "conducted in the sincere spirit of inquiry after truth, without fondness for dispute or desire of victory"? Every Friday night, starting when he was 21, Benjamin Franklin brought together 12 men from disparate backgrounds to discuss matters of the day. Every three months, one of the members of the club, known as the Junto, was required to offer up an essay, prefiguring, in some oblique way, the writing workshops of today.

In the mid-1990s a quartet of English professors at Duke University formed a writing group. Alice Kaplan's *French Lessons,* Cathy Davidson's *36 Views of Mount Fuji,* Jane Tompkins' *A Life in School,* and Marianna Torgovnick's *Crossing Ocean Parkway* were the result. Those women read one another's works in ways that made each memoir better and more accessible to larger readerships.

Here's another Duke story. Some 30 years ago, my friend Peter Klopfer trained for a marathon with three other middle-aged academics. During their weekly runs, they took turns talking about their fields. Henry, a physicist, explained how quarks were discovered. Peter, a zoologist, lectured about mother–infant attachment. Seth, a topologist, would draw mathematical figures in the dirt when the group stopped for water, and Orrin, a geologist, would drive the course the night before in order to coordinate his talk with appropriate geological illustrations.

The questions they asked one another, Peter says, were in many ways more helpful and interesting than those they would get from their departmental colleagues.

While some small part of me recognizes that not everyone's idea of bliss is covering 20 miles on a Sunday morning, the idea appeals because, like Franklin's Junto, the members were from different disciplines. They forced one another to speak beyond jargon, to explain, without dumbing down, the complexities and implications of their work.

There are, I know, dissertation-support groups and departments where junior faculty members meet to share work. There may even be places where posses like Peter's—with senior people from across disciplines—meet. If so, I'd like to hear about them.

Because such sharing is, I believe, the way to produce scholarship that is good and readable and that transcends the monograph. It's the way to find smart readers who will remind you that nothing goes without saying, that coded language is the refuge of the lazy and the weak, and that people outside your field may well find your material interesting, if you help them along the way.

Most university press editors are not schooled in the disciplines in which they publish. When professors whose work I was interested in publishing at Oxford University Press asked me where I had done my training in classical studies, I was happy to reply that I hadn't been trained in the classics, but in publishing. That, I argued, worked in their favor. Most people know how to talk to scholars in their own disciplines.

I am perplexed by those who do not seek trusted readers. One friend, a professor who thinks of himself as a writer rather than an academic, seems proud that he never asks anyone to read unpublished work. How much better would his books be, I wonder, if he did? If someone asked him to move along more briskly, or suggested cutting self-indulgent passages?

Bartering has become a lost art. If we keep in mind that asking someone to read a manuscript is a burden, it's good to come armed with a reward. (Cookies work for me.) The nature of a writing group is that of a collective. It functions if everyone gives according to her abilities, and gets according to her needs. I've been in groups where people show up only when their own work is being discussed. That is called mooching.

What if we thought of ourselves as teammates, each bringing different skills, but all invested in the game of making books and scholarship as good as they can be?

There are a lot of people on a football field. Each has a job—even if it's taking two steps and knocking the fluff out of someone. Though it can be bruising, having the fluff knocked out of your writing is not a bad thing. Especially if there's someone wearing your colors to help you to your feet.

If I ever found my own personal left tackle—someone to ease my way and protect me from being squished—I would probably marry him. There's a reason left tackles are so expensive; good ones are hard to find. Universities are replete not only with beefy football players, but with the kinds of people who can help protect our blind sides. We need only seek them out, be brave enough to ask for help, and then offer something in return.

Rachel Toor is an assistant professor of creative writing at the Inland Northwest Center for Writers, the MFA program of Eastern Washington University in Spokane. Her most recent book is *The Pig and I: How I Learned to Love Men (Almost) as Much as I Love My Pets* (Plume, 2006).

Her website is www.racheltoor.com. This article appeared July 2007 in the Chronicle Careers column of the online edition of the *Chronicle of Higher Education*.

The Three S's:
Structure, Solitude, and Silence
by Beryl Singleton Bissell

NOT LONG AGO, a friend and fellow writer, Patry Francis, asked me to talk a bit about how life in the cloister prepared me "for the solitary life of a writer." Although I've been asked many questions about my book and how I wrote it, I've never fielded this question before. I've been mulling it over for several days now, wondering how best to answer as its complexity surprised me, and I was stumped.

In cases of "stump," I go do something else—like take a walk or attempt to finish the hat I've been trying to knit for two years or I head to the kitchen (a place I normally avoid because I'd much rather write than cook). Yesterday, as it was the first warm and sunny day we've had here on the North Shore of Lake Superior where I live, I decided to garden and had such a grand time grubbing around in the earth, planting bright annuals and weeding out dandelions, that I stayed outside until the black flies appeared in search of supper.

As I gardened, I mulled over the question of how cloistered life prepared me for the solitary life of a writer and realized that I was having difficulty because the cloister had both positive and negative qualities—and the negative contained modifiers.

The first "how" that comes to mind is the way we lived in the monastery. For those of you who might not know much about cloistered or monastic existence, one of its underlying tenets is the importance of silence. Silence provides the monk or nun with a "place" to live in the presence of God. The cloister walls provide the seclusion, the rule of silence provides the atmosphere, and the quieting of the mind creates the actuality. So here, in this one word "silence," as practiced in monastic life, we have several factors at work: structure, solitude, silence (what I refer to as the three S's).

I believe that good writers need all three S's to turn out good pieces of work. I didn't realize the three S's importance as a writer until I had the opportunity to go away for two weeks to a writing retreat for women. There, separate from my daily life, living in silence, and having structured writing time, I wrote more in two weeks than I had during the two prior years.

Many writers will tell you the same thing. Like the monk or nun who leaves the world to seek a place apart in which to find God, writers do their best work in a place away from or separate from their homes (a room of one's own). In that room they are not distracted by the daily (dog, duty, diapers, dianthus, disasters, etc.). Alone they confront the empty sheet of paper, silent they listen to their muse, structured they work at their writing. I have a writing shed next to the garage with no access to phone or Internet. It is there that I write what I cannot write elsewhere.

So what about the negative impact of cloistered life on me as a writer? In the cloister I lost my voice. By voice I mean not the use of tongue and vocal chords but the loss of the ability to think things through. To have opinions that might differ from those of others. To express doubt. To challenge belief. To search for one's own truth.

This loss of voice should not exist in cloistered life. It does not belong in a place dedicated to the God of truth. So, here is where I must insert those modifiers that I mentioned earlier. I didn't lose my voice because of the cloister but because I was a cloistered nun in the '60s when thinking for oneself was not permitted. Our superior did all our thinking for us and in obeying her we were obeying God, and because I was a woman in a pre-Vatican II Catholic Church little value was placed on women's roles save as "servant of."

I didn't realize how much I missed having a voice of my own until I returned to the world and had to start thinking for myself, where I was frightened and hesitant to express myself. I maintained silence, was timorous and obedient and docile—and I was angry and I didn't know why.

During the process of learning how to write, I discovered that a very strong voice of my own lay tucked deep within me. It took a long time—20 years apprenticeship learning to express myself—to summon that voice. And now that I've found my voice again and have learned to use it, I nourish and encourage it through the practice of the three S's of silence, solitude, and structure.

Beryl Singleton Bissell is the author of the memoir *The Scent of God,* chosen as an April 2006 Notable Book Sense selection by the American Booksellers Association. Patry Francis described the book, the story of a passionate young woman who enters a cloister at age eighteen, as "a rich, sensual, and marvelously told tale by a woman who leaves the religious life, but never stops embodying its virtues: humility, faith, and above all, joy." The *Minneapolis Star Tribune* described it as a "riveting memoir of devout faith and forbidden love" and named Bissell to "Best of 2006 Minnesota Authors."

This piece first appeared as a guest post in June 2007 on Patry Francis's blog, http://simplywait.blogspot.com. Bissell's own website is www.berylsingletonbissell.com.

Starting

by Lois Lowry

I HAVE JUST TYPED page eleven of a new book. Is it astounding that it takes a person three days to write eleven pages ... and at that, eleven pages that will ultimately be re-written again and again?

Of course today I also answered email, and I went and got my hair cut, and I went to the post office to mail my granddaughter a birthday gift, and I did the *New York Times* crossword puzzle, and I am about to get out of this chair to go and make an apple pie because the apples are *there* and ripe and cry out for a pie to be made.

But each day, as I do such chores, I think over what I have just written ... maybe two pages, or three ... and then, when I go back, it is to change and clarify and delete and expand and explain.

So I have not written eleven pages. I've probably written, oh, I don't know, maybe forty pages. Of which eleven remain.

In those eleven pages, I so far have introduced five characters: all of them important, one vital. Two others are sleeping, off stage, so we know of their existence but haven't met them yet. One other is in hiding but we know she is there.

Because this is to be a book that follows others, there is a tiny bit of back-story included. I hate that part, to be honest, and always try to write a new book without needing too much of it. When I was a kid, I always wanted to shout, "I *know* Carson Drew is a lawyer! Don't tell me *again* in every book!" But of course there is always the reader who comes to it fresh, without knowledge. So I make the best of it and try to do the filling-in in an interesting way.

I'm eager to get back to the hiding woman, though. She's new. And intriguing, even to me.

The Neglected Horse and the Undiscovered Room

I have two recurrent dreams, but I have never, until last night, had them in combined form.

One I have talked about before. Briefly: in the dream I have bought, or rented, or somehow acquired a new house and am moving into it. I discover a door—or sometimes it is a staircase—that I haven't known about, and it leads to a wonderful, previously-undiscovered room.

Many people tell me they have had this dream. (I should add, though, that they always are women).

No one else I know, though, has had the actual experience, the way I have. When I bought this old farmhouse (I am in Maine as I write this), I had only seen it once. But I hired a painter and sent him paint samples with an outline drawing of the house interior, and instructed him which color to use in each of the ten rooms. He called me to ask what to do about the eleventh room. Gulp. I hadn't known there was an eleventh room.

(The eleventh room is now the studio where I work. The paint color is called "Rain Barrel" by Benjamin Moore.)

The Neglected Horse dream has not come true the way the Undiscovered Room dream did. Thank goodness. In this one, I am responsible for a horse. He stands in a pasture. But he is very, very thin because I have forgotten about him and he hasn't been fed for a long time.

(When my kids were growing up, we had horses, and they were in a pasture behind the old house we lived in ... or, in bad weather, in the barn. But they were always fed. It was my son Grey's responsibility, and he went out early, early every morning before school bus time, and fed the horses.)

Anyway: last night the horse reappeared, and again I had forgotten him, hadn't fed him, felt terrible about it. But in last night's dream I met someone who had a beautiful horse farm, well tended, and who said I could house my horse there and he would be well taken care of. It was a great feeling of relief.

At the same time that I was making arrangements for the horse, in the dream, I was also trying to unload from a vehicle some furniture that I had acquired for a guest room in my house. It was difficult, unwieldy, and also disheartening because it was ugly and inappropriate furniture.

Then, suddenly, and with the same feeling of relief that I felt about the neglected horse, I realized that it was unnecessary because there were already two beautifully furnished guest rooms that I hadn't known about.

Okay. So what was that all about?

Well, over the years I have come to realize that both the horse and the rooms, in different ways, represent work and creativity. As it happens, I am about to start working on a new book. I have two books finished and awaiting publication but have not yet turned my attention to a new one. It is the horse standing in the pasture, wondering when I will feed him.

It's not surprising to me that when I came to Maine, as I did yesterday, intending to spend a few isolated and uninterrupted days starting a new book ... that the dream horse found a clean stable where he would be tended and fed. And that the dream house, too, has well-furnished rooms waiting for guests.

Isn't the subconscious an amazing thing?

Different Dreams

Many, many, *many* years ago I wrote a book called *Autumn Street*, which remains one of my personal favorites, perhaps because it was (is) autobiographical (though written as fiction) and the little-girl narrator—I called her Elizabeth—in a small Pennsylvania town in the early 1940s is actually me.

Although the child protagonist/narrator is very young, it is not a book for young children. It deals with loss, and with anguish, and with a young child's groping toward coming to terms with those things (writing this, the classic *A Death in the Family* by James Agee comes to mind because it grapples with the same themes).

I thought this morning of a short paragraph from *Autumn Street* and went and looked it up. Here the two little girls—Elizabeth and her slightly older sister, Jessica—are in bed in the room that they share, and have been talking. Then, after a silence:

> *"Good night, Jess," I whispered, but she was already asleep, breathing softly. I realized then, for the first time, that her dreams would always be different from mine.*

In truth, I do remember a moment from my early childhood when I had that sudden awareness—psychiatrists have a term for it, but I have forgotten what it is—that I was separate from others, and individual, and unique. (My memory is not the scene I created in the book, but took place outside, and near a magnolia tree beside my grandparents' house, so that I am very aware, thinking of it, of bruised and velvety pinkish-white blossoms on the ground, though I can't bring back any other details.)

Anyway, the reason I went back to the "different dreams" paragraph in *Autumn Street* was because a reader, referring to my post titled "The Neglected Horse and the Undiscovered Room," has reminded me that many of us do have the same mysterious dreams.

She writes:

Good grief, I've had that horse dream too. I've never owned a horse, never wanted one. Why is it a horse? Why isn't it the "neglected dog or cat" dream, the forgotten ferret, the overlooked hamster? Why horses?

I have over the years talked to a number of people who have the "undiscovered room" dream ... and of course *all* of us probably have the "Exam coming up and I haven't studied, haven't even gone to class" dream. But I have not before met anyone who dreamed of the Neglected Horse.

And her question is interesting. Why horse?? A horse is an archetypal creature, I suppose. And so *large*. No averting your eyes from something so massive, the way you could from a dying hamster or a starving kitten.

So: all of this is just to say, thinking back on *Autumn Street* and that moment of awareness-of-self, that although it is true that her dreams would always be different from mine ... still, clearly, there is something that connects us to one another, and there are parts of our unconscious life that we do share.

And I think that is what we look for, often, in fiction that we read: the moments of identification, of kinship, of reverberation.

Lois Lowry is the author of over 20 novels and twice winner of the Newbery Medal. A native of Hawaii, she now divides her times between Cambridge, Massachusetts, and a home in Maine. In her books, Lowry has tackled difficult topics including adoption, mental illness, cancer, racism and more. She throws her characters into thought-provoking situations, and says that she measures her success as an author by her ability to "help adolescents answer their own questions about life, identity, and human relationships."

In 1979, Lowry began her "Anastasia" series of books with Anastasia Krupnik, about a ten-year-old girl who wants to be a writer. Lowry would go on to write seven sequels and five books about Anastasia's brother Sam. In 1980, she published her novel *Autumn*

Street, in which the main character is a girl named Elizabeth, whose father is away at war.

Lowry won her first Newbery Medal in 1989 for *Number the Stars.* She won again in 1993 for *The Giver,* a book that has occasionally been the target of banning attempts. *The Giver* is set in a future society where those who are not deemed acceptable are "released," i.e., put to death. Undaunted by the controversy, Lowry expanded the themes into a trilogy with the subsequent books *Gathering Blue* and *Messenger.*

On her website at www.loislowry.com, she says: "I try, through writing, to convey my passionate awareness that we live intertwined on this planet and that our future depends upon our caring more, and doing more, for one another."

This piece combines three posts from her blog (www.loislowry.typepad.com) from late 2007: "Starting," "The Neglected Horse and the Undiscovered Room" and "Different Dreams."

Critiquing a Friend's Manuscript

by Susan O'Doherty

Dear Dr. Sue:

What do I do when friends ask me to read their manuscripts, and I hate what they've written? This has happened more than once.

—R

Dear R,

Most published writers have to deal with this situation eventually. I wish there were a simple, universally applicable solution. So much depends, though, on the quality and closeness of the relationship, and on the personal and professional stakes for the writer in question.

For example, consider the case of a valued colleague whose substandard manuscript could be ruinous to his career. We have an obligation to save the people we care about, and those to whom we owe favors, from professional disaster or humiliation.

On the other end of the spectrum, it's often possible to fudge our response to more distant connections, especially if they have nothing to lose by showing their work. Your lawyer acquaintance's courtroom thriller isn't likely to derail her partner-track aspirations no matter how weak the plot or clichéd her observations. In these cases, I would suggest the vaguest possible response short of an outright lie. "I don't think I'm the best reader for this—I have trouble following legal logic, and I get queasy at descriptions of bloodshed" is usually preferable to "How can you bear to churn out such derivative dreck?"

Recommending an alternative reader can be helpful as well, as long as the objective is to connect the writer with someone who enjoys the genre and would welcome the opportunity to be of use, not to pass the buck.

Between those two extremes, though, lies a great deal of gray area. What happens when a gifted, emotionally fragile friend asks your opinion of the novel she hopes will mark her comeback, and you find it flabby and trite? What if it's your father-in-law who has written the clichéd thriller?

Here are some general guidelines to help you calibrate your response to the needs of the writer and the demands of honesty and friendship:

> Remember that all literary opinions are subjective. You may hate what your friend has written, but other readers, editors, and critics could hail it as a masterpiece. It's helpful to emphasize this perspective when delivering a critique: "I don't understand why Hamlet didn't just skewer Claudius when he had the chance" is easier to hear than "The plot meanders all over Denmark before getting to the action."

> Business managers endorse the "hamburger method" of conveying criticism: sandwich the "meat" (your main objection to the work) between two supportive "buns." Even the most dreadful potboiler must have at least two praiseworthy aspects—it helps to identify and emphasize these to cushion the unappetizing gristle you are asking your friend to chew and digest.

> When feasible, suggest a possible solution to each identified problem. "I couldn't buy Ophelia's last scene—her reaction seemed way out of proportion" goes down better when followed by, "What about sending her to rehab instead?" Even if your friend finds your suggestion ludicrous, you have made it clear that you consider the manuscript salvageable and worthy of further work (assuming that this is the case).

> Keep in mind that all writers identify with their work, most to a greater extent than they let on or even realize. "I want you to be brutally honest" is usually unrecognized code for "I'm in desperate need of reassurance." This isn't to say that you must compromise your integrity or artistic standards to cater to your friends' insecurities, only that a true friend will strive to communicate important truths in a way that allows the recipient to maintain dignity.

Finally, consider the honor that these requests represent. Try to cultivate gratitude for the accomplishments that have brought you to this place of authority, and for your friends' admiration and trust. If you respond from this place of appreciation and generosity, chances are you will find the words your friends need to hear.

Susan O'Doherty is the author of *Getting Unstuck Without Coming Unglued: A Woman's Guide to Unblocking Creativity* (Seal Press, 2007). Her work has appeared in numerous literary magazines and in the anthologies *Sex for America: Politically Inspired Erotica* (HarperPerennial, 2008); *About What Was Lost: Twenty Writers on Miscarriage, Healing, and Hope* (Penguin, 2007); and *It's a Boy!* (Seal Press, 2005). Her popular advice column for writers, "The Doctor Is In," appears each Friday on M.J. Rose's book-promotion blog, Buzz, Balls, & Hype; this post appeared on that blog December 2007.

O'Doherty's website is www.susanodohertyauthor.com.

Lewis, Tolkien, and the Inklings

by Diana Pavlac Glyer

THERE'S A RUMOR going around that C.S. Lewis was an irritable introvert, isolated and lonely and scared to death of girls. Maybe it comes from some grim stereotype of smart people or college professors or, maybe, published writers. That whole image is completely wrong. Lewis wasn't an introvert. Or a loner. No—he was a large man with a booming voice, a hearty laugh, a robust enjoyment of everyday life. And that is why he was a man with friends.

It makes sense if you think about it. His writing is so warm. His ideas are so engaging. His approach is so inviting. The lively, personal voice that emerges from the written page reflects the heart of a man who lived his life in community. Every season of Lewis's life was marked by strong personal connections. He was very close to his brother, Warren. As the two boys grew up together, they wrote stories and illustrated them with maps and watercolors. Later, he became good friends with Arthur Greeves, a neighbor, and they shared boyhood secrets and favorite books. In college, Lewis became a member of a small circle of serious poets, and from that literary circle, he and Owen Barfield emerged as fast friends. When he started his first teaching job, he got to know a bright young linguist named Tolkien. They discovered common ground in their love of Norse mythology.

Lewis's entire life, early and late, was marked by this kind of sustaining friendship. And right in the middle of his life, at the very heart of it all, was a group of fellow writers called the Inklings. The group started informally—Lewis and Tolkien enjoyed one another's company, and so they cultivated the habit of meeting on Monday mornings for beer and conversation. Lewis wrote about it in one of his letters: "It has also become the custom for Tolkien to drop in on me of a Monday morning for a glass. This is one of the pleasantest spots in the week. Sometimes we talk English school politics: sometimes we criticise one another's poems: other days we drift into theology or the state of the nation; rarely we fly no higher than bawdy and puns."

Lewis and Tolkien continued to meet, week after week, to talk and joke and criticise one another's poetry. Over time, these literary critiques proved to be so interesting and so useful that they invited other writers to join them. The group just kept growing. Eventually, a total of 19 men became members of the Inklings. Their meetings moved from Monday mornings to Thursday nights. Late nights. The members arrived around 9:00, or 9:30, or even later.

When half a dozen members had assembled, Warren Lewis would produce a pot of very strong tea, the men would sit down and light their pipes, and C.S. Lewis would call out, "Well, has nobody got anything to read us?" Someone always did. Out would come the rough draft of a story or a poem, and the others would settle down to listen, to encourage, to critique, to correct, to interrupt and argue and advise. They'd continue this way, reading aloud, energetically critiquing, until two or three in the morning. And meetings went on like this every week for nearly twenty years.

The range of manuscripts that these men brought to meetings was rich and remarkable. Lewis read *Out of the Silent Planet*, *The Great Divorce*, *The Problem of Pain*, *Miracles*, and others, many of them chapter by chapter as they were written. He read some of his poetry, including "Donkey's Delight," and, at one point, he shared a long section of his translation of Virgil's *Aeneid*. He also read *The Screwtape Letters* to the group, and the Inklings loved them. According to one of the members, *The Screwtape Letters* "really set us going. We were more or less rolling off our chairs."

Tolkien brought along each new chapter of *The Lord of the Rings*, week after week, as each one was written. He also shared original poetry, excerpts from "The Notion Club Papers," and sections from *The Hobbit*. Others read poetry, plays, literary studies, academic papers, biographies, histories. Charles Williams read his novel *All Hallows' Eve*; David Cecil read excerpts from his biography *Two Quiet Lives*; Owen Barfield read a short play about Jason and Medea; Warren Lewis read *The Splendid Century*, a history of France.

What practical difference did it make that these writers worked together as they drafted and revised each piece? There are dozens of examples: projects kindled, poems retooled, essays clarified, ideas abandoned, and even whole entire novels redirected. One example of a major shift can be seen in a comment that Lewis made about Tolkien's *Lord of the Rings*.

Tolkien had begun *The Lord of the Rings* reluctantly: *The Hobbit* had sold well, and so his publisher had asked him to write another book like it. Tolkien made his beginning confidently enough, with Hobbit jokes, feasting, fireworks, mischief, and family spats.

But after a few chapters, things stalled. Tolkien was stuck. On 17 February 1938 Tolkien writes, "The Hobbit sequel is still where it was, and I have only the vaguest notions of how to proceed" (*The Letters of J.R.R. Tolkien*, p. 29). Five months later, on 24 July 1938, he is in exactly the same spot. He says of the story, "It has lost my favour, and I have no idea what to do with it" (*Letters* 38).

Although Tolkien offers a number of explanations for his difficulties, it is clear that at this point, he is fundamentally uncertain about the nature of the book. He writes, "I am personally immensely amused by hobbits as such, and can contemplate them eating and making their rather fatuous jokes indefinitely; but I find that is not the case with even my most devoted 'fans'" (*Letters* 38). As this comment shows, Tolkien still saw his *Hobbit* sequel as being much like the first book: aimed at a young audience, built around humor and pranks, and modeled somewhat on the structures of a folk or fairy story. Readers and critics alike have noted that even in the published version, the first three chapters of *The Lord of the Rings* retain something of this quality.

At this point in Tolkien's composing process, on 24 July 1938, C.S. Lewis made an important observation. Tolkien records, "Mr Lewis says hobbits are only amusing when in unhobbitlike situations" (*Letters* 38). It appears that as a direct result of this comment, Tolkien began to consider a more ambitious purpose, an "unhobbitlike" seriousness to his new story.

There is even more evidence that points to the part that Lewis played in changing the story away from the frivolous and toward a more serious purpose. In a letter to one of his readers, Lewis makes it plain that he urged Tolkien's story in this specific way. Lewis writes, "My continued encouragement, carried to the point of nagging, influenced him very much to write at all *with that gravity* and at that length."

The change in tone and purpose is clear in Tolkien's revision of a key passage in chapter 3. In the first draft, the story goes like this: three hobbits named Bingo, Odo, and Frodo have left Hobbiton and are walking through the Shire. Suddenly, the sound of hoof beats draws near. They scurry off the road and hide in a little hollow, crouched tight beneath the roots of a tree. "Round a turn came a white horse, and on it sat a bundle—or that is what it looked like: a small man wrapped entirely in a great cloak and hood so that only his eyes peered out, and his boots in the stirrups below."

The horse and rider stop near Bingo. "The figure uncovered its nose and sniffed; and then sat silent as if listening. Suddenly a laugh came from inside the hood." It is Gandalf, who calls out, "Bingo my boy!" as he throws aside his wrappings.

In manuscript, the story breaks off at the bottom of this page. After Tolkien first drafted it, he went back and rewrote this passage. Here is the same section again, as it appears in *The Fellowship of the Ring*:

> *Round the corner came a black horse, no hobbit-pony but a full-sized horse; and on it sat a large man, who seemed to crouch in the saddle, wrapped in a great black cloak and hood, so that only his boots in the high stirrups showed below; his face was shadowed and invisible.*
>
> *When it reached the tree and was level with Frodo the horse stopped. The riding figure sat quite still with its head bowed, as if listening. From inside the hood came a noise as of someone sniffing to catch an elusive scent.*

It is clear that this description of a Black Rider draws many of its details from the original description of Gandalf, including the great cloak and hood, and that sniffing sound. But things have shifted radically. Gandalf is gone: a mysterious Black Rider appears instead. The mood is quite altered. Once personal and playful, the whole feel of it is now much darker. Frodo's response to this strange figure is an "unreasoning fear."

The sudden appearance of this Black Rider raises two questions that are key to the direction of the story. First, what is the nature and purpose of this evil creature? And second, if this isn't Gandalf, then what could have happened to their friend? Finding answers to these questions will determine the necessary direction of the events that follow. With this new apparition, the tale has turned.

But not only has the hobbit adventure changed—Tolkien's experience as a writer has changed as well. At last, Tolkien seems to catch his stride. Soon afterward, he reports that the story "is now flowing along, and getting quite out of hand. It has reached about Chapter VII and progresses towards quite unforeseen goals" (*Letters* 40). There is a clear break from the tentative and uncertain tone of the past. Now the manuscript flows along and has taken on a life of its own—*it* is flowing, *it* progresses, *it* has reached chapter 7, *it* is getting out of hand.

Even the title has changed. It is no longer "The New Hobbit": Tolkien now refers to his story as "The Lord of the Ring [sic]" (*Letters* 40). It is clearly something new, distinct from its predecessor, and moving toward a different purpose. These radical changes occur within a month of Lewis's observation that "hobbits are only amusing when in unhobbitlike situations" (*Letters* 38).

Less dialogue, more narrative. Less hobbit talk, more danger. It is evident that Lewis's comment has had a powerful influence on Tolkien's story.

This is only one example of how the Inklings advised one another—and advice was only one of the many ways that they interacted. They criticized and encouraged and modeled and collaborated. Listening to drafts and offering energetic feedback occupied the better part of every Inklings meeting. Nothing could be more simple—a small group of tweedy British men, meeting week after week in Lewis's rooms at Magdalen College, sitting on the shabby grey couch, drinking tea, reading and talking. But as they met together throughout the 1930s and 1940s, extraordinary things began to happen. They generated enormous creative energy. They forged strong personal connections. And together, they helped bring to light some of the greatest literary works of this past century.

Diana Pavlac Glyer is a professor of English at Azusa Pacific University. She has been widely recognized for her work on C.S. Lewis, J.R.R. Tolkien and the Inklings, including contributions to *The C.S. Lewis Readers' Encyclopedia* and *C.S. Lewis: Life, Works, and Legacy*. She is the recipient of the Wade Center's Clyde S. Kilby Research Grant (1997), APU's Chase A. Sawtell Inspirational Teaching Award (2002) and the Imperishable Flame Award for Tolkien Scholarship (2007).

You can read more about creative writing and the Inklings in Glyer's book *The Company They Keep: C.S. Lewis and J.R.R. Tolkien as Writers in Community* (Kent State University Press, 2007), from which portions of this article are drawn. For more, visit: www.theplaceofthelion.com.

Travel Writer Personalities

by Tim Patterson

TRAVEL WRITERS are a weird bunch of people who tend to think too much. They travel and write to make a living (or a vague approximation of one), but sometimes it seems as if they don't enjoy either activity.

They write fact, they write fiction, and sometimes they write both in the same paragraph. They consistently come up with the most creative and original excuses for missed deadlines in the entire publishing industry.

What types of people are drawn to travel writing? What types of people succeed? As I contemplate an extended foray into the profession and look for role models, I wonder—who are these people?

I've come up with six possible types of travel writers:

The Intrepid Monk

Many of the truly great travel writers are loners, monastic personalities who speak softly and carry a very big notebook. Pico Iyer is a classic example. One of the very best active travel writers, Iyer is a teetotaler who lives simply and anonymously in a Japanese suburb and does much of his writing in an actual monastery.

Iyer's writing is precise, lyrical, and permeated with heartfelt personal emotion, but as a person, he is most comfortable blending into the crowd.

The intrepid monks of travel writing don't spend all their time scribbling quietly at the back table of tea shops. They are, after all, intrepid. They take risks.

They venture far from the guidebook page. They are unconventional and unassuming, and though they write from a personal perspective, their personality is unobtrusive enough to never get in the way of the story, and the deeper themes of place, culture, and interconnection that give weight and meaning to their prose.

The Epic Adventurer

These guys (and ladies) always up the ante. They may be good writers, but their writing is always secondary to the sheer audacity and creativity of their next adventure. The covers of their books often feature themselves—clinging to the edge of a cliff, or gripping an oar in the face of an Arctic storm, lips locked in an expression of grim determination and masochistic delight.

The unique angle, or hook, of their stories often involves some sort of stunt, an added layer of difficulty that has nothing to do with the territory they traverse. "Across The Yukon ..." a title might read, "... by Tricycle!"

If Epic Adventurers also happen to be excellent writers, like Mark Jenkins or Rory Stewart, their work can easily become a classic of the genre. Otherwise, no matter how far they push the limit, their literary careers rarely last longer than the initial rush of adrenaline.

The Naked Introvert

Naked introverts spend an inordinate amount of time fretting about their constipation, and then write about it in excruciating detail. They are funny, honest, and extremely self-deprecating.

Naked introverts are especially well-suited to writing about travel because travelers are bumbling fools, and naked introverts are most entertaining when they find themselves in awkward and uncertain situations.

David Sedaris is the archetypal naked introvert, and I can't think of another writer whose byline I'm more excited to find.

The Walking Party

Walking parties don't query editors—they invite them out for beer, which turns into Tropical Karaoke Night, which turns into shots of tequila to greet the dawn. The next week the walking party emails the editor a story with "Cheers!" in the subject line.

The editor, having gotten over her hangover, can only remember that she had a great time and figures she must have signed off on the story. When the story is published, the walking party invites the editor out to celebrate, and the cycle repeats itself.

Walking parties are fun to hang out with. They network naturally, and like to leave inside jokes on editors' Facebook walls. David Farley is one walking party I've been lucky enough to meet.

He's writing a book about his quest to find the missing foreskin of Jesus Christ. See—you just laughed, didn't you. That's how walking parties work.

The Public Relations Professional

The PR Pro is seldom a good writer. She doesn't need to know how to write. She has contacts with half the tourism professionals in the state of Florida. She knows how to play the publicity game.

She has a stock of exactly eight adjectives with which to describe a new beach resort, but rarely bothers to use more than three of them. She is highly organized, has never heard of Alexandra David-Neel, and probably makes more money than any other category of travel writer.

The Guidebook Writer

Guidebook writers actually fall into two categories: the expert and the fool. The expert knows the territory he covers like the back of his hand. He may even be writing the entire guidebook, and he's capable of doing a great job.

After a few editions though, jaded by a lack of royalties and the monotony of the work, the expert gets lazy. He doesn't bother to fact check or visit properties he reviewed five years ago. Finally, he stops returning his editor's emails, at which point the editor hands the ball off to ... the fool.

The fool is young, bright-eyed, and bushy-tailed. He or she is probably intelligent, especially if working for Let's Go Guides, and is absolutely thrilled to be on assignment as a professional travel writer.

The thrill lasts until the eager young writer gets off the plane and realizes he doesn't speak the language, doesn't have a clue about the culture, and needs to turn in an exhaustively researched compendium by the end of the month.

At which point the fool checks into a youth hostel, crawls into the top bunk, pulls the sheets over his head, and emerges only to throw himself on the mercy of the unfortunate English speaker at the Tourism Information Office.

Which type of travel writer do you enjoy reading?
Which one is most like you?

Tim Patterson is a frequent contributor to MatadorTravel.com and writes a regular column for Brave New Traveler's website. As a travel journalist, he focuses on off-beat destinations, long-term travel, cultural awareness and environmentally conscious tourism. He travels with a sleeping bag and pup tent strapped to the back of his folding bicycle, and is more likely to recommend an organic farm or backcountry fly-fishing hotspot than a spa package at a luxury hotel.

While he has had many articles appear in print media such as *Get Lost* magazine, most of his articles and travel guides are published online.

This article first appeared on the Brave New Traveler site (www.bravenewtraveler.com) January 2008. Patterson's own website is www.rucksackwanderer.com.

What Am I Supposed To Be Doing?

by Fred Ramey

I DON'T KNOW if you've noticed, but every time a new bit of technology arrives, publishers start waving their arms in the ether and hollering up and down the halls of Manhattan realizing again how little they know about what comes next: How do we publish "books" in the world of the new media? How will readers want their "books"? What are we publishers supposed to be doing?

In the high-hum of all this prognostic worrah, it was a relief last month to enter the part of my semi-annual work cycle that is actually, well, editing.

I set to work on a novel we're slated to release in the fall of 2007, a sizable book, an historical novel. I had some questions about the early pages of exposition, questions about whether there was too much back story early on, even questions about punctuation. And then there was a bigger issue—about character, about what a woman would or wouldn't do in this circumstance and that one over a troubled life in a difficult time.

My author and I began an email, UPS, and telephone exchange about all that, an exchange that lasted for days. I love the trajectory of the novel, but I felt one character might make decisions that were different from those the author had allowed. (I knew this was because I had fallen in love with the character, but I probably shouldn't say that out loud.) And as I began to explain what I thought about her, I began to map out the novel—began to see how each character seems to relate to the terms of the story, what they might really want and need from one another, how the book as a whole appears to be structured—how, for me, it means.

All this to explain to myself as much as to the author why I feel this way.

In that process, I found myself saying things about the story that I didn't know I knew. And then it struck me that, right or wrong, my own response to the novel had developed slowly over the course of reading it three times. Or was it four? And I remembered that the reward of publishing is to find the book that becomes richer each time you read it.

In the world of rapidly changing questions about publishing technology, I have the luxury to work with books that should be read more than once.

When I recalled that, I knew what it was that publishers are supposed to be doing.

Fred Ramey and Greg Michalson formed Unbridled Books in 2003, an independent press dedicated to publishing literary works that are moving, beautiful and surprising. Unbridled's books make frequent appearances on the Book Sense lists and in the Discover program at Barnes & Noble. Recent titles include: *The Pirate's Daughter* by Margaret Cezair-Thompson, *Hick* by Andrea Portes and others.

Ramey and Michalson have been publishing together since 1992 when they opened the fiction line at MacMurray & Beck. Together, they have published titles that won or were short-listed for the PEN/Faulkner Award, the PEN Hemingway Award, the Book Sense Book of the Year Award, American Book Awards, the American Academy of Arts and Letters Rosenthal Award and the National Book Award.

Their website is found at www.unbridledbooks.com. This piece is drawn from a post from Ramey's Publisher Blog at Unbridled Books.

Midlister:
Embracing the Term
by Sean McLachlan

SOME WRITERS loathe the term "midlister," thinking it conjures up images of second-best failures. They prefer to think of themselves as literary stars in the making.

I embrace the term "midlister" because that's what I am. Most serious writers who keep at it never make the bestseller lists. They become midlisters, like me. They juggle several different projects at a time, wearing several hats in order to maximize their chances of securing a deal. It ain't pretty, but that's the way the publishing industry is. If you're an aspiring author, my life is your realistic expectation.

Am I interested in getting an agent and writing a breakout book? Of course. I'm actively searching for an agent, and I'm working on two different breakout books at the moment. All midlisters worthy of the title "writer" strive to break into the stratosphere of big-time publishing. It's the dream that keeps us going.

That and the fact that no other job is nearly as fun.

Is midlist writing purgatory, as the subtitle of my blog ("Midlist Writer: Welcome to Literary Purgatory") says?

Yes and no. My subtitle is only half serious. Yes, midlisting involves getting paid late, struggling with inadequate advances and apathetic marketing people, and the general frustration of knowing you deserve better. But purgatory, if you know your Catholic theology, is finite. It will end some day. I know I'll get a few rungs higher. I've climbed several already.

And purgatory isn't so bad. I get to research interesting topics, see my name in print, travel the world, and avoid cubicle Hell. I used to work in an office. I'd rather rob banks than go back to that.

Is staying too busy on a lot of different midlist projects a bad move for a writer? Yes, it can be. That's why I reserve a sizable chunk of my time for my fiction. I've never sold a novel. I've sold a grand total of one novella, one novelette, and one short story. As a percentage of my total writing income, my fiction sales come out to way below one percent. But my dream is to write both history and novels. I'm halfway there. When I look at my fiction I know I picked the right career. Some day my novels will be published, and that's when I truly get to express myself to the reading public.

There is a certain unfair stigma in some writing circles to being a midlister. If I need to use a pen name to rise higher, so be it. I'll be in good company, and I don't really mind if the name Sean McLachlan isn't on the cover of my breakout novel. I don't write for fame; I write for self-satisfaction. Everyone I care about will know it's me anyway.

Until that happens I'm stuck on the midlists, where I get to satisfy my somewhat academic curiosity about the world by writing history and travel, and whatever else I can successfully pitch to an editor. Plus I get the satisfaction of actively pursuing my dream. How many cubicle slaves can say that?

Purgatory is okay. It's warm here, but not too hot. And there's always the promise of Heaven.

Sean McLachlan worked for ten years as an archaeologist before becoming a full-time writer specializing in history and travel. He is the author of *Byzantium: An Illustrated History* (Hippocrene, 2004), *It Happened in Missouri* (TwoDot, 2007) and *Moon Handbooks London* (Avalon, 2007), among others.

For more about him and life in the publishing industry, visit his blog, Midlist Writer (www.midlistwriter.blogspot.com), where this piece appeared March 2008.

Diary of a Novel

by Will Weaver

THIS IS A JOURNAL about writing a novel. I've published nine of them with Simon & Schuster, HarperCollins, and Farrar, Straus and Giroux, and have always meant to keep a log. My new novel (second in a series, actually) is written for boys who love cars and hate their English classes. However, all novels are more alike than they are different, so here goes …

July 5, 2007. Novel deadline looming. But it's difficult to write much before the Fourth of July in Minnesota. It's just too nice out of doors—green grass, bird-chirping, loon-calling upper Mississippi on-the-river living. But Wes, my editor in New York, wants the second Motor series novel by the end of August, so I have to get rolling. The contract says delivery on November 1, but things have been informally moved up. I'm happy to push harder and try to deliver in August.

But a series is not an easy thing. Each novel has to stand alone, yet intersect with the previous book. The first, *Saturday Night Dirt*, took an ensemble approach—multiple points of view, all focused to one Saturday night at the race track. Wes wants a more singular point of view—a main character—in this one. And he might be right (editors usually are).

July 6. Am going with Trace Bonham, 16, from *Saturday Night Dirt*, as the main character for the new novel. He'll "own" the book. His story.

Working title is *Super Stock Rookie*. I set the stage for this at the end of SND, when Trace's driving skill is noticed by Cal Hopkins, well-known Late Model driver.

Now I have to set about ruining his life. I think this will be a Be-Careful-What-You-Asked-For kind of story. Novelists have to be tough on their characters. It's easy to be too easy on them.

July 7. Spent a couple of hours working on the plot and cast. My process is to briefly summarize the plot, and name and describe my characters. A third of a page or less for the plot summary. The characters need only a few sentences of description, mainly about their personalities. Delicate decisions here, especially on plot. Snares abound at this stage. A bad decision can cost me weeks worth of work later on.

My "donnee'" (great French literary term for the "given" of the novel): Trace tries out and is selected to drive for a new team, a team all about marketing a new product. I'm interested in several things here: how drivers move up from the local tracks to the pro level; how the forces of sponsors and marketing dominate auto racing; and—more interesting—the effects of success on a kid who might not be ready or even want it. I particularly like the matter of Trace being chosen as much for his looks as for his driving skill.

July 9. Have chosen a racing team name and product. "Team Blu" is behind a new energy food to be marketed to teens. Their strategy is to a choose a "kid from nowhere" and make him and their product well known: "Out of the Blu."

Risky business plot-wise, but hey, this is fiction. Plus following my movie *Sweet Land*, I have good contacts in Minneapolis advertising biz who can help me with how new product marketing works. I really could care less about that marketing side; I'm interested in how things bear on my characters, on Trace. How he deals with new people who are not like him at all. Fiction writing is all about revealing the true nature of your character's character.

July 10. I'm rolling with the chapter break-outs. By this, I mean I've started listing—briefly—what's going to happen chapter-by-chapter. Just a few sentences, up to a short paragraph. Sort of like Melville, "Chapter Seven: Ahab Sights the White Whale," but a bit more. Lots of the old novels had names for each chapter—not a bad way for the author to stay on track.

July 11. Some new character types are wanting in, and I've made room for them. The make-up of Team Blu was sort of predictable: young advertising types from Minneapolis. In contrast, today's light bulb (I hope): to give Trace a car/crew team made up largely of "real" racers from southern Indiana and beyond. Some good ole boys, both smarter and dumber than they look. They see a good dollar to be made on Team Blu, and have bamboozled the Team Blu marketing types with their drawl and race-talk/name-dropping. They will crew for Trace.

A thought on my process: when I first start a novel, I can't sit and work on it for more than an hour at a time. But gradually my "seat time" (to use a racing term) increases. When I'm fully up to speed—when the novel is real in my head and I'm writing out of that realism—I can work for hours, and come back again for a second shift in the evening. But those first days are agonizing.

July 16. Note-taking and chaptering (is that a word?) continues. I have nine chapters blocked out with a short paragraph of summary for each. I know from experience that those current nine chapters will probably end up being 12 or more.

July 17. Day One on the new novel. It's like starting a marathon: stiff, edgy, no rhythm, no feel for the road. Three very rough pages.

July 19. Two "shifts" today, with the prose starting to loosen. The first day's three pages turned out to be skeleton thin; by going back and adding flesh (mainly more imagery and detail), they grew to five pages—and pushed me nicely into new material. That's part of my daily process: begin a new day by revising what I wrote yesterday. I recommend it.

July 20. Got an email note from Wes. We had a good chat about the novel, which he really wants in August, "for all kinds of reasons." Say no more, I said. Now back to your regularly scheduled broadcast, i.e., me out of here to go write fiction.

July 22. Took Saturday off for a family reunion, but got a couple good pages done on Sunday before the races. My (real) driver, Skyler, finished third in the Modified feature—his best race yet. There's quite a bit of intersection between that actual racing team and my racing novels, in terms of technical details.

Detail from last night's race: "The track was so dry the lights were shining off the dry slick." —Skyler

After five days, I've hit page 20. A decent pace at the start, but I'll have to pick it up to make my August deadline. As predicted, my first chapter split into two.

July 26. Limping along, still not feeling the rhythm, and lots of details to fill in. My initial drafts are always thin; they need more texture, more imagery and detail. In a way, each draft is like a camera or binocular or a lens of some kind, sharpening its focus. I write to make the scenes intensely real to myself.

Took a day off to go actual racing in Grand Rapids, Minnesota, on a very hot Wednesday night. We finished last, but it was our first race under the lights and on true dry slick conditions. Skyler continues to impress with his instincts and technical driving skills. He spun out in turn three, did a full 360, and got back on the gas and headed down the straightaway without missing a beat. A fun night, but the heat (90s and 75 percent humidity) and four hours of sleep took it out of me; couldn't write a word the next day until 3 P.M.

August 1. I'm through four chapters, closing in on page 50. I'm liking it. So much so that I'm not going to jinx it by talking about here.

August 8. Have entered chapter 6, about page 75. Chapter 5, with Trace heading to Minneapolis to sign with Team Blu, has a nice shape. A chapter should have a rounded feel to it, with some stand-alone qualities. Am set up nicely for Chapter 6, wherein Trace goes back to Headwaters, sans Street Stock (his contract has lots of exclusions, including no "independent" driving).

I'm more interested in the descriptive qualities of this chapter—which can be deep and tonal. Without his car, he will see his home track in new and different ways, noticing things he has always overlooked.

This matter—the set-up for description—is the key to good prose. Think of Tim O'Brien's piece "The Things They Carried"—he gets by with extremely close-up, nearly obsessive description because of the alienation of the men from their environment ('Nam). Same, at a lower level, with Trace: his comfort zone is ending.

August 9. Tough to write today. Had a commentary appear in the *Minne-*

apolis Star Tribune today, "War, Language and 'Heroes'," in which I make the argument that our returning soldiers, just because they were in Iraq, are not all heroes. I'm gonna take some heat on this one, but writers write what others don't. Writers say what others won't. If we (writers) are not in trouble on occasion, we're not doing our job.

Will take the weekend off to go the Bayfront Blues Fest in Duluth, MN, a calculated absence from the writing desk. It's important, when writing, to be as well rested as possible. One should be (ideally) brimming over with thoughts, ideas, energy and the desire to write. This is hardly ever possible. But recognize when the well is empty, and take a break.

August 15. Too much sun and the Blues. But a long weekend away from the novel was good. Back at it haltingly on Tuesday. Four good pages today and better prospects for tomorrow.

Page 75. The novel is reaching that dangerous middle part, when things can go flat. It's the novelist's most difficult task—to sustain the arc of plot and reader engagement through the middle zone. What's needed is major plot lift, as in *Memory Boy* (shamelessly referencing myself) wherein the Newell family, having escaped disorder, chaos, and environmental collapse in the city, finally arrive at their cabin "up north"—only to find it occupied by squatters. That twist gave MB an injection of energy sufficient to carry it through to its ending.

August 19. Page 85 today. Rolling along nicely. Have a nice shape to Chapter 6 that includes Trace back at his old track, sans car, and at loose ends. Managed to make use of the season and the Perseid meteor showers. Tip #97: don't ignore using the weather—why not make it a player? So much modern fiction is written indoors, so to speak.

August 21. I'm getting worried. My page count needs to be higher, and a five-day vacation is looming. I don't see how I'll finish by month's end. I've thought of taking my laptop along (a train trip to Glacier Park, then some hiking with my wife and another couple), but they put up with enough from me, the fiction writer.

I've come to see, over a career of twenty-some years of work, that there's a vast, world-wide conspiracy against the act of writing. I'm not unserious here. Life does not wish to be slowed down, sped up, manipulated, excerpted, or fiddled with. It wants only to roll on like an end-less river to some far-off sea. Happy people cast their boats in the water and just go with the current. Writers don't. They beat on against the tide (F.S. Fitzgerald writing at the end of *Gatsby*).

August 24. Got myself to page 95, then hit the wall. I need to be sharp for this trip. And no, I'm not taking my laptop. Not taking my laptop. Not taking my laptop.

September 1. Back after a head-clearing trip to Glacier Park, lovely at summer's end. Took the train out, rocked and rolled through North Dakota and Montana, with plenty of naps, glasses of wine, cards, read-ing (Alice Munro's "short" stories), and conversation.

But now back to matters at hand: the last short half of my Super Stock novel. I've been worrying about too much plot, and resulting believability issues. But that anxiety evaporated last night during a viewing of the latest Bourne movie. Action films have defaulted to a kind of short-hand code for Realism. Jason Bourne hotwires a new Audi in three seconds—impossible of course—but acceptable to view-ers. So why worry about stretching the limits just a tad in a YA novel? Would a 17-year-old nobody driver really get picked to drive a new Super Stock, and be paid good money to boot? He would—if I get just enough details right about his good looks, the car, and the market-ing machine behind the team. It could happen, right? And if it could, that's Realism.

September 2. Have been agonizing about a plot-line, the matter of the Trace's Super Stock being built "down south" (Indiana), and the south-ern-leaning Bubba-type crew. But I think it will work, thanks to a con-versation with my first and best editor (and wife) Rose. She has a way of cutting through the fog and keeping me on track.

Together we talked the plot back onto the straight and narrow road forward: the Southern crew was hired for a reason—to give Trace an advantage, but that only creates more trouble for him.

This was what I and all novelists do: create characters, then put them in trouble. The rest of the novel is them wriggling their way out.

95 pages.

September 6. Am trying to avoid southern clichés with my car crew, and at the same time get maximum value from north-south culture clash. Much of literature, plot-wise, is based on "And then a stranger came to town …" That or some kind of intrusion into the pastoral, which will certainly be the case when Trace's top-dollar car and hauler arrive at Headwaters Speedway. I anticipate some irony: my south-Indiana crew [is] used to more modern speedways, and think they're in Hicksville.

Hey, novelists have to have fun, too.

September 8. Just about over the hump (a literal narrative rise) at 110 pages, but laboring. Many second thoughts about this whole project: I should be writing "serious" adult fiction. Am I wasting my literary talent on teen car novels?

Then I'm reminded of how thinly the chain of literacy is stretched—broken in some cases—and how many kids and adult don't read. There are two approaches to Literature: the first is to treat it like a museum, wherein the Great Books are housed and guarded by critics and intellectuals; we can visit the books and pore over them, but we cannot hope to live up to their gravitas. The second is literature as a living, breathing organism, one that belongs to all of us, one in which we can all participate—if only we find something to read that catches our attention and speaks directly to us.

There's the challenge: to catch people's attention in this Century of Distraction. At no other time have young people had so many demands on their ability to sit still and focus on a single endeavor, such as reading.

My ideal reader in this Motor Series is the boy wearing the cap in the back row who can read but doesn't like to. But once he reads *Saturday Night Dirt* and the Motor Series, he goes on to *Vision Quest* (Terry Davis), *My Losing Season* (Pat Conroy), *A Fan's Notes* (Fred Exley) … then onto Ralph Ellison and Flannery O'Connor and Harper Lee and David Sedaris and … you get the picture.

Of course, it assumes that he doesn't get humiliated by his friends for being found with a book. But gradually, reading lifts him out of the very small orbit of his life, a life that he comes to see as a confinement, even a trap, one from which he has managed to escape—and into the full complexity of the world as a thoughtful, open-minded citizen.

Back to work on Trace Bonham and his Super Stock.

September 15. I've been hard at it. Close to the end now, at 145 pages, a "non-scary" length, as Wes put it. Finishing a novel is like a 50-mile hike in, say, Glacier Park. Lots of terrain, so much space that it's easy to forget one has a home. Life becomes a march, with the only truth that one will never get there (wherever that is) if he doesn't keep moving. Then, suddenly, the pass is crested and the trail is mostly downhill. I remember that I have a Jeep waiting in the parking lot. On the final slope there is an exhilaration, but no rush to the conclusion.

In fact, there is tendency to slow down a bit, to make this last. After all, isn't this where I live now, on the trail?

September 17. "Done." Finished the draft at 9 P.M., and streamed it all to Wes by 10 P.M. so it would be on his desk this morning. I'm fried today—didn't sleep well last night, largely from the usual, part-of-the-territory anxieties: the novel is stupid and poorly written. But once I get some sleep and exercise my confidence ought to return.

Anyway, time to let go. 160 pages in eight weeks. I'm headed into the woods.

Will Weaver writes fiction for adults and young adults. Born in northern Minnesota, he grew up on a dairy farm. His novels and short stories have earned the praises of reviewers from coast to coast for their unflinching realism.

Red Earth, White Earth, his debut novel (Simon & Schuster, 1986), was produced as a CBS television movie in 1989. *A Gravestone Made of Wheat & Other Stories* (Simon & Schuster, 1989) won many awards and saw the title story produced as the independent feature film *Sweet Land.*

Will Weaver has also written novels for young adults. A number of his books have been honored as Best Books for Young Adults by the American Library Association.

Formerly an English professor at Bemidji State University, he lives in northern Minnesota, where he is a full-time writer and avid outdoorsman, enjoying hunting, fishing and canoeing. This piece is excerpted from a September 2007 post on his blog, On Writing, found at his website, www.willweaverbooks.com.

On Rejection:
or, Dear Author, After Careful Consideration

by Bret Anthony Johnston

WE HEAR that rejection preys upon and depends upon the writer's ego; seemingly informed people tell us that successful writers appropriate rejection and use it as fuel, that they co-opt the editor's or agent's malice, stupidity, or worst of all, indifference, and they cure it until it becomes a kind of treat, something akin to beef jerky. And we hear that those who reject our work are not rejecting us, they're not rejecting our souls because if we could get our souls on the page, we wouldn't get rejected at all; instead we'd get flown first-class to Sweden to accept the Nobel Prize for Literature. They say this because most writers, especially beginning or unpublished writers, freak out over rejection. To the good men and women offering this consolation and advice, I say, okay, yes, sure, but you've obviously never ridden a skateboard.

Think of it this way: After you start sliding on the middle of your board down a handrail that runs the length of 12 brick stairs and realize your back foot has slipped off and in less than a millisecond your "eggs" will be "scrambled" on the banister, then a form letter from a second-rate agent takes on a less pressing, almost appealing meaning.

Like skateboarders, writers live by rejection; like writers, any skater worth his salt must have the single-minded tenacity of a wiener dog. Learning how to spin and not over-rotate Caballerials, in which you cannot see anything except sky or ceiling for most of the maneuver, requires the same prolonged dedication as submitting to glossies and finer literary journals. Eventually, you will land with the board under your feet, your weight centered, and with an unparalleled surprise and elation, you will ride away. But in the first hundred or so tries, you're going to fall, and you're going to want to return to easier tricks—things like frontside grinds, or paying mortgages or having babies or performing brain surgery, in the dark, on yourself.

This is a long, meandering manner of saying writing—let alone getting published—is as frightening as it is difficult. And in many ways, these two endeavors demand perfectly divergent skills; the tough-skinned, hard-won confidence that it takes to survive rejection after rejection is the polar opposite of the necessarily vulnerable and acutely sensitive work of writing an affecting piece of prose. (In other contexts, however, maybe the demands aren't quite so dissimilar; for writers reject their own work everyday, deeming this paragraph not worthy, this sentence too lax or long or confusing for inclusion in the finished manuscript.) So, then, it comes down to trust. Writers who second-guess themselves because they've received yet another rejection from the editor who's been so encouraging in the past will very often fall victim to not trusting their work or its process; that is, they will deny themselves that essential, empowering privilege: the privilege of bad writing, the privilege of, in Anne Lamott's famous words, writing "shitty first drafts."

Perhaps it would help to think of publishing as a process as well, a process as idiosyncratic, wanton, and bewildering as writing a publishable story. If one cannot trust editors or agents—and editors and agents should only be trusted after they've agreed to represent or publish you—then one can certainly trust the *process* of publishing. You can take a Zen-like solace in sending out manuscripts, and place faith in the admittedly unfounded idea that all good work will find an audience. Writing, I believe, is an act of faith, an act of courage. Publication, that last, absolutely necessary separation of the writer from his work, is the means that justifies the end; beyond our dreams of film options, glowing reviews, our names in prestigious tables of contents, publication becomes a simple key that opens the door to what we really and truly want: readers. Henry James says all writers are readers moved to emulation, and I'd humbly add that we read and write out of a tremendous curiosity in other human beings; it's a cry from the heart, a protest against our own mortality, and we believe there are more of us out there. Stated another way, if you keep sending out stories, you're eventually going to get good news when you open your SASE. It's stilting, laborious, and compromising work—like those first attempts to ride a skateboard without, as we say, "eating hell"—but the readers are worth it, we know that, and you're not alone. As a way of attesting to our community of rejection, I'll close by sampling from rejection slips I've received over the years:

> Dear Mr. Johnston, Having a talking cow in a story is nothing short of disaster.

> This lovely story suffers from bland language and perhaps not enough plot.

> (For the same story as above): I'm distracted by the narrator's voice and I feel that the overly prominent plot overshadows all else.

> Honestly, Mr. Johnston, this may be one of the finest stories I've read in twenty years, but because of backlog pressures, I'll have to pass.

> Got a real kick out of seeing my grandmother's first name in this story. She was a real twit, that one. Liked to soak peanuts in her Pepsi.

> On a standard form rejection, the word "Over" was scrawled at the bottom. When I flipped the paper, there was nothing there.

> On 9/20/2000: I'd be delighted to publish your story and make your writing known to the larger world.

> 5/14/2002 (Same magazine as above): Sorry for the long delay, but I wanted to let you know the magazine is in a permanent state of suspension. You're free to send the story we accepted elsewhere.

> Stories devoted to the geriatric theme theme (sic, the editor wrote the word twice) run across my grain, and over the years I have seldom published a piece of fiction written in that vein. In any case, I don't think your story was a successful piece of work. My troubles with the backlog continue here. I'm doing my best not to add anything to it, especially fiction or poetry or nonfiction, before the spring. If you would like to submit another story by April 15, I'd get around to it.

Finally, this last selection marks the only occasion on which I've corresponded with an editor who's not accepted the story in question:

> I feel you may lay it on a bit thick with the dying donkey.

> My response: What dying donkey?

Bret Anthony Johnston is the author of the acclaimed *Corpus Christi: Stories* (Random House, 2004), which was named a Best Book of the Year by the *Independent* of London and the *Irish Times* and received a number of prizes, including the James Michener Fellowship. He is also editor of *Naming the World: And Other Exercises for the Creative Writer* (Random House, 2008). His work appears in magazines such as the *Paris Review,* the *New York Times Magazine* and *Esquire,* and in annual anthologies such as *New Stories from the South.* In 2006, the National Book Foundation honored him with a new National Book Award for writers under 35.

A skateboarder for almost 20 years who spent a number of years on the professional touring circuit, he is currently the Director of Creative Writing at Harvard. His website is www.bretanthonyjohnston.com.

This essay first appeared in the literary magazine *Shenandoah.*

A Writer by Any Other Name

by Giles Turnbull

"WE NEED A SHORT BIO of yourself to accompany the story, just some background for readers. Thanks."

I spent two hours staring at the screen.

I'm a professional writer, or at least that's what I say to people. I ought to be able to come up with a short paragraph about myself. It should only take a moment to write.

My first effort is automatic:

> Giles Turnbull is a freelance writer based in Bradford on Avon, England. He has a website at gilest.org.

Well, it's accurate, you can give it that. But there's not much *spark*, is there? Not much of me. Where's the humor? Where's the person? Where, in particular, is the biography? These two sentences are just statements of fact, things my mother could tell you—but also things *anyone* who's vaguely heard of me could tell you. We need some added value, here, something that lives. Some biology for the biography.

> Giles Turnbull is a freelance writer based in Bradford on Avon, England. He has a website at gilest.org. He has written for the BBC, The Guardian, The Daily Telegraph, MacUser, *O'Reilly Publishing, and many others.*

Oh, please. "And many others?" Who am I trying to fool with that sort of weasely rubbish? Of course there have been others, but not many, and most of them were years ago. Some of them have gone bust. A lot of the stuff I wrote in the past is stuff I would rather forget. Just as your photographic technique improves with experience, so your writing improves over time, and you look back on your earlier work and wince—physically, recoil—when you see how *bad* it is. You wonder how you ever made it this far.

Giles Turnbull lives in Bradford on Avon, England. It's a small town where everyone knows everyone else, and he likes the community feel.

Bradford straddles a hillside, sprawling out into the valley below where 18th- and 19th-century entrepreneurs built a canal and a railway line. Once it was rich, a small industrial town thick with smoke; but industry outgrew the confines of the valley and moved away, and now all that's left is the architecture, the narrow streets, and the tourists.

Just last weekend, while doing a hasty climb up and down Glastonbury Tor, I fell into conversation with an architect. We discussed Bradford and our respective reasons for moving there, and it turned out our reasons were identical: we both wanted to live somewhere that offered freedom from the tyranny of the car. This town has most things you need for daily life, all of them within walking distance no matter where you are. The train line to Bath—and in the other direction to Salisbury, then to London—offers everything that Bradford can't provide.

It's anything but a sophisticated place. Do I want people to know about it? Does my living there—and mentioning so in my self-summary—give anyone any further insight into me and my professional career? And anyway, why should I be giving away my location? It's almost as if I *want* to be stalked.

Giles Turnbull is a writer who lacks ambition and will go out of his way to make people like him. He avoids confrontation, is hopeless with numbers—

Wait. Stop. This is not supposed to be therapy.

They want a "short bio," that's what they said. What's a biography? A story of a life. They want a short story of my life.

Not everyone seems to have as much trouble with this. Our Prime Minister, Gordon Brown, gets the luxury of 19 paragraphs. His bio opens with: "Born in 1951, Gordon Brown is the second of three sons. He grew up in the town of Kirkcaldy, an industrial centre famed for its linoleum and mining industries."

I could use that as a template, perhaps:

Born in 1970, Giles Turnbull is the second of two sons. He grew up in the town of Folkestone, a coastal town in decline, no longer famous as a fishing port, holiday destination, or for anything else really.

Accurate, but a little unfair. Folkestone is a town like most others: As a teenager, I couldn't wait to get away from it. As an adult, I have a soft spot for its elegant architecture and the beauty of its beaches, even if they do get covered in genuine flotsam and jetsam from the busy sealanes of the English Channel. It feels right to mention where I grew up, because the town shaped me, much like Kirkcaldy shaped Mr. Brown. Perhaps, though, the emphasis should remain on writing:

> Giles Turnbull was raised by his mother in a coastal town. He attended a good school but didn't really excel at anything except writing, which might go some way to explaining how he ended up writing third-person biographies of himself on a rainy January morning.

Too clever by half. Too much up its own backside. There's more bio in there, but it's a self-obsessed sort of bio. What we need is something with a little more humility.

> Giles Turnbull's pitiful scratches have been earning him a meagre living for a while now, and it's a wonder his family puts up with it.

Too much humility.

> Giles Turnbull started writing at school and is still at it. You'd think some-one would have told him it was break time by now.

Too much *stupid*. I need some more inspiration. Hold on, while I grab some paperbacks from the bookshelf.

Inside the front cover of his science fiction black comedy *Making History*, comedian and actor (and author) Stephen Fry (and geek, let's not forget that) writes of himself:

"Stephen Fry was born in 1957, and after a year or so of compara-tive silence, began to talk coherently in 1960. His first written work, 'Mummy,' was awarded the Sunnyvale Primary School Gold Star for Neatness in 1961."

JD Salinger's *Catcher in the Rye* has no biography at all, not even a blurb on the back cover. There's nothing on *Doctor Zivago* either.

Another sci-fi author, Iain M. Banks, writes this inside the front cover of *Look to Windward*:

"Iain Banks came to controversial public notice with the publica-tion of his first novel, *The Wasp Factory*, in 1984. *Consider Phlebas*, his first science fiction novel, was published under the name Iain M. Banks in

1987. He is now widely acclaimed as one of the most powerful, innovative, and exciting writers of his generation. Iain M. Banks lives in Fife, Scotland."

Did he really write that, or was it his agent? If it was his agent, was he embarrassed by the superlatives? Did he blush or argue, or consider re-writing the paragraph so that at least it didn't repeat the syllables "public" twice, and so close to one another, in the first sentence?

> *Giles Turnbull's first published article was a wedding report in the local weekly newspaper. He got the names of both bride and groom correct.*

Yes, I got my first wedding report right, but some of the later ones wrong. I always thought this was a strange task to give to an intern. The wedding captions are a popular part of any newspaper—popular for the newlyweds and their families, of course. The journalists hate writing them. Once you've written 20 dull-as-hell captions about Sarah and Matt and how they met through their mutual friend Debbie, and are so in love and looking forward to their honeymoon in Florida, you've written them all.

I can understand never wanting to write another ever again; I can't understand asking the spotty 19-year-old intern to do them. One error, you see, and you get the entire family on the phone.

"You spelt Matty wrong!" they yell, all of them.

"It's M-A-T-T-Y, not Matt!" they cry, quite justifiably. My 19-year-old self cringes and wilts under the onslaught of outrage, wanting above all to avoid the confrontation (see?). But it's "Matt" in the newspaper, now. The error is in danger of becoming fact. Decades from now, other journalists might be wanting to track down Matty—once he's been arrested for triple murder, perhaps—and my mis-typed copy (yes, typed, on a typewriter, not a computer) found in a library will throw them off the scent. Perhaps Matty's family will thank me then.

They'll be able to find me, of course, because the net will be littered with short bios about me. Short, terrible bios.

> *Giles Turnbull has made many errors in his professional career and begs your forgiveness if you have been slandered or libeled by any of them.*

Let's not invite litigation, shall we?

Giles Turnbull writes words for money. He is married and has a child. He lives in a house.

Actually I quite like that one. It's a bit clinical, though.

Giles Turnbull finds it hard to write a meaningful bio, despite being a professional writer for some 15 years now. That's horrifying. It's frightening.

Yes, it is. Already, I've spent longer writing the bio than I did writing the article it is supposed to sit alongside. I must never admit this in public. Imagine the ridicule.

Giles Turnbull is a—well, you know all that now. His website is www.gilest.org, and you can find him on Twitter and Flickr and all the usual places.

This piece first appeared February 2008 in *The Morning News*, a daily online magazine (www.themorningnews.org).

Authorial Worries

by Holly Black

WHEN TWO of my dearest friends were gearing up to have their first novels released and because I am not a nice person, I decided to make a list of all the things writers worry about.

Not that my friends should worry, of course.

Everything will go fine for them.

> Contract sent to wrong address.
> Contract stolen by gypsies who finish book and turn it in.
> Roommate thinks contract is junk mail and throws it away.
> Contract actually from Satan. You sign anyway.
> Book not completed by contract date.
> Book completed by contract date, but terrible.
> Only copy of book blows out of car in friend's hilarious re-enactment of *Wonder Boys.*
> Editor hates completed book.
> Editor loves completed book, except for main character.
> Editor loves completed book, except for plot.
> Editor takes one look at book and leaves publishing.
> Editor moves houses. You are assigned new editor that hangs up on you.
> Book too good. Secret publishing cabal plots your demise.
> Freelance copyeditor leaves tin-foil covered apartment. Voices tell her to replace the word "the" with the word "lambchop."
> Cover terrible.
> Cover great, but for a genre you hate.
> Cover great, but with new title and your name misspelled.
> While revising, call lover by name of character in book during intimate moment.
> While revising, call lover by name of villain in book during intimate moment.

> While revising, call lover by name of minor character that dies in the first chapter.
> Bookworms infest printers!
> Printers print book with invisible ink.
> Next Harry Potter book (or other blockbuster) sucking up all available paper. Your book printed on paper towels.
> Bad reviews.
> No reviews.
> Aliens destroy earth because they hated your book so much.
> Stellar reviews of book that sounds nothing like your book of the same title. Possibly the one written by gypsies?
> Your book becomes very popular. It is being read aloud instead of *The Eye of Argon* at conventions nationally.
> Book accidentally shelved with dictionaries.
> Book accidentally shelved with porn.
> Book accidentally shelved with porn, but sells like hotcakes.
> Book shelved in humor. Editor tells you this is no accident.
> Publisher does not send you on tour.
> Publisher sends you on tour to Bermuda Triangle.
> No one comes to booksigning.
> Many people have come to booksigning, including your mom, but at podium you realize you are naked.
> Many people come to signing because they mistake you for another author.
> Two people come to signing. One dozes off. The other interrupts your reading to ask for your editor's cell phone number.
> You misspell names of small children at signing. They cry.
> Death occurs before sequel. (Good for sales of first book.)
> Book does not earn out advance.
> Book earns out advance, but agent uses the money to buy one-way ticket to Disneyland and suitcase full of silly string.
> Book is banned.
> Book is controversial, but no one bans it. Suspect it is because no one read it.
> Book sells bazillions of copies. Fans break into house and steal your cat.
> Book sells fine, but you are only remembered for a humorous list.

Obviously, the list is incomplete. I'm sure you can come up with more.

Holly Black is the bestselling author of fantasy novels for teens and children. Her works include co-writing the bestselling *Spiderwick Chronicles* with Caldecott Award–winning artist, Tony DiTerlizzi. The first two books, *The Field Guide* and *The Seeing Stone* were released in 2003 by Simon & Schuster, with the next three, *Lucinda's Secret* (2003), *The Ironwood Tree* (2004) and *The Wrath of Mulgarath* (2004), following in quick succession. To date, the books have been translated into 32 languages.

The illustrated *Arthur Spiderwick's Field Guide to The Fantastical World Around You* (2005), *The Notebook for Fantastical Observations* (2005) and *Care and Feeding of Sprites* (2006) expanded the Spiderwick universe. A new related series has been launched, Beyond the Spiderwick Chronicles.

Black's first book, *Tithe: A Modern Faerie Tale* (Simon & Schuster, 2002), was called "Dark, edgy, beautifully written, and compulsively readable" by *Booklist*, and was included in the American Library Association's Best Books for Young Adults. Black has since written two other books in the same universe, *Valiant* (2005), recipient of the Andre Norton Award for Excellence in Young Adult Literature, and *Ironside* (2007).

This piece first appeared April 2005 on her LiveJournal blog, found at her website, www.blackholly.com. *The Eye of Argon* novel mentioned on the list is a famously atrocious piece of writing, attributed to a young novelist, often read as a humorous activity at science fiction/fantasy conventions.

One More Song

by Patry Francis

TUESDAY, MARCH 18, 2008. Well, it's a good thing I didn't worry before my surgery. It's a good thing that I reveled in every moment of being at home, rather than spoiling it by mentally leaping into "what might happen." Because as it turns out what might happen arrived all on its own.

My recovery was on track until Sunday when I became seriously ill. Doctors were summoned (one even racing down the hallway), tests were taken, conferences were had. The consensus was even more desperate than the way I felt. My surgery had failed, and would need to be repeated today.

Fortunately, by yesterday, I was feeling much better. A young Vietnamese man arrived to take me by wheelchair to radiology. It felt like a real outing. Running three and a half minutes late, and obsessively punctual, my high-spirited driver gave me the kind of thrill ride I haven't had in years. We practically did wheelies around the corners.

Wheee!

Once I got off the ward, I marveled at the healthy people I saw, and all the incredible things they could do without a second thought. They walked fast, carrying backpacks or heavy satchels, while nattering on their cell phones about what they were doing that night.

A woman enjoyed a bagel and coffee at her desk. Then around the next turn, a frustrated young mother chased a toddler while balancing a baby on her hip. A man, talking in the hallway, complained that his supervisor was compelled "to micro-manage everything."

In another time, I have done all these things, I have been all these people (though I don't think I've ever used the word "micro-manage").

(Remind me to try it.)

My popular driver was greeted enthusiastically by co-workers everywhere. "How ya' doin'?" they asked.

"Same old. Same old," he responded the first three times.

That was when I spoke up. "Look at you. You're racing. You're whistling. You're calling out to your friends. You're not Same Old anything. You're *wonderful*."

He laughed out loud. When he met the next friend, he didn't even wait to be asked how he was.

"You know how I am today? I'm *wonderful*."

My destination was a spot in an empty hallway where I was to wait for the radiologist. I was sitting there thinking of everything I'd seen on my ride when unexpectedly, someone behind me belted out the old Billie Holiday classic, "Good Morning Heartache." It was a damn good rendition.

I turned around and saw an old man in a wheelchair, waiting as I was. He continued to sing, and when he was finished, I clapped.

"Do you know that song?" he asked.

Oh yes, I know that song. All too well.

But then I thought about all the people I'd seen that day. I thought about how blessed they were. All of them. And how blessed I was, too. Blessed to be loved by my family and friends, to be cared for by an amazing team of doctors and nurses. Blessed to meet my buoyant young wheelchair driver, and to be able to see the world around me as I traveled. And especially blessed by an old man, sitting alone in a hallway, who had the fortitude to turn his troubles into a song.

Saturday, March 22, 2008. This morning, after ten days in the hospital, my nurse told me I had become the official mayor of the floor. But if they're going to hang a sign outside my room, I would prefer it say "Writer in Residence." I never was much for politics. As a writer, I tend to grow empathy for even the darkest of characters. Clearly, I'm unfit to govern—even among my own creations.

So. After days of sipping clear liquids, watching TV, surfing the net, reading books and emails (which I can't answer from the hospital for some reason) a strange urge came over me. It was the urge that has dominated my life. Stories bubbled up; a poem began to form. I thought of the novel I would begin after the one I'm working on was finished, and behind that, I glimpsed the shadow of another.

How strange, how marvelous that it should follow me here! Even when my brain is still thick with anesthesia! Even when I ignored it in favor of TV and magazines! Still it follows. Still it comes.

As for my medical status, I'm well enough to walk to the kitchen and make tea, well enough to joke with the staff, and to get excited about the new "surgical soft" diet that's been ordered for lunch. (It's been a long ten days on jello and broth.) Now it's pretty much a waiting game. Waiting to learn if the surgery will hold. Waiting to eat normally again. Waiting, waiting to see the imperfect incredible place known as home.

Saturday, March 29, 2008. Last night, I couldn't sleep. Maybe I'd been spoiled by three nights in my own bed. Or maybe as Lisa Kenney once wrote to me, night is just a particularly vulnerable time for people in the hospital.

Around eleven, my roommate, a young woman from Panama, got a call. It seemed her three-year-old son was having trouble sleeping, too. He needed his mother to sing to him to sleep, just like she always did.

And so she did. It turned out to be a long concert, as the boy continued to beg for one more song, not wanting to let go of the connection to his mother's voice.

I'm not sure how long it took for him to fall asleep, but I slipped off to the sound of her voice after about the third song.

Today, as I was watching *The Power of Song,* a documentary on PBS about Pete Seeger, I smiled as I remembered the night before.

At the end of the documentary, Pete said we don't sing enough any more and it's a huge loss. People used to sing when they walked and when they built roads and bridges and when they cleaned their houses; and subtly they lifted up the world around them with their song—or comforted it, as a sick woman, singing to her child stilled and illuminated my hospital room last night.

I've never had a voice as strong as the man I heard singing "Good Morning Heartache" last week, or as light and high as my roommate's, and I can't play the banjo like Pete Seeger. But I can tell you one thing; I will leave this hospital (hopefully tomorrow) determined to sing my song and to sing it with all the force I have in me.

Coda. Not long ago, I wrote about a whole community of writers and bloggers who believe that stories can change the world, a community who believe that the fate of fictional characters, or the meticulous or messy arrangement of words and motion and feeling into a poem or an essay is worth whatever sacrifice it takes.

I was listening to Philip Pullman being interviewed by Charlie Rose. I found myself nodding when he said (and I'm paraphrasing badly here; he was far more eloquent) that he wrote because we live in such a fabulous, miraculous world and he wanted to remind his readers how precious it is.

In other words, he writes not because he's a mad egomaniac, as we writers are often reputed to be, but because he feels he has something to give and he wants to give it.

When you come right down to it, is there another reason to begin this epic struggle with self, with words, with blank pages and empty screens? If we truly wrote "for ourselves" as so many writers say with understandable defensiveness, why move beyond the safety of our private journals?

Why post on a blog, or god forbid, seek publication—subjecting ourselves to the crazy-making mix of rejection, elation, despair, intoxicating praise and bitter criticism? Why invest so much time and hope if we didn't believe we had a story to tell that someone—maybe just one person—really needed to hear?

Why do it, if not to share, as Pullman said, our love for this startling and wondrous world we find ourselves in, and the even more startling goodness that the people in it often rise to exhibit?

Patry Francis is author of *The Liar's Diary* (Dutton, 2007) and runs a popular blog for writers, Simply Wait (http://simplywait.blogspot.com). This piece combines several posts on that blog in early 2008.

APPENDICES

Editor's Afterword

by Philip Martin

WELCOME BACK to *The New Writer's Handbook*, an annual compilation of eclectic and, I hope, thought-provoking short articles with advice for writers on craft and career. The annual part of the effort offers writers a source for regular professional development. The eclectic part means I've tried to scour many out-of-the-way sources, plunging into the depths of blog archives and exploring related disciplines, as well as offering outstanding selections drawn from some of the biggest and most familiar sources: *The Writer* magazine, *Writer's Digest*, the ASJA *Monthly* (American Society of Journalists and Authors newsletter), the SCBWI *Newsletter* (Society of Children's Book Writers and Illustrators), and such.

The problem with advice: it can be overwhelming, endless, repetitive, contradictory, sometimes stretched paper-thin, and often comes from someone who wants to sell you their services. This is inherent in the advice business (after all, we're charging for this book). On the other hand, there is a ton of free advice floating across the Web, some of it very good—if you know where to look. But you might have to wade through a ton of blog blather to find it.

So here's my advice about advice:

1. Be a good listener. Keep an open mind. Fresh ideas are good for the creative soul.

2. Accept that you'll learn in small chunks, a bit here and there. No one really has a magic bullet or comprehensive program. Look to improve in small, steady ways.

3. Limit your time. Pick effective sources: the best blogs, a magazine or two, membership in selected organizations, a few best books.

4. Don't swallow everything you hear. The proof is in the pudding, as the saying goes. The outcome—is there a benefit to you?—is the only real measurement.

5. Embrace complexity. I often describe writing as a type of human cultural ecosystem. Every writer who survives finds a niche. Each figures out how to cooperate with others, while also competing for limited resources. We adapt to larger changes in climate, nutrients, and cycles of drought and flood, disasters and lush seasons.

   The complexity means that advice that works for one writer may not work for the next. Successful techniques are often dependent on niche. Find a good niche and grow into it.

6. Embrace opposites. One aspect of a sophisticated mind is the ability to hold two contradictory ideas in the mind, accepting that both can be "true" (or at least useful). Combining different or hybrid approaches, ideas, philosophies, techniques in your writing can often develop new, original, and very appealing results.

7. Look across genres. Can a nonfiction writer learn from a novelist? An academic professor from a commercial copywriter? A writer of books for adults from a writer of books for children? Certainly.

8. Look across disciplines. Writing shares much with other neighboring disciplines: business, technology, art and design, psychology, cultural studies.

9. Write. Don't wait for inspiration. As Raymond Carver noted, Isak Dinesen (Danish writer Karen Blixen) said that she worked every day without hope and without despair. She meant that writing was not a matter of wishful thinking, but of what you do, one day at a time.

10. Test and measure results for yourself. Throw away what doesn't work, and keep turning toward what works best. Once you have noticed what works better and what doesn't, move your resources (time, clear thought, focus) to those things that work the best. And away from those pursuits that work poorly. This is immensely important to your success.

One of the oddities of the writing world is that it allows you—in some ways glorifies the tendency—to continue in fruitless ways. If you were in the restaurant business—because you love to cook, you have a true passion for food—you would face substantial overhead costs, so great that unless you pushed hard towards what worked, you'd soon have to close. You'd have to learn marketing, customer service, good pricing practices very quickly, or fail.

For writers, that's less true; the overhead is so minimal. A computer, some paper, and not much else besides time, time, and more time. So a lot of people bumble about, repeating mistakes, persistent (that's good), but not progressing (that's bad). They would like to do better, but they just don't consider seriously enough how to correct mistakes and learn all the key practices.

To grow as a writer, be more honest about evaluating what works. I'm a firm believer in outside feedback. Ultimately, it's not a matter of whether *you* like your work. The tough question: do *others* like, read, buy your work—or at least invest some of their own resources into publishing it? If not, it's a hobby at best. To gain tangible success, you have to listen more to others and what they think of your work. And that's a good thing for most of us as writers, as communicators, as creators of work to be read.

Yes, there is a niche for you. How will you go about seeking it, finding it, growing into it? Whether your niche is writing blockbuster medical thrillers like Tess Gerritsen, or being a copywriter/fly fisherman like Tom Chandler, or an Inklings scholar like Diana Pavlac Glyer, or a writer of books for young readers like Lois Lowry, or whatever ... you can learn to do better, over time. If you apply yourself seriously.

That's the trait all successful writers share. Like Karen Blixen, they work without hope and without despair. They have good days and bad days. They are passionate, they love their stories, they believe in their skills, but they ask, always, how to improve everything they write.

And they work. And they grow as writers with each piece.

As will you.

Publication Credits

Abrams, Rhonda

"Great Faith. Great Doubt. Great Effort." is copyright 2007 by Rhonda Abrams and is reprinted by permission of the author. The article, first published April 13, 2007, appears on her website of advice for business entrepreneurs, www.RhondaOnline.com.

Babauta, Leo

"Five-Minute Decluttering Tips" is copyright 2008 by Leo Babauta and is used by permission of the author. The piece is drawn from a longer article posted April 3, 2008, on his Zen Habits blog (http://zenhabits.net), "18 Five-Minute Decluttering Tips to Start Conquering Your Mess."

Bell, Susan

"The Pen and the Artful Edit" is from *The Artful Edit: On the Practice of Editing Yourself* and is copyright 2007 by Susan Bell. The excerpt is reprinted by permission of the publisher, W.W. Norton & Co., Inc. For more, visit the author's website at www.artfuledit.com.

Bissell, Beryl Singleton

"The Three S's: Structure, Solitude, and Silence" is copyright 2007 by Beryl Singleton Bisell and is reprinted by permission of the author. Her website is www.berylsingletonbissell.com. This piece first appeared as a guest blogger piece, June 3, 2007, on Simply Wait (http://simplywait. blogspot.com), a blog by Patry Francis.

Black, Holly

"Authorial Worries" is copyright 2005 by Holly Black and is reprinted by permission of the author. The author's website is www.blackholly.com. The piece first appeared April 7, 2005, on her LiveJournal blog (http:// blackholly.livejournal.com).

Bourret, Michael

"A Day in the Life of a Literary Agent" is copyright 2007 by Michael Bourret and is reprinted by permission of the author. The article appeared March 2007 on the blog of the Dystel & Goderich Literary Management agency (http://dglm.blogspot.com).

Bransford, Nathan

"First Person or Third Person?" is copyright 2007 by Nathan Bransford and is reprinted by permission of the author. This post appeared July 9, 2007, on his blog (http://nathanbransford.blogspot.com).

Chandler, Tom

"Two of a Writer's Best (and Least Known) Friends" is copyright 2006 by Tom Chandler and is reprinted by permission of the author. It first appeared as a post December 11, 2006, on his blog, The Copywriter Underground (http://copywriterunderground.com).

Clark, Tony D.

"Business Card as Offline Home Page" is copyright 2007 by Tony D. Clark and is reprinted by permission of the author. The piece was posted on his blog, Success from the Nest (http://successfromthenest.com), March 28, 2007.

Crispin, A.C.

"Multiple Queries: Playing the Waiting Game" is copyright 2007 by Ann C. Crispin and is reprinted by permission of the author. Her website is www.accrispin.com. The article first appeared April 15, 2007, on her Writer Beware blog (http://accrispin.blogspot.com).

Day, Kay B.

"Back Up Those Files Now" is copyright 2008 by Kay B. Day and is reprinted by permission of the author. The article first appeared February 27, 2008, in the *The Writer* online (www.writermag.com).

Delaney, Stephen

"Sweat the Small Stuff" is copyright 2006 by Stephen Delaney and is reprinted by permission of the author. A version of this article first appeared in the January 2006 issue of *The Writer*.

Eisler, Barry

"Resonance in Titles" is copyright 2007 by Barry Eisler and is reprinted by permission of the author via his agent, Daniel Conaway of Writer's House. The author's website is www.barryeisler.com. The piece first appeared as a two-part series of posts, March 22 and 25, 2007, on the Buzz, Balls, and Hype blog produced by M.J. Rose (http://mjroseblog. typepad.com/buzz_balls_hype).

Faust, Jessica

"A Word on Pitching a Novel" is copyright 2008 by Jessica Faust and is reprinted by permission of the author. The excerpt from the query within the piece is copyright by Heidi Willis and is included with her permission. This piece appeared February 12, 2008, on the BookEnds literary agency's blog (http://bookendslitagency.blogspot.com).

Firke, Lisa
> "Three Creative Exercises" is copyright 2008 by Lisa Firke and is reprinted by permission of the author. The article is drawn from a series of creative tips titled "Blockbusters and Balancing Acts" on her website, Hit Those Keys (www.hitthosekeys.com).

Francis, Patry
> "One More Song" is copyright 2008 by Patry Francis and is reprinted by permission of the author. The piece combines posts from January and March 2008 on her blog, Simply Wait (http://simplywait.blogspot.com), found on her website, www.patryfrancis.com.

Frishman, Rick, and Robyn Freedman Spizman
> "Describing Your Book's Benefits" is copyright 2006 by Rick Frishman and Robyn Freedman Spizman and is reprinted by permission of the authors. It is an excerpt from their book, *Author 101: Bestselling Secrets from Top Agents* (Adams Media, 2006). The piece also appeared in Frishman's newsletter for writers, *The Author 101 Newsletter*. For more, or to receive their Million Dollar Rolodex of resources, visit: www.author101.com.

Galbraith, Colin
> "Marketing Your Freelance Writing Business" is copyright 2008 by Colin Galbraith and is reprinted by permission of the Daily Writing Tips blog (www.dailywritingtips.com). His own website is http://freelance.colingalbraith.co.uk. This piece also appeared May 9, 2008, on Freelance Switch blog (http://freelanceswitch.com), titled "5 Tips for Marketing Your Freelance Writing Business."

Gerritsen, Tess
> "Action Is Boring" is copyright 2007 by Tess Gerritsen and is reprinted by permission of the author. The piece appeared November 19, 2007, on her blog, found at her website, www.tessgerritsen.com.

Glass, Ira
> "Storytelling Techniques" is copyright 2008 by Ira Glass and is reprinted by permission of the author and the producer/publisher, Current TV. This article is a transcribed excerpt from a video featuring Ira Glass of *This American Life*, from Chicago Public Radio. The video is produced by Current TV as part of their Storytelling Module of resources for contributing producers. For the full video, see http://current.com/make/training?section+storytelling. Current is "the world's peer-to-peer news and information network," the first network to feature Viewer Created Content (vc2), which now comprises over 1/3 of its programming.

Glyer, Diana Pavlac

"Lewis, Tolkien, and the Inklings" is copyright 2008 by Diana Pavlac Glyer and is reprinted by permission of the author. The article includes passages from her book, *The Company They Keep: C.S. Lewis and J.R.R. Tolkien as Writers in Community* (Kent State University Press, 2007), used by permission of the publisher. Portions were drawn from a December 12, 2007, blog entry by Glyer on www.cslewis.com, on its blog, http://booksbycslewis.blogspot.com. For more on Glyer's work, visit: www.theplaceofthelion.com.

Grow, Gerald

"The Metaskills of Journalism" is copyright 1996 by Gerald Grow and is reprinted by permission of the author. It appears with other articles on his website, www.longleaf.net/ggrow.

Hale, Shannon

"Writing and Mothering: How I (sort of) Do Both" is copyright by Shannon Hale and is reprinted by permission of the author. It appears on her website, www.squeetus.com, in a section of articles for writers.

Hanley, Kate

"Simple Stretches for Writers" is copyright 2008 by Kate Hanley and is reprinted by permission of the author. It appeared in the February 2008 issue of the ASJA *Monthly*, the newsletter of the American Society of Journalists and Authors (www.asja.org).

Hart, Melissa

"Creative Nonfiction" is copyright 2008 by Melissa Hart and is reprinted by permission of the author. The article first appeared in a slightly shorter form in *The Writer* magazine, April 2008.

Henkin, Joshua

"Autobiography or Imagination?" is copyright 2007 by Joshua Henkin and is reprinted by permission of the author. The piece appeared October 3, 2007, on his blog, found on his website, www.joshuahenkin.com.

Johnston, Bret Anthony

"On Rejection: or, Dear Author, After Careful Consideration" is copyright by Bret Anthony Johnston and is reprinted by permission of the author. The article appears on his website (www.bretanthonyjohnston.com) and was first published in the literary magazine *Shenandoah*.

Jones, Bronwyn

"Better Writing Through Design" is copyright 2007 by Bronwyn Jones and is reprinted by permission of the author. This article first appeared July 31, 2007, in the online magazine *A List Apart* (www.alistapart.com).

Kome, Penney

"Writing Humor" is copyright 2008 by Penney Kome and is reprinted by permission of the author. The article first appeared March 11, 2008, as a post to a listserv for journalists, WriterL, moderated by Lynn Franklin.

Konrath, J.A.

"Sling Your Web" is copyright 2007 by J.A. Konrath and is reprinted by permission of the author. His website is www.jakonrath.com. The article first appeared in *Writer's Digest* magazine, October 2007.

Kooser, Ted

"Ordinary Things" is copyright 2008 by Ted Kooser and is published by permission of the author. Portions of the article are drawn from his book *Poetry Home Repair Manual: Practical Advice for Beginning Poets* (University of Nebraska Press, 2005). Thanks also to ideas drawn from a Winter 2005 interview by Dan Cryer that appeared in *UU World* magazine. "Father" is from *Delights and Shadows* (Copper Canyon Press, 2004). "August" is from *Sure Signs* (University of Pittsburgh Press, 1980). The poem that begins "The quarry road tumbles before me" is from *Winter Morning Walks: 100 Postcards to Jim Harrison* (Carnegie Mellon University Press, 2000). Kooser's website is www.tedkooser.com.

Larson, Kirby

"Keeping the Faith" is copyright 2007 by Kirby Larson and is reprinted by permission of the author. The piece is based on an entry, December 3, 2007, from her blog, found at her website, www.kirbylarson.com.

Liu, Cynthea

"Status Queries" is copyright 2008 by Cynthea Liu and is reprinted by permission of the author. It is first appeared as a blog entry on her website, Writing for Children and Teens, as "Status Queries: When and How to Do It" (www.writingforchildrenandteens.com) in June 2006.

Lowry, Lois

"Starting" is copyright 2007 by Lois Lowry and is reprinted by permission of the author. Her website is www.loislowry.com. This piece combines three posts from late 2007 from her blog (www.loislowry.typepad.com): "Starting," "The Neglected Horse and the Undiscovered Room" and "Different Dreams."

MacGregor, Chip

"Competitive Titles" is copyright 2007 by Chip MacGregor and is reprinted by permission of the author. The article was posted August 7, 2007, on his blog of advice for writers on his website, www.chipmacgregor.com.

Martin, Philip

"Developing a Sense of Place" is copyright 2007 by Philip Martin and is reprinted by permission of the author. The article, the first half of a two-part series, appears on his website, www.greatlakeslit.com.

"Boost Your Personal Brand Online" is copyright 2008 by Philip Martin and is reprinted by permission of the author. The article appears on his website, www.greatlakeslit.com.

"Editor's Afterword" is copyright 2008 by Philip Martin and is included by permission of the author.

McDaniel, Ron

"Evaluating Blog Results: Does Your Blog Suck or Succeed?" is copyright 2007 by Ron McDaniel and is reprinted by permission of the author. The piece appeared September 17, 2007, on his Buzzoodle Blog site (http://blog.buzzoodle.com). The post was originally titled "Your Blog Results Suck—Or Do They?"

McKenna, Maryn

"To Blog or Not To Blog" is copyright 2008 by Maryn McKenna and is reprinted by permission of the author. The piece is based on a post January 4, 2008, on WriterL, a listserv for nonfiction writers moderated by Lynn Franklin.

McLachlan, Sean

"Midlister: Embracing the Term" is copyright 2008 by Sean McLachlan and is reprinted by permission of the author. His website is www.freewebs. com/seanmclachlan. The piece is based on a post March 14, 2008, on his Midlist Writer blog (http://midlistwriter.blogspot.com).

Miller, Meghan

"Dialogue: Say What?" is copyright 2008 by Ellora's Cave Publishing, Inc. and is reprinted by permission of the publisher. This piece was posted February 1, 2008, on the publisher's blog, Redlines and Deadlines (http://redlinesanddeadlines.blogspot.com).

Moran, Stephen

"Common Faults in Short Stories" is copyright 2008 by Stephen Moran and is reprinted by permission of the author. It appeared February 21, 2008, in the *Willesden Herald* blog (http://willesdenherald.blogspot.com).

O'Connor, Barbara

"Show, Don't Tell: Before and After" is copyright 2007 by Barbara O'Connor and is reprinted by permission of the author. Her website is www. barboconnor.com. This piece is based on a blog entry, "Before and After," that appeared November 21, 2007, on her blog, www.greetings-from-nowhere.blogspot.com.

O'Doherty, Susan

"Critiquing a Friend's Manuscript" is copyright 2007 by Susan O'Doherty and is reprinted by permission of the author. Her website is www. susanodohertyauthor.com. This post appeared December 28, 2007, in her column, The Doctor Is In, featured in the blog, Buzz, Balls, and Hype (http://mjroseblog.typepad.com/buzz_balls_hype).

O'Hanlon, Bill

"Baby Steps" is excerpted from the book *Write Is a Verb* by Bill O'Hanlon, copyright 2007 by Writer's Digest Books. Used by permission of Writer's Digest Books, an imprint of F+W Publications, Inc. This excerpt appeared in *Writer's Digest* magazine, February 2008.

O'Neill, Alexis
> "School Visits: How Much To Charge?" is copyright 2008 by Alexis O'Neill and is reprinted by permission of the author. Her website is www.alexisoneill.com. This piece first appeared in the January/Febuary 2008 issue of the SCBWI *Bulletin* (newsletter of the Society of Children's Book Writers and Illustrators).

Patterson, Tim
> "Travel Writer Personalities" is copyright 2008 by Tim Patterson and is reprinted by permission of the author. His personal website is www.rucksackwanderer.com. This piece appeared January 25, 2008, on the website of Brave New Traveler (www.bravenewtraveler.com).

Porinchak, Eve
> "Sock Monkeys and Stegosauruses" is copyright 2007 by Eve Porinchak and is reprinted by permission of the author. It was posted August 21, 2007, on the group blog The Disco Mermaids, found at www.discomermaids.blogspot.com, featuring Porinchak and fellow writers Robin Mellom and Jay Asher.

Poyer, David
> "The Matrix of Multi-Character Development" is copyright 2008 by David Poyer and is reprinted by permission of the author. Portions of the material appeared in an article, "Crafting the Braided Narrative," found on his website, www.poyer.com.

Rafter, Michelle Vranizan
> "Asking the Hard Question: Top Ten Interview Tips" is copyright 2008 by Michelle Vranizan Rafter and is reprinted by permission of the author. The piece appeared on her blog, WordCount (http://michellerafter.wordpress.com) on February 5, 2008.

Ramey, Fred
> "What Am I Supposed To Be Doing?" is copyright 2008 by Fred Ramey and is reprinted by permission of the author. This piece is drawn from a post from Ramey's Publisher Blog at Unbridled Books, www.unbridledbooks.com.

Reidy, Jean
> "Ten Ways To Land a First Assignment" is copyright 2008 by Jean Reidy and is reprinted by permission of the author. The article first appeared in *The Writer* magazine, March 2008.

Reissenweber, Brandi
> "Revision Strategies" is copyright 2008 by Brandi Reissenweber and is reprinted by permission of the author. A slightly shorter version of this article first appeared in *The Writer* magazine's online Q&A column.

Sant, Tom
  "Fluff, Guff, Geek, and Weasel" is copyright 2008 by Tom Sant and is reprinted by permission of the author. The article is drawn from his book, *The Language of Success* (AMACOM, 2008), and appeared in his free newsletter, Dr. Tom's Tips, which is available from his website, www. hydeparkpartnerscal.com.

Scanlan, Christopher "Chip"
  "Why I Blog" is copyright 2006 by Christopher Scanlan and is reprinted by permission of the author. The article was posted February 18, 2006, on his online column, "Chip on Your Shoulder" at Poynter Online (www. poynter.org).

Skloot, Rebecca
  "Querying" is copyright by Rebecca Skloot and is reprinted by permission of the author. This article is drawn, with the help of Elaine Vitone, from materials Skloot developed for *The Creative Nonfiction* MFA *Student's Playbook*, a guide to building a portfolio of published work from the Creative Nonfiction Writers' Professional Development Society, University of Pittsburgh. A longer version of the article appears on her website at www.rebeccaskloot.com.

Stawar, Terry L.
  "Five Steps to Successful Email Interviews" is copyright 2007 by Terry L. Stawar and is reprinted by permission of the author. This article first appeared June 11, 2007, as "The E-View: Five Steps to Successful Email Interviews for the Nonfiction Writer," in the online newsletter *Absolute Write* (www.absolutewrite.com).

Taylor, Laini
  "Brainstorming" is copyright 2008 by Laini Taylor and is reprinted by permission of the author. The piece is drawn from posts on her blog of advice for writers, Not For Robots (www.notforrobots.blogspot.com).

Toor, Rachel
  "My Left Tackle" is copyright 2007 by Rachel Toor and is reprinted by permission of the author. This article can be found on her website, www. racheltoor.com, and appeared July 27, 2007, in the Chronicle Careers column of online edition of the *Chronicle of Higher Education*.

Trunk, Penelope
  "Seven Ways to Get an Agent's Attention" is copyright 2007 by Penelope Trunk and is reprinted by permission of the author. It appeared April 22, 2007, on her Brazen Careerist blog (http://blog.penelopetrunk. com).

Turnbull, Giles
  "A Writer by Any Other Name" is copyright 2008 by Giles Turnbull and is reprinted by permission of the author. His website is http://gilest.org. The piece first appeared February 13, 2008, in the *Morning News* (www. themorningnews.org), an online magazine.

Weaver, Will
"Diary of a Novel" is copyright 2007 by Will Weaver and is reprinted by permission of the author. This piece is excerpted from a September 29, 2007, post on his blog, On Writing, which can be found at his website, www.willweaverbooks.com.

Westerfeld, Scott
"First Page Test" is copyright 2007 by Scott Westerfeld and is reprinted by permission of the author. This piece appeared June 11, 2007, on his blog, Westerblog (http://scottwesterfeld.com/blog).

Yansky, Brian
"The Serious Nature of Comic Fiction" is copyright 2006 by Brian Yansky and is reprinted by permission of the author. The piece is drawn from an article that appears on his website, www.brianyansky.com.